M000312409

CARIBBEAN WRITERS ON
TEACHING LITERATURE

CARIBBEAN WRITERS ON TEACHING LITERATURE

LORNA DOWN AND **THELMA BAKER**

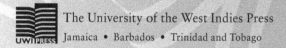

The University of the West Indies Press
Jamaica • Barbados • Trinidad and Tobago

The University of the West Indies Press
7A Gibraltar Hall Road, Mona
Kingston 7, Jamaica
www.uwipress.com

A catalogue record of this book is available from the
National Library of Jamaica.

ISBN: 978-976-640-738-4 (paper)
978-976-640-739-1 (Kindle)
978-976-640-740-7 (ePub)

Book and cover design by Robert Harris
Set in Scala 10.5/15 x 24

Printed in the United States of America

FOR MY MOTHER, VERONICA EARLE,
WHO TAUGHT ME TO LOVE BOOKS
&
FOR THE BAKER FAMILY

Contents

SECTION 3. MILLENNIALS, THE GLOBAL AND NEW TECHNOLOGY:
THE THIRD GENERATION OF CARIBBEAN TEACHERS

Foreword

Caribbean Writers on Teaching Literature is a series of interviews which provides insights into, and strategies for the teaching of literature through the personal experiences of teachers and writers of literature from the English-speaking Caribbean and the Caribbean diaspora, experiences which together span three generations and approximately six decades. The writers' own enthusiasm for the subject, and their individual enjoyment of teaching literature should be inspiration for teachers and students alike, who often approach literature with some amount of uncertainty. The book is a valuable contribution to the library of books on the teaching of literature, especially with respect to teaching Caribbean literature. The Introduction describes the editors' journey which led to this book and provides theoretic context for the contributors' reflections.

The editors, Lorna Down and Thelma Baker, are themselves teachers of excellence and in this series play the dual roles of editors and contributors. Lorna Down was a lecturer at the Mico University College, then transitioned to the School of Education at the University of the West Indies at Mona, where she lectured in literature and literature education. Thelma Baker taught literature at Merl Grove High School, Kingston, Jamaica, and was known for the quality of her literature teaching. She was also a tutor of literature at the University of the West Indies, Mona. Both editors worked on behalf of the Joint Board of Teacher Education, Mona, as external examiners for literature and literature education as taught at Jamaican teachers' colleges. As they carry out the role of editors, therefore, they do so using the lens of experienced and highly accomplished experts in this field. They, like their fellow contributors, have a deep passion for literature.

Caribbean Writers on Teaching Literature is a fitting contribution to the teaching of literature, which tends to present an enormous challenge to many teachers. Not surprisingly, also, many students find studying litera-ture a difficult task. On one level, literature may be viewed simply as a body of written work set in a particular period or culture. Like painting or music, it is an art form, operating on emotional, imaginative and creative planes, but using the medium of language to communicate. At a more fundamental level, it is a mirror of life and a response to writers' urges to express themselves on life issues. This aspect of literature is reiterated throughout many of the interviews in this book. Victor Chang describes literature as raising valid questions about life, and crossing over into life, while Kelly Baker Josephs expresses the view that literature helps students understand themselves more fully. Carolyn Cooper extends that thought in another direction, explaining that students need to understand not only the context of the text, but also need to have their own context understood in relation to the issues raised by the material under study. Indeed, students' personae, their personal experiences and perspectives on life issues impact their responses to different writers and literary genres.

The teaching of literature explores and interrogates cultural concepts and messages, as well as the language used to communicate these ideas. For some, therefore, literature may be viewed as a difficult subject of study. From the perspective of the teacher, this difficulty could also emanate from student disinterest. From time to time teachers complain that students read very little and often reject literature both as subject and as entertainment. A number of the writers in this book share their frustration at the reluc-tance of their students to read, of students wanting to be told what to write or what book will tell them what to write. The disinterest is not surprising in a society where education is seen primarily in terms of its potential to generate wealth. In other words, it is deemed to have a functional role which discounts the value of the humanities. As a consequence, a number of universities have lamented the trend of declining enrolment in literature courses among other areas of the humanities (Flaherty 2015; Haven 2010).

But there is, I believe, consensus on the worth of literature. At one level the representational language of literary texts involves the learners and en-gages their emotions, as well as their cognitive faculties. Literarture helps learners to use their imagination, enhance their empathy for others and develop their own creativity. At another level the study of literature develops an understanding and appreciation of culture, fostering private interpersonal and intercultural attitudes and values (Pieper 2006). At yet another level it develops the ability to analyse in order to evaluate and make judgements, enhancing the generalization of knowledge to similar and relevant contexts. Perhaps more than any other subject, it promotes academic literacy and fosters metacognitive functions. The experiences and views shared by these eighteen teachers of literature, a number of whom are themselves writers, show that they share this view of the power of literature.

Caribbean Writers on Teaching Literature presents interviews with eighteen contributors which delve into understandings of, and practices in the teaching of literature in general. In the process, these individuals are also invited to share their experiences in teaching Caribbean literature in particular. Most of those interviewed currently work or have worked in institutions in the region, though some have had teaching experiences outside of the Caribbean.

A body of work in literatures of English that can truly be described as Caribbean emerged in the mid-twentieth century. While writing from the region preceded this period and in fact goes back to the eighteenth and nineteenth centuries, these works were largely written by visitors to the region and were Eurocentric in focus and theme (Dance 1986). Ledent (2007) pins the beginning of this emergence to the arrival in the United Kingdom of the *Empire Windrush*, the boat that in June 1948 brought 492 Jamaicans to the United Kingdom. This was the start of a large exodus of post-war Caribbean people who settled in Britain and among whom were a number of writers and artists. From this group came an outpouring of creativity. They were prolific in writing about their experiences in the country of their former colonizers as well as of their Caribbean home, which Ledent feels they saw with more clear-sightedness from a distance. Out of these experiences, therefore, came distinctive modes of writing which merit critical treatment similar to that of any other literary period or group. Caribbean literature is no longer confined to the geographic region of the United Kingdom, however, nor deemed to be exclusively writings by persons born in the Caribbean; rather, it also embraces individuals born outside of the Caribbean but who write from the perspective of their Caribbean heritage. Edward Baugh, in his interview, reminisces on his experiences when the University of the

West Indies decided to change the focus of the Department of English from one which primarily taught the literature of England to one with a broadened focus, resulting in a name change to Department of Literatures in English and, by such a change, enabling the inclusion in its repertoire of Caribbean literature.

Caribbean Writers on Teaching Literature, then, looks at the issue of the teaching of literature but from a novel perspective. It invites the reader to share in the experiences of these Caribbean teachers and to learn from them. It provides a glimpse into how these teachers of excellence have approached their teaching. The love, passion even, for literature rings out across all the interviews. These teachers love literature and would wish to share this love with their students. They seem to come alive with the material they teach. Edward Baugh talks about his theatre-style lecture performances, while Victor Chang recounts using costuming to make a point. The material also shows how important it is for the teacher to reconnect with the text, no matter how many times they have taught a particular book or poem. The interviews exposed the reader to pedagogy, from the conventional to the unusual. The interviews offer strategies to bridge the divide between the "popular" and the "literary", and even suggests how to actively use the "popular" to explicate and unravel the meaning of literature. An interesting component is the interviewer's use of Elaine Showalter's seven teacher anxieties to provide perspective on the vulnerabilities of these eminent teachers of literature.

F. Scott Fitzgerald wrote, "That is part of the beauty of all literature. You discover that your longings are universal longings, that you're not lonely and isolated from anyone. You belong."

Marcia Stewart
Manager, Joint Board of Teacher Education, School of Education
The University of the West Indies, Mona Campus

Acknowledgements

We would like to thank Edward Baugh, Victor Chang, Carolyn Cooper, Norval Edwards, Brian Heap, Kelly Baker Josephs, Mark McWatt, Mervyn Morris, Sharon Phillips, Velma Pollard, Sandra Robinson, Samuel Soyer, Aisha Spencer, Maureen Warner-Lewis, David Williams and Ann-Marie Wilmot, our teachers, poets and writers, for their willingness to share their experiences and the insights they have gained in teaching literature. Regrettably, Victor Chang died shortly before the publication of this book. We give thanks for his significant contribution to the teaching of literature and to this work. We also thank Sonia Roberts, then senior secretary in the School of Education, the University of the West Indies, Mona, for her careful transcriptions of most of these interviews. Her enthusiastic response to the interviews also underlined for us their value. We acknowledge as well Marcia Stewart, friend and colleague, for her significant contribution to the manuscript. We are also grateful to Shivaun Hearne, the editorial and production manager of the University of the West Indies Press, for her editorial acumen. Equally important has been the support of our families, in particular Mervyn and Keisha-Ann Down, Allicia Dunn, and Barbara O'Connor.

Introduction

LORNA DOWN AND THELMA BAKER

The sheer pleasure of reading a good book is unforgettable. To pass on this love for books, of magical and mystical experience with a literature text, is the often unspoken and undocumented vision of the teacher of literature. Yet creating that magic in the classroom has often been simply fortuitous. Reflecting on successful and unsuccessful lessons of literature – those we have taught, those we have participated in and those we have observed – we yearned to distil such times into a text that we could share.

That search initiated the journey to *Caribbean Writers on Teaching Literature*. We increased our informal conversations on teaching literature, and we began our research in the field with observing student teachers and talking with experienced teachers of literature. We listened. Some of these stories were humorous and wise. Others simply reflected a need to know more about the craft of teaching literature and ways teachers pass on their love of literature. We also began to journal our own experiences. We researched books on teaching literature and found many helpful ones – from those detailing activities to those discussing approaches in a more formal way. In fact, we found such books on teaching methods for literature few in comparison to the tomes on literature criticism and theory. These few books also included those with specific material on selected texts or writers – here the emphasis was on theme, style, structure, language. What eluded us were books on how a teacher could foster the somewhat mystical connection between books and readers.

1

We wanted a "living text", one which would emerge from the field itself, from teachers who were engaged in the teaching of literature. Gradually what developed was the idea of teachers talking with each other, sharing their literature experiences, in a text. So we invited experienced teachers and writers to share with us their stories about teaching literature. There are eighteen interviews (not all those we asked to be interviewed accepted, and some we wanted but could not ask, because we wanted a regional reach and not one island dominating). Our teacher interviewees are drawn from around the English-speaking Caribbean and among the Caribbean diaspora. All of them are published writers (of literary or non-literary texts, or both). We feel that working from both sides – reading as well as writing – these interviewees bring to the discussion a certain richness. Some of the interviewees had taught us; we had collaborated with others on various projects. Together they, like us, belong to an academic circle of literature teachers who love reading, listening to and writing literature.

Initially we planned to invite each teacher to use the transcribed interview as a basis for their narrative on teaching literature. This changed mainly as a result of four factors. One was the response to this idea by one of our interviewees, Kelly Baker Josephs, who asked, "Why not keep the interview format?" Second was the unsolicited response of the person transcribing the interviews, Sonia Roberts. An English major, she would comment on how interesting the interviews were and how she found hearing what some of her past teachers felt fascinating and, in some cases, entertaining. Third was the publication of Hyacinth Evans's text of interviews of six educators, loudly signalling that a book of interviews could work. One interviewer also spoke to how the oral tradition of the Caribbean and social media generally have created a public that desires "orality" even in written narratives.

In addition to these, we "discovered" Judy Kravis's text *Teaching Literature*; it was a validation of our project, a book on teaching literature. It showed the possibilities for a book on this subject that allowed a great deal of space on literature-teaching methodologies, with little or no interruptions with exposition and discussion on literary theories and books. The field and lecture halls were already filled with those. Instead, we wanted teachers to hear from master teachers, colleagues and friends on how and why to teach literature, and to join in the conversation. It was a conversation that we had already been engaging in for many years over coffee. Moreover, we had been encouraging our pre-and in-service teachers to practise being reflective practitioners.

We say that Kravis's text was an ironic validation; it affirmed for us the need and place for narratives about the teaching of literature, the pedagogy of literature. The format of "narratives" she had used mirrored, somewhat, the format that we have chosen – interviews, conversations. It was good to see that another literature teacher and enthusiast had also recognized the value of hearing directly the voices of those with expertise. Yet despite the similarities, we felt that our book would also produce a new experience, a sharpening of sensations, new delights and new insights into teaching literature. Caribbean literary pieces – poetry, prose and drama – are acknowledged widely and have contributed much to world literature. Similarly, our works of criticism, of theory have extended the field in significant ways. Yet what has been missing is the voice of the practitioner, the teacher of literature. There are a number of books on teaching literature, but the Caribbean perspective on teaching approaches and methods has been to a great extent limited. This book aims to fill that gap, to present the voices of Caribbean teachers and lecturers as they speak to their art.

These interviews are the primary text. They are organized in three sections: three movements, three generations of Caribbean teachers and writers talking literature. Our introductory comments, instead of a theoretical discussion, serve like the lighting in a play, to illuminate and highlight specific aspects. The book then becomes a site for readers to listen to the voices of fellow teachers of literature in an unmediated way or with little academic commentary; here, then, we re-create the rich conversations which we have had on teaching literature and which have honed our own teaching.

Using a set of basic questions in regard to methodology, style, philosophy, teacher-readiness and preparation, and vision, we explore what makes for effective teaching of literature. An array of voices offers us diverse perspectives, together proclaiming that teaching literature is an art. Teaching literature, then, is more than possessing a list of activities, using a set of strategies. By a stroke of good fortune, we have been allowed to participate in the creation of this art through these shared experiences as well as our own.

3

Edward Baugh in his interview speaks of wanting his students to come to literature the "true way". Baugh is not making any narrow, prescriptive, Cleanth Brooks et al., New Criticism kind of declaration. "True way" is used in a nuanced and open sense – one which suggests space for the learner to complete the meaning, to make sense of the texts being studied. Using Baugh's comment metonymically, we invite the readers to read this text in the "true way", recognizing that they bring to it their own perspectives, knowledge, expertise and experience, and that by adding these to the conversations, they will engage in completing the narratives in these interviews. We might even speak of such a reading as constructivist. These interviews provide for what Sumara (2002) calls "literary anthropology"; here the willing reader can find truth and insights and gather ideas which have emerged from the lived experiences of teachers in classrooms and lecture rooms. Like a Mervyn Morris poem, these interviews are tightly condensed bearers of multiple truths. They reflect at core Kravis's declaration of a love of literature: "[we] have some long love of words, even dependency on words read, written", she declared (Kravis 1995, 1) in the introduction to her intriguing book of narratives on teaching literature.

In recent times, the field of literature pedagogy has seen the publication of a number of important books, such as Beach and Myers (2001), Beach et al. (2006); Bowell and Heap (2001); Bryan and Styles (2014); Collie and Slater (1990); Kravis (1994); Milner and Milner (2008); Showalter (2003), and Sumara (2002). They all respond to the need for a variety of teaching approaches and methodologies that will engage students in the reading and appreciation of literature, that will help students develop a love for literature. These books raise issues such as the place of literary theory and critical material in teaching literature; they reflect on the displacement of the primary texts by literary theories and its impact on students' reading of fiction, poetry and drama. Judy Kravis (1995, 5), in fact, suggests that the various "isms" – formalism, structuralism, and deconstruction (which she sardonically notes "doesn't need an ism") – reflect "the dilemma of the critic in the tower, the theorist in orbit", one for whom literary theory has been set "on the kitchen table next to the salt". The consequence she implies is that of students being so encumbered by the secondary texts of criticism and theories that they lose sight of the primary texts. She also suggests that when our libraries are filled with secondary texts, and primary texts are absent, we send a message about the importance and value of the latter texts.

The issue is this: How can we teach literature so that students are encouraged to read and appreciate fiction and poetry? Grace Paley (1995), too, broached this question, asking if the right types of questions for literature texts were being raised. She reflected on the narrowly focused questions that were asked about the stories she had written and suggested that the questions needed to evoke students' "personal" response to the text. They should be as sufficiently broad as "Do you like this story?" and "What do you think it's about?" Otherwise, the teaching of literature can become a tedious exercise. All of this despite Rosenblatt (1996) and her work on reader response.

How to engage students has thus led to an emphasis on literature providing meaning, helping us to interpret the world, create our identities and locate ourselves in the world. Sumara (2002) speaks to the success that he has had with his creation of a teaching approach which he terms "literary anthropology". Here learners explore literature through creating a "commonplace" of literature texts, other materials (for example, newspaper articles), and artefacts, as well as their [the learners'] comments. The text is literally "embossed" with the learners' comments and their artefacts. Read and re-read, it acquires layers of comments over time and becomes a commonplace book for the learner, who in rereading these comes to understand more clearly themselves and their world. Sumara asserts that literature texts can be sites for developing insights and creating identities. Developing insights emerges from the hard work of interpreting one's relations with people as well as one's relations with objects, which people have made. Such "objects" include narratives that describe and explain experiences. Sumara's approach is based on reader-response theories and on the idea that texts do not simply reflect experience but constitute in and of themselves an experience. This interesting interpretive practice of teaching literature is one we, the editors, have also tried with varying levels of success. What is clear is that as students engage with such a practice, they become more conscious of why reading matters and, equally important, how to read analytically and creatively.

Another approach to teaching literature that highlights its value as a tool for meaning making is an inquiry-based teaching technique. Beach and Myers (2001) propose that students are encouraged to reflect on their participation in their world through examining representation of social worlds in literature texts. Here the conventional practice of using literature to teach language is flipped, as learners' critiquing of their world becomes the entry point for the study and appreciation of literature.

The approaches so far illustrate an underlying key education principle – that of student-centredness, or participatory learning. It's a theory of learning that Beach et al. (2006), in *Teaching Literature to Adolescents*, tell us is derived from the progressive movement in education in the 1920s that challenged the teacher-centred model. They, however, limit its meaning, interpreting it as a theory that leaves the responsibility for learning up to the student. In effect, it is student-focused learning that aims to encourage students' participation, to encourage students' discovering knowledge and constructing meaning. In that situation, teachers act as facilitators, as they treat the learner like an active maker of meaning and one who possesses knowledge (that they may sometimes be ignorant of having).

The student-centred approach is even more emphasized today, as nations around the world attempt to meet the United Nations General Assembly's 2015 Sustainable Development Goals for the year 2030. Education is recognized as an important driver in this movement. The relatively recent development of Education for Sustainable Development (the United Nations devoted a decade to it, 2005–2015, and has since continued its development in the Global Action Programme) emphasizes a student-centred pedagogy as well. It is based on the principle that learners learn through doing, that the active participation of the learner is necessary for effective learning. Moreso, the learner is treated as being actively involved in the making of a society (Down 2011). The teacher of literature needs also to attend to this principle in order to create effective literature lessons.

It is important to note as well that the text often determines the approach. Editors Bryan and Styles explore this idea in their recent publication *Teaching Caribbean Poetry*. The writers discuss this in relation to experiential triggers and connectives which aim to link the poem with the experience of reader. They also explore communicative and language awareness strategies, informed by reader-response theories. (See Bryan, Down, Hudson and Spenser, in Bryan and Styles 2014, 107–15.)

In the teaching and learning situation, however, the learner is only one element. Equally important is the teacher. Conventionally, education at the tertiary level has taken place mainly through lectures. Sometimes these have been balanced by small-group tutorials, which allow for greater student participation. The lecture mode encourages a teacher-centredness. Showalter's (2003) text on teaching literature addresses this issue by focusing on the teacher. Incorporating different teachers' voices in her text, she discusses their feelings in that role, the role of the "sage on the stage", and uncovers their unease and sometimes "triumph" there. She speaks to the deliberate strategies of involving students in that mode. Most notable is her identification of seven teacher anxieties – a useful guide for teachers' self-reflection and transformation.

Clearly, ongoing research is needed in "best practices" in the teaching of literature. The changing landscape and contexts of learners, teachers and books demand this. The new generation of Twitter, Facebook, WhatsApp, Instagram – the techie generation, whose preference is for instant, sound-bite morsels of text – calls for new approaches. In this situation, many of us who teach literature, who are "tech migrants", are all in some ways like Morris's "crippled schoolmaster". Yet there is an art to teaching literature that transcends periods. The study of varying literature pedagogies will enable us to refine and enhance our practice of teaching literature in order to develop lovers of literature.

Caribbean Writers on Teaching Literature offers a platform for a rich dialogue on how to teach literature to diverse student populations, to different generations. Each interviewee opens up an aspect of teaching literature. All of them are writers and literary critics, and a number are celebrated poets. They are involved in the production of literature as well as its teaching. Edward Baugh, Mark McWatt, Mervyn Morris, Velma Pollard and David Williams are poets who teach and write about literature. Complementing the poets are Thelma Baker, Victor Chang, Carolyn Cooper, Lorna Down, Norval Edwards, Brian Heap, Kelly Baker Josephs, Sharon Phillips, Sandra Robinson, Aisha Spencer, Samuel Soyer, Maureen Warner-Lewis and Ann-Marie Williams, who have written articles or texts on literature and also teach. Passionate about literature, they highlight its value and necessity for enriching the quality of life in our societies. Our interviewees have been drawn largely from the tertiary level, though all of them have also had experience teaching at the secondary level.

This collection of interviews embodies the experience of teaching literature. The collection re-enacts the creation of the literary experience in the lecture room and in the classroom, as each interviewee recalls what it is like to prepare for the literature lecture, to create interesting and meaningful experiences with literary texts and figures, and all within the larger context and understanding of the purpose and value of literature regionally and globally. These individuals also reflect on memorable as well as challenging experiences in teaching, as they strive to engage their students.

What has clearly emerged from this collection of voices, each distinctive, is a *pedagogy of connectivity*. Each generation of teachers has contributed uniquely to this teaching approach. Thus the collection is organized into three sections – three generations of teachers forging a new idiom for an approach that emphasizes connections between the text, the context and the students, so that a community of readers may evolve. It is a community sensitive to place, and to self and others. *Caribbean Writers on Teaching Literature* is intended to preserve a rich cultural heritage of a pedagogy of literature that is ultimately about students connecting to self, others and their world. Each of the three sections features an introduction discussing this pedagogical approach.

We invite readers to enter this unique circle of storytellers, to listen to the different voices, to bring their own story to the circle, and then see how together we can rekindle in our students a deep love of literature. Let us allow the best of this art form to inspire us.

SECTION 1.

THE WIDENING STUDENT-CENTRED VISION
The First Generation of Caribbean Teachers

In these new nations art is a luxury." So wrote Derek Walcott in 1998. What must it have been like teaching that art! The first native Caribbean teachers of literature at the University of the West Indies included Jean Creary (D'Costa), Winnifred Risden and Jean McLaughlin, and the list for literature education included John Figueroa. They who were schooled in the Western classics; who knew, as Walcott expressed it in *What the Twilight Says* (1988), the literature of empires, Greek, Roman, British, yet also knew intimately "the patois of the street and the language of the classroom". These teachers must also have experienced the "elation of discovery". Among this first wave of native teachers are our interviewees Edward Baugh, Mervyn Morris, Velma Pollard and Maureen Warner-Lewis. Though they had joined the staff of the University of the West Indies after these teachers – Baugh in 1965, Morris in 1970, Pollard in 1975 and Warner-Lewis in 1970 – they may also be considered part of the group of pioneers.

Significantly, the teaching of Baugh, Morris, Pollard and Warner-Lewis has spanned a couple of decades. The interviews capture, therefore, the distilled wisdom of their years of teaching different generations of students, different periods in the development of literature and literature education, and different political, social and economic realities. It was this group that oversaw the major change from a literature programme that had been only that of "the literature of empire" to one in which literature texts by Caribbean writers formed a substantial part. Kenneth Ramchand, in fact, designed and introduced the West Indian literature course for the English Department at Mona. These teachers also helped to usher in the name change from the Department of English to the Department of Literatures in English, which corresponded with a move to effectively challenge the primacy of British literature, as the literature programme changed to include Caribbean literature as well as literature from other parts of the world.

At the core of this, and the focus of this text, is the pedagogy that has emerged from teaching in a region during its various political periods – pre-independent to post-independent, colonial to postcolonial and postmodern. It is a pedagogical approach that pushes for connections – student, text and context. Whereas most of the literature pedagogical texts focus on one or two of these elements, these four foundation teachers bring all three elements together. Moreover, they have passed on to a second and third generation of teachers, many of whom they have taught, this pedagogy of connections.

There is no doubt that literature teaching, like literature, has been influenced by its time, its period. A people, with a history of living in a fragmented society, of heritage lying in other places, naturally longed for "home", for "roots", for connections to place and people, and to self. Much of Caribbean literature has explored these concerns. In a comparable way, the pedagogy of the literature emerging from this region centres on the making of connections, for a people and society, and, more specifically, connecting students to self, others and place through the study of literary texts and their contexts. Baugh speaks of such teaching and learning of literature as making a "web of connections".

In other words, these teachers, even as they introduce literature texts through various contexts of gender, linguistics, history, structures and myths, among others, are aware of the "global connectors" of place, history and culture. Teaching from that awareness, they help the learners acknowledge their global connectors and explore their sense of self and place. Teachers, in turn, acknowledging and affirming their students, take learner-centred pedagogy to another level.

It is more than the "sage leaving the stage" and focusing on student participation, though this is included. What we see at core is the teacher respecting all students and acknowledging their knowledge and possibilities. Morris, in fact, tells us that respect for all students is critical. He truly listens as they share their response to the texts being studied. And he creates an environment in which they feel comfortable to say what they think. Moreso, it is about paying attention to where students believe they are (in terms of abilities, knowledge) and not just where they are.

This pedagogy based on making connections also means teachers creating a space for the original voices of their students to be heard. A colonial legacy no doubt also left its imprimatur on the teaching approach and academic expectations of native teachers. To find one's voice in spite of imposed sounds and rhythms or to negotiate a clearing through colonial structures and styles required extraordinary courage. We see such courage reflected in an approach to teaching literature that allows students to

12

develop a confidence in their literary skills; to realize that they can abandon mere adoption of and accommodation with established critical viewpoints. This opens the way for them to discover new insights from the literature studied and engage in creating new metaphors and new literary styles and forms.

In this way, old hierarchies of lectures and students are overturned, and the teacher becomes the experienced guide, or facilitator, deliberately creating space for the development of the literary sensibility. Sole mimicry as the path to success is shut down. The student is never "nothing" – a void to be filled. Instead teachers see themselves as co-creators with the students. Making way for the emergence of new voices, these teachers are ready to birth the new poets, writers and dramatists. That is the vision underpinning their teaching of literature – a vision that shapes the quality of the learning and teaching in their classrooms and lecture halls.

Moreover, students know that their voices will be heard and welcomed, sensing, even if not fully understanding, that vision. They are thus prepared to engage deeply with the text – the poem, the drama, the fiction – to have a "literary experience". Baugh expresses it this way: "I'd like them to feel that the novel or the poem is an experience." The reader and the text meet each other. The students have thus come to literature "the true way", as Baugh explains.

There are two important strands highlighted in this teaching and learning of literature. On the one hand is teacher recognition of students' capabilities and the landscape they will travel through literature. On the other hand is the teachers' knowledge of what is required, the "lenses" needed for such a journey. They had garnered this knowledge more from their life experiences than from texts and such knowledge provided the key to unlocking the literary work. So Warner-Lewis shares the importance of recognizing recurring patterns structure – not only the what of the text but the how and why. Pollard discusses the significance of language, the linguistic elements of the text as revealing meaning. Morris emphasizes the sound and movement of the text – its rhythms, its ambiguity and verbal riches. Drawing on his own work as poet, he discloses how even an image can point in multiple directions. And Baugh cites the danger of erasing the text through readings imposed on it. It is as if the knowledge gained from

surviving a history like that of the region – of recognizing recurring patterns, linguistic and language machinations, rhythm flows, ambiguity and
erasure – had found its way into the pedagogy of literature.

Thus the question of context – of the teachers themselves, the students
and, of course, the literature text – could not be dismissed. This forms, too,
the web of connections in which the teaching and learning of literature is
positioned. Pollard affirms that texts do not exist in a vacuum; she insists
that a text always has "stuff" behind it. She speaks of interesting ways of
bringing that context into the classroom, while recalling a terrible ironic
incident where context was ignored in the study of a particular text. Warner-
Lewis also explores the value of having information on the writer, their
social and historical background and special concerns. She reflects as well
on the importance of developing awareness of the physical context of the
text, its geography and landscape, as with the use of films.

Also revealed is the significance of the students' cultural context for
learning: why does performance matter so much, or orature, or music?
Our teachers in this section discuss the importance of acknowledging and
validating cultural norms, not in a simplistic way but through the creation
of a discriminating ethos. They speak to how this invites students to relax
into literature, to develop their critical reading lenses and extend the levels
in which literature in all its diversity can be appreciated. Respecting and
caring for the students leads to a respect for what they possess, deepening
their experience of it and training critical eyes to view such "artful" posses-
sions. As a result, students are exposed to the value of the wide-open field
of literature. Illustrative of this is Warner-Lewis's discussion of her course
on orature.

Centring the text is primary, however. The connections lead into and out
from the text. In an era where discussion of literary theories often displaces
the fiction, the poetry and the drama, we are reminded of the importance
of the actual literary text. Threading throughout the interviews is the view
of literature as pleasurable. Implicitly stated is the desire that students will
come to share this view as they become immersed in the text, something
that is really only possible when the text itself is highlighted and not marginalized. Equally important is their approach to the text that shows it as a
site to interpret lived situation (Sumara 2002). Engagement with the text

is therefore at the heart of their teaching. Emphasized are varying practices of interpreting the text. Such interpretive practices are shown, moreover, to allow for the emergence of insights that shape personal and communal identities. Teaching literature is, among other things, the making of a self and a people.

Important in this web of connections is the teacher. Showalter interestingly focuses on teachers' anxieties. Knowing one's anxieties clearly prepares one to deal with them. Showalter insists that acknowledgement of anxieties will enable more productive relationships with students and, as a result, lead to more effective teaching of literature. Significantly, not all the teachers interviewed spoke to teacher anxieties; yet, all referred to teacher dispositions, a more inclusive subject.

Teacher dispositions are seen as making a major difference in teachers' choice of methodology. Baugh, Morris, Pollard and Warner-Lewis show how a teacher's passion and love of literature influence tremendously their relation to the text and how this ultimately influences the students' attitude to the subject. Baugh speaks, therefore, of the teacher finding that point of connection to the text and the importance of that for effective teaching. Morris remarks on the "burden of knowledge" demanded by particular texts and, therefore, the teachers' responsibility to know the text. If not, he asserts, "there are things that you are going to get horribly wrong". What is revealed is the importance of teachers respecting the art itself and the work of teaching it.

There is the shift, then, from teaching to student-learning. The teacher recognizes that teaching is an art too – it is really about creating a site for students to become engaged, "have fun" with the texts and share in the absolute pleasure of discovering new readings of a text. Morris affirms this as he points to the ultimate compliment that a teacher can receive from a student: that of a student's acknowledgement of how much they are now able to understand as a result of a teacher's facilitation.

Pollard introduces another perspective concerning "the burden of knowledge" a text may demand, when she tells us that "the more you know [about literature] the more you can enjoy it". She alludes, in effect, to the breadth of knowledge that the teacher may need to possess for effective teaching – knowledge of literary criticism as well as knowledge drawn from other disciplines. Emphasized is the care the teacher needs to take in the art of teaching literature: selection of teaching strategies, research, immersion in the text, attention to language. "You push the simile until it becomes the thing" is how she describes a literature class observed. Yet it metonymically captures an effective teacher's relation to the teaching of a literature text.

In reflecting on the literature pedagogy of this first generation of native literature teachers, it is clear that at the heart of such pedagogy is deep respect for the student, the art of literature and the learning design itself. Attending to students, validating them, affirming them, allowing them space to voice their response to the text – these are a necessary first step for effective teaching. It is understanding, too, that the teaching of literature is teaching about and for place and people. So students are introduced to literary practices that help them connect at varying levels to the text. The literature text is, moreover, treated as a literary experience, and so students learn how through the arts they can connect with self, others and place. Students, too, are guided into seeing texts as more than the "what"; they are taught also that its "meaning" is closely tied to its structure, its patterns, its language and its context. Perhaps what is most important is learning that the teachers need to teach the text from a position in which they connected with the text, its context and the students.

Baugh, Morris, Pollard and Warner-Lewis have thus laid an important foundation for literature pedagogy. These lecturers have taught and or worked with all the other interviewees. What this second wave of Caribbean teachers has done with this foundation is seen in the next section of *Caribbean Writers on Teaching Literature*.

Edward Baugh

"You have to feel that literature matters."

"I'd like them to feel that the novel or the poem is an experience."

Professor Edward Baugh, lecturer, poet and literary critic, has taught at the University of the West Indies since 1965. His tertiary teaching started six years earlier, in September 1959, at Victoria College (now Victoria University) on Vancouver Island, where he taught for one year. He began teaching at the UWI in January 1965 at Cave Hill, Barbados, and in 1968 he moved to the UWI's Mona campus in Jamaica, from which he retired in 2001. He taught for over thirty-three years at the UWI, Mona. What many may not know, however, is that his teaching began much earlier than 1959, at his alma mater, Titchfield High School. A sixth-former at the time, Baugh received the news that he had won a Jamaica Government Exhibition and would, in a few months, enter the University College of the West Indies. So during those months, at the invitation of his then principal, he taught at Titchfield High School. Baugh recalls that his first experience there was teaching Latin to first-formers. He points out that he himself had learned to relate to Latin as literature because of the newly arrived headmaster's teaching approach. Up until that time, he had studied Latin, had done well in the Latin examination, but had never really understood it. For him, observing teachers, both "good" and "bad", provided him with a foundation for teaching effectively. Another high school teaching stint came much later, after he had completed his master of arts at Queen's University in Canada. Kingston College, a high school for boys in Kingston, Jamaica, became the beneficiary of his additional years of experience. And it was while teaching there that he received a Commonwealth Scholarship to pursue doctoral studies at the University of Manchester, on completion of which he was appointed at the UWI, Cave Hill.

Baugh has published a number of poetry books and critical literary texts, including *Black Sand: New and Selected Poems* (2013) and *Derek Walcott: Memory as Vision – Another Life* (1978).

Q: Professor Baugh, it has often been said that teaching literature well has a lot to do with preparing for the lecture, for the class. How do you prepare for your lectures?

Edward Baugh: The answer to how I prepare for my lectures would, of course, depend on what I am going to lecture on. For example, if I am going to give a lecture at the beginning of a course on a particular author, then more than likely I would begin by having a lecture which is some sort of general introduction to that author, whereas if I am going to prepare to lecture on a particular book, like a novel or some poems, which is what mostly the day-to-day work is, then the preparation is different.

If I am teaching a course on a particular poet, I would give some general sense of the poet, so I would start with that kind of lecture. When I reach the stage of giving lectures week after week on poems, I try to make the students relate to the poems, not just by giving general information about the poems, but by going through the poems with them. Whichever kind of lecture I am doing, and of course it goes without saying, I think beforehand what it is I want to say, what kind of line I want to take, and, for the given lecture I try to get some sense of a structure in my head and make notes to reflect that. I am not one of these people who write out the lecture word for word and then read it. I work from notes. Every now and then I might look down on my paper and read a few sentences strung together, but generally it is notes, and it is a matter that I try to think, say, if I am dealing with the poems, not so much of telling them what they are to think about the poems, though the teacher inevitably does that, but of trying to get them to see how the poem works. I mean, I don't know if there is a difference, but the whole idea is that the students must relate; they must become familiar with the poem or with the novel and go through the experience of relating to it. Then, from another point of view, at another level, when I prepare for a given lecture, I always try to make sure that I have more than enough to say. For instance, with poems, I will try to cover, say, three poems closely in a given lecture. I would prefer to be in a situation where I can't cover the three, or I don't manage to cover the three, rather than be in a situation where I cover the three and there are ten minutes left – so that almost invariably the next time I will be picking up, continuing and finishing off something I did the time before. Those are some of the things about preparing for classes.

Of course, I read the novel or the poem, not just read it, but I read it over and over – though not with novels, as you can't read novels so many times – and then with a novel, I would focus on, say, bits of it, because with novels, I like the students to look at the page, but you can't look at every page of a novel, so I would decide on what bits I would pick out in order to lead them into a sense of the whole novel.

Q: How would you describe your own style of teaching? You have talked about preparing for the lecture, but looking back or even reflecting now on how you teach, how would you describe your style?

E.B.: Well, I suppose for good or ill, one would have to say it's a kind of performative style. In other words, one does not want to make performance distract from substance, but one wants to convey some kind of vibrancy, so that every lecture for me is a kind of performance. Although I'm not setting out to perform, I almost invariably get so involved and so caught up about my feelings and about what I'm talking about, that it comes out in a way that involves animation and gesture and so on. I also like to keep it at a kind of talking-to-other-people level, not a grand theatrical thing but a more intimate kind of level. Those are some of the points I would say about my style. On the business of the performance, one of the things that always pulls me up short when I'm lecturing is that I might suddenly realize that, let us say, two young women sitting beside one another are sort of smiling or even giggling, and at first I think that they're not paying attention to me, and then it hits me that what they're amused at is me. I have mixed feelings, because of course you are glad to know that they are concentrating, but you also wonder if they are being distracted by the performance, so to speak, if they are really paying attention to what I'm saying. I never know, but at least that makes me aware that there's some sort of animation in my style.

Q: Yes, you have a theatre style really.

E.B.: Well, I can't really help it, and as I said, when I speak of performance, even if you are not going to be gesticulating or very animated, the truth is, and people wouldn't believe it, but for every single lecture in a class that I've been teaching for ten weeks or so, I am keyed up beforehand. Just as if I were in a play backstage waiting to go on, I'd be keyed up. It's when I start [teaching] that I relax. My big fear, whether I am making a speech or giving a lecture or whatever . . . what I have to feel before I start, is that I do have something to say. That might seem a silly thing to say, because one always has something to say, but I don't want to say just the routine things. Therefore, until I feel that I have caught that little connection point, that little spark, I don't feel confident. So that sometimes – and this has been a reassurance over the years – I've gone into a lecture when I feel I am totally unprepared, not having anything to say, and most times I come out of that lecture feeling on a high that it has gone exceedingly well.

Q: Let's return now to the actual teaching. When you look back at your teaching, can you recall things that actually worked very well for you? How did you, for example, encourage your students?

E.B.: I don't know how I encouraged them. I feel that I did encourage them when afterwards, or later in life, they meet me and say things that mean they had been encouraged. I even meet people nowadays who are in a crowd, and somebody whom I don't recognize will say, "I was in your class and you did so and so and I will never forget X or Y."

Q: Can you think of things that you deliberately did in order to help the students understand particularly difficult poems, or sections in a novel?

E.B.: Well, with the poems, and I suppose this is part of my teaching method, one of the things that I try to get them to do is to relate to the poem as an experience. One of the challenges that I found increasingly in later years is that so many of them simply want to be told what to say in an exam about a poem or an author. So my great challenge always is to make them come to this knowledge the true way, which is by relating to the poem and discovering that if they do that, they have a wonderful experience, and out of that comes things they can say about the poem – although the things

20

they can say are always there from the beginning, but it is how you relate to the experience that matters. So, for instance, with a poem, one of the things that I do is read the poem aloud, which I believe is a valuable thing, and one of the ways in which I have influenced them is by getting them alert and alive to the poem by hearing it read aloud. One of the sad things about the teaching of poetry in schools is that often the reading of it aloud is lacking. So I read it aloud, and then ask, "Okay, so what is happening here?" And I know the importance of that, because somebody will quickly put up a hand and not tell me what is happening but will try instead to tell me what the theme of the poem is, and I will say, "No, no, you've gone too far. The question is: What is happening here? Where are we? Are we in Moscow, or are we in Port Antonio? Is it a cold day? Who is speaking? Who is the person speaking to?" And we work through the poem in that way. The result is that often they will come up with insights that I had not even thought of.

Q: I always had a sense, though, that one had to be very scholarly in one's response to your questions.

E.B.: Well, perhaps to that extent I might have failed, because I did not want scholarship so much as sensitivity. However, I suppose that feeling that you had, along with others, might come from the fact that perhaps I was able to say so much, which could only have come from long reading and so forth, which then set up in the mind of the student that this is how they ought to [approach literature] too.

Q: This is something that teachers really need to consider. Let's return, however, to your focus on students being sensitive to the poem and "experiencing" the poem. Is this influenced by the fact that you are also a poet? In other words, does your own writing influence the way you teach?

E.B.: I think it must do, certainly with poetry, because one of the things that I am always trying to sensitize the students to is that poems don't just happen. A good poem is something that has been worked at. Students, or most people, will so easily read a poem and take for granted a particular word or image, and I am always trying to ask them why, for instance, does the poet say the person "stalked" rather than "walked" – I mean the person walked, but walked in a certain way. I try to get them to understand that the poet could easily have said "walked", and it would still have been a good poem – but the poet said "stalked", so the poet had made a decision. Thus, my writing of poems sensitizes me to that aspect of the poetry, which I then pass on to them, so that the more they can appreciate that everything involves, even unconsciously, a decision [by the poet], the better they can relate to the poem. So in that sense, at least, I think my own writing of poetry is relevant.

Q: When you look back at your teaching over the years, what memorable moments can you recall?

E.B.: There were loads of them. What I always remember – and it wasn't a particular class – is when I first came to Mona to teach in 1968, I taught for many years Romantic and Victorian literature, and one of my memories of satisfaction was teaching the dramatic monologues of Robert Browning . . . and I remember how many of my former students responded, which lifted me. But, alas, in the whole change of the syllabus and so on, all that went. Up to the other night I was thinking that maybe if I were young again, I could invent a course in the dramatic monologue, because then we could include Browning, Caribbean poets and some of my own poems which are dramatic monologues. I had moments of happiness and satisfaction in the days of the BA degree offered for evening study, where English classes consisted of mainly mature women who were teachers. . . . These students had a seriousness of purpose, a desire to learn, the kind of involvement that many students just take for granted.

Q: Yes. Let's talk now about teaching literary theory. You introduced it in the MA programme, and you taught it. Could you please share with us your thoughts on teaching theory?

E.B.: I regard theory as fun – because it is taken deadly seriously! I taught it; and I taught it, I hope, with some kind of passion. But I never once felt that one had to be steeped in theory in order to be a research scholar, because that notion became the *sine qua non* – that you couldn't write a thesis unless the first chapter set out the theory and cited all the theorists. But people had written excellent theses in generations before which did not do that. There was an author who said we cannot live in theory [and] we cannot live without it. In other words, everybody is a theorist; everything I say implies a theory. I'm an eclectic in that, and I have fun with it, and I have learned all sorts of things from it. What I suppose I believe and try to convey is that theory does not pre-date or precede literature. Theory is like grammar with language; grammar does not precede language – grammar is what you notice in language as a sort of structure by which you can explain it. Similarly, with theory; in a sense I think it is important to disabuse people of the idea that you need theory as theory . . . Like this idea of dismissing the author – the idea that the author is really the product of the structures of meaning. What was always interesting to me is that in the heyday of theory, what it helped people to understand was what they were doing when they related to a work of literature; not that [theory] determined it, but it helped them to understand it. Just as with grammar and English – so many people mistakenly think that you have to learn the grammar of a language before you learn the language.

Q: This takes me to another aspect of literature. Do you see literature as having a political function? Did you ever approach literature in that way?

E.B.: That's one of those important questions, and I suppose some critics of mine would say that I didn't sufficiently treat literature as political, but I want to say that in one sense all literature is political. For instance, this notion of people who think that somebody is not being activist enough in their own poetry or in their teaching of literature and so on. They say, "Oh, he's just 'art for art's sake'", but I've always thought people who were great advocates of the notion of art for art's sake, like Walter Pater and Oscar Wilde, that what this notion meant to them really was art for *life's* sake. With regard to saying that all literature is political, in a poem titled "Truth and Consequences" (relating to a scene from Shakespeare's *Julius Caesar*), I suggested that in a way every line of poetry is political; every line commits you, even the people who sit on the fence – and, as a matter of fact, I would like to write a poem about the courage of sitting on the fence, because the normal view is that those who sit on the fence lack courage. So I'm not political in the sense of taking partisan political sides, but I'm also not a protest poet, because I don't think literature works in that way. It works on people by raising their consciousness, to their sense of the possibility of the human mind, and the sense of the pain of people, even though I have [written] poems that are political in some ways, like "Nigger Sweat" and others.

Q: Yes, I get your point about the politics of literature. It's interesting too what you've said about how literature works. I now want to ask you a question fairly close to this one concerning postcolonialism and a postcolonial approach to literature and Caribbean literature. In terms of your developing courses and teaching literature, how much emphasis did you give to that?

E.B.: Let me start by saying that I don't know if people notice it, but I make a point of avoiding what I call theoretical jargon. So, for instance, the word "postcolonial" in my criticism will hardly appear, although some of the things I am saying may be seen in this light. One does not really need the word, and the word has become a "tyranny" – and because it has a certain set of concepts fitted on to it, once one uses it, it's as if you're imposing those concepts on the writer you are talking about. The challenges with Derek Walcott, for instance, who is obviously postcolonial in all sorts of ways, is, once you've boxed him into that, you miss certain things. To the extent to which the word came to be used in a way of rejection – of "oppositionality", to coin a word – Walcott's relationship with Europe was never that, but it was never as some people seem to think, sucking up to Europe. He was never rejecting the things he learned, but he was never tamely accepting them – he was being himself. In other words, postcolonial became such a tyrant of a word that every so-called postcolonial was required always to be simply rejecting, so I studiously tried to avoid it. There are other words which I try to avoid using – "hegemony" is one of them – because these words tend to become boxes.

Q: I want us to talk about the importance of Caribbean literature. I realize that many students automatically accept Caribbean literature as the norm, whereas when I went to school, there was no "Caribbean literature". That was much later, and there is [now] a kind of taking for granted of all of this literature by Caribbean writers. But on the other hand, I am just wondering if teachers of literature on this side of the world ought not to ensure that we still do non-Caribbean literature. I'm talking about the balance between Caribbean and non-Caribbean literature.

E.B.: This is something I've been thinking about a lot, particularly as it relates to my department. After careful thought, years ago the three departments met, and after some time, we agreed to change the syllabus. When I was a student at Mona, what I was taught was the literature of England from *Beowulf* to T.S. Eliot; and of course West Indian literature in a sense did not exist. It was decided to revise the syllabus and shift the emphasis, and the shift was suggested in the renaming of the Department of English, which would still carry the notion that the literature being taught is the literature of England, but the emphasis was broadened, and the name was changed to the Department of Literatures in English and set up in terms of the genres – poetry, drama et cetera. As the courses were redesigned, a lot of the old courses that we once had were discontinued. For instance, I used to teach, with great joy, Victorian literature, and I deliberately stayed away from West Indian literature, because everybody [colleagues] wanted to teach it. I have a sort of curious history, because I'm known out in the world for my criticism of West Indian literature, but I hardly ever taught it . . .

Regarding the question about what is West Indian literature, one of the things I found very curious is that we tend to think naturally that a West Indian writer must be somebody who is a born West Indian, but then we know there are writers like Paule Marshall, who was born in New York, and Stewart Brown, born in the United Kingdom, whose poetry was once in an anthology of West Indian poetry. It is curious to me that in the world of painting, for example, in Jamaica this distinction is not made. If you pick up a book about Jamaican painting, it will include non-Jamaicans without any explanation or excuse, yet in literature this inclusion would have to be justified. So my short answer to your question is yes, I think maybe there should be more emphasis on non-Caribbean literature.

Q: What do you see as some of the challenges of teaching literature?

E.B.: Well, I've mentioned one or two of them already, but one which I con-sider challenging is the student who simply wants to be told what to say or wants to be referred to a book. At the beginning of a course I will hand out a list of secondary reading of ten or twenty books, which, I say, if you can get them in the library, they will help you, but I try to do that in a way that says *you have to read the text*, and one of the challenges nowadays, I guess, has to do with money, but it also has to do with attitude. For example, I've been teaching for the past few years a Derek Walcott course, and one of the first things I have to do when the course starts is, somehow, without berating them, start impressing upon them to get the book. One of the excuses will be that they can't afford it, and it shows something about attitude, because if they read the book, or are told about the book, they think they don't have to buy the book. So that is a huge challenge.

Q: Do you have any advice about how to deal with this?

E.B.: I should say, by the way, that what is always wonderful is that quite a few of them *will* have bought the book, but one way of dealing with it would be that if I had enough money, I would dish out texts, or if I had an extra copy . . . I once gave a girl one, and she was kind of overwhelmed. So if the department managed to acquire some copies, they could do the same. But I don't know what else one can do, because there are students who eventually go into the exam without having bought the text. What some of them do is photocopy, but all they photocopy, of course, is the particular poems you are dealing with in class, when what I am saying to them is *you have to have the book*. It's not just the poems we talk about in class but the other poems, and you will have the book forever after.

Another challenge, a practical challenge nowadays, which is disheartening, is the business of attendance, because you will be teaching a course of twenty students, and they all profess enthusiasm, and you will find that no two successive lectures will have the same people in it. But they lose out, because what I have created is an integral thing that is built up by a cumulative process, and, as I've said, I'd like them to feel that the novel or the poem is an experience. I'd also like them to think that the course is an experience, but there is no way it can be an experience if they come, at most, to every other class.

Q: It's a different approach, I think, to study.

E.B.: It certainly is, because I can't remember in the old days it was like that.

Q: When I was a student here, there was a lot of passionate discussion about the poetry of Brathwaite and Walcott. People generally saw Walcott as being very difficult to learn. Has the situation changed?

E.B.: I don't really teach Brathwaite, but I teach Walcott, and it's always that Walcott is considered difficult, and one of the satisfactions that I've got all these years is that students will come to me afterwards and say, *you know, I* *thought Walcott was so hard, but you've opened him up to me.* So that has been of great satisfaction. Another point I would like to make on Walcott and Brathwaite is that I think in some ways that [teaching] Brathwaite is more difficult. People begin by assuming that because Brathwaite is all about Africa, he isn't difficult, but they find that when they go to study him, he can seem quite abstruse – and while his language, in a lot of his poetry, is clear, in the later poetry it takes a lot of thinking, studying and even re-search. If you are reading about the Masai, for example, you have to go and read up on things. But people tend to believe that his poetry sounds like it's easy to relate to, but it's not exactly "easy". Another interesting thing about Brathwaite is that he is big on orality, but he has also developed a style that depends heavily on the visual. You have to see how the poem is displayed across the page, which is not oral at all, and sometimes depends a lot on the computer and what you can do with the computer, which is not oral either, and so the situation is complex.

Although Walcott can be difficult, one of the things I try to show them – and it is part of the appreciation of poetry in general – is that one of his outstanding characteristics is his use of imagery, the layering. You can get so many layers of connotation in the image. In teaching Walcott, I always have to stress, and sometimes some of them did not appreciate it, the differ-ence between the denotative meaning of words and the connotative mean-ing. And the same thing applies in poetry in general; the connotative is of more importance, although the denotative is necessary.

Another challenge is that of punctuation, where a poem is written with-out punctuation marks, and the students will interpret this as one that moves along quickly, but the fact may be that it sometimes does the op-posite – and they try to make statements to which I respond by saying that if there is nothing worth saying about punctuation in the poem, then don't say it. But they were taught that you must say things about imagery, punctuation, and so on, so they say things. I have to stress that it is the poem in front of them that will really dictate the kinds of things they need to say. Another challenge I have, for example, in teaching Walcott, is that naturally in order to teach, you have to arrange things. That is why essays are written in paragraphs. It helps you to take in ideas and structure them. So I may talk first about poems that deal with Caribbean history and slavery and so on, and then poems that deal with universal topics. What starts to happen is that they, the students, read four or five poems about slavery and colonialism – and then we go to another poem [which is unrelated to Caribbean history], but they will "find" slavery and colonialism [in it], because their heads are now full of that – to which I have to say *no, those things are not there, you are including what is not there*. So, going back to challenges in teaching, those were some of the specific practical challenges. And talking now about novels, one of my methods when I teach novels – and you cannot go through the novel in detail in class – is to pick out a page and go through it in detail and show them how you could work through that passage to bring in the whole novel.

Q: Do they respond satisfactorily, even though some of them have not completed the reading?

E.B.: At least what I have done is make them focus on a page which they would not otherwise have focused on. What I have tried to show them is that if they stop and look at any page closely, then the whole novel is in that page.

Q: My last question. What has been for you, as a teacher of literature, the joy of teaching literature?

E.B.: What can I say but just teaching it! The point is that I love literature, so the joy is being able to stand up in front of people and talk about it.

Q: Is that an end in itself, or is that a means to anything?

E.B.: Well, it can't be an end in itself. The end is to help them in some way to be better people. It may sound vague and attitudinal, but that is the end; otherwise why have I spent my life teaching literature? In other words, one is always resisting this. This is the challenge to teaching literature, that there is this feeling out there that it is only some hobby that people do; so always one labours under that consciousness. I have a poem I wrote recently which is called "What's Poetry For?" It eventually talks about how frustrated I became in trying to find some fetching answer – and so the poem ends, *and so we slunk away, the poem and I, to nurse our dream of heaven, a place where no one asks what's poetry for.*

It all came out of a PBS [programme] that used to have five-minute segments on days where they interviewed a poet . . . and one night I was watching the programme, and the poem was excellent, and just when the programme was closing off, the interviewer asked, "So what would you say that poetry is for?" I was sure the man knew, but he floundered around and said nice things. That was what provoked my poem.

Q: Any final word of advice to people entering the field of teaching literature?

E.B.: One thing I would say to begin is that you have to love literature – you have to feel that it matters. I guess it is possible that somebody may be a good literature teacher who doesn't love literature and doesn't feel that it matters, but that is hard to imagine.

Mervyn Morris

"Listening is the most important part of tutoring –
listening and re-directing as far as you can."

Professor Mervyn Morris first taught literature in 1957, after graduating from the University College of the West Indies (the precursor to the University of the West Indies), at Munro College, a boarding school for boys in Jamaica. At that time he taught mainly the middle forms – and not only literature, but mainly English language. He left after a year to pursue studies from 1958 to 1961 in England. On his return to Jamaica, he served for a year as an assistant registrar at the UCWI/UWI. In 1962 he returned to teaching, this time as senior English master at Munro. His teaching was interrupted for only a few years, when he became warden of Taylor Hall at Mona in 1966. In 1970 he began lecturing in the Department of English at the UWI, Mona. He retired in 2002.

Morris, who was appointed Poet Laureate of Jamaica in 2014, has published volumes of poetry and critical literary texts including, *I been there, sort of: New and Selected Poems* (2017) and *Miss Lou: Louise Bennet and Jamaican Culture* (2014).

Q: Professor Morris, would you say that you have a particular style of teaching literature?

Mervyn Morris: Teaching literature or teaching creative writing? I suspect I'm better at teaching creative writing than any other kind of teaching – but then you mean teaching literature; let's focus on that. In the university context, there is lecturing and there is tutoring, and those are somewhat different skills.

Q: Tell me about how you see yourself as a lecturer and then as a tutor.

M.M.: I think I'm a useful lecturer, and I sometimes lecture from notes, but I often write out the lecture and read it, though I try to be alert to my audience. Well, I think the most fundamental training if you're doing literature should be in what to do if you are confronted with a text with nobody telling you about it. In other words, ideally, if you keep focusing on texts, you will probably find that people become more and more comfortable with reading what they haven't heard anything about. I think the real challenge in teaching literature is to help people to read independently so that they are quite comfortable to say what they think, giving reasons and evidence from time to time. I enjoy tutoring very much. I suppose because there is more interchange. I know that lecturers – and some very good lecturers – can build interchange into their lectures.

Q: You used to do this, actually. That's what I remember about your lectures.

M.M.: Well, yes, by stopping and asking questions and so on.

Q: Yes, more than that – teasing out responses from us.

M.M.: Yes, well, sometimes you're there and you see something on a face that is saying, *I don't think that makes sense*, in which case you would try and see what it is you said that was not very sensible. One of the things about lecturing – and it's much truer of tutoring – is that you have to pay attention to who the students are and where they are in relation to what you are doing, so that it's not just a matter of engaging them, it's a matter of paying attention to where they think they are. Sometimes a student will give a body language sign that says, "Why are you going on like this on this point, and do you really think it's of any importance?" – and then you try to relate to that. I was wrong to say that lectures are not interactive – they can be interactive, but I much prefer the tutorial situation where, if the tutorial is going very well, the tutor may say very little, and what the tutor does is listen and redirect and make sure that everyone is having fun while learning.

Q: Yes, let's talk more about having fun as part of teaching. When Dennis Scott taught me at drama school, he told us that we have to make sure to focus, to upgrade the student, to clarify and to provide kicks for them. I remember, too, that we thought of you and your classes as always having this element of fun. Do you plan for it? Or is it just part of your personality?

M.M.: Well, I think it should be fun if you can manage that. But no, I didn't plan for it usually, and in fact the best fun usually doesn't come from anything the tutor would have thought of before, but from the tutor or others in the room being alert to what is actually going on in the room. So that's one of the things. But another thing, of course, which is even more important, is that, as you know, teaching is the encouragement of learning. In other words, it's not [so much] about what you teach, it's about what people learn. One of the most important things about helping people learn is that sometimes there are people who don't realize how bright they are or can be, and, if you are really listening, you will often find that some students who are, by all the statistical records, average, from time to time have terrific insights, and if you move the insights around, the students who thought of themselves as being just one of them there would probably feel better about themselves. Listening is the most important part of tutoring – listening and redirecting as far as you can. The worst tutorials are the ones where students seem unwilling to talk.

Q: Can you recall memorable moments, sessions, periods of teaching – and what made them memorable for you?

M.M.: Well, lectures – and I don't know why this has come up into my head, because I never even published an article on it – but I think one of the best sets of lectures I've ever given was to first-year students, on Lovelace's *Wine of Astonishment*, which is a book I like a lot. It's an important book, and so well organized. People, I think, responded well to it. I remember that one of my bright students later (and he didn't tell me this; somebody else did) was expressing disappointment after hearing me lecture in another year, because the kind of care and thoroughness and interest, I suppose, that I had managed on that earlier occasion wasn't quite there on some of the other occasions. The absolutely crucial thing is the extent of the preparation, so that sometimes while you give a lecture that you think is adequate, it is not something that you care greatly about, and it may also be something about which you know that other people have written quite well, so that you do some synthesizing to point towards criticism the students may find helpful. But that's rather less exciting, I think, than when you find a work you admire and are able to take it apart in a way that you haven't seen it taken apart.

Do you know a lecture that I remember very vividly? Gloria Lyn on *Interim* by Neville Dawes. It is a book I like, and I thought that she did an extremely good job on that. It's mostly about preparation.

Q: How do you actually prepare? What do you do?

M.M.: You mean lecturing?

Q: Yes, and even tutorials.

M.M.: The ideal preparation for tutorials is to have reread the text fairly recently; not much else matters to me. But of course if it's a text that you've also been lecturing on, you would probably be very clear that there are certain areas that you want them to focus on. For example, if you are talking about Lamming's *In the Castle of My Skin*, you certainly want them to be aware of the various shifts in the storytelling approach. Read and reread. There is also some very necessary "journeyman" stuff. That is to say, if it's a text that is well travelled by good criticism, then you want to at least introduce them to the criticism, without letting them feel that they don't have to go and read it themselves.

Q: Could you please elaborate?

M.M.: Introduce them to the criticism without being so full in your introduction that they think they don't have to go and read it. It's important to stimulate their interest, and to leave them work to do, but also not to do it for them, because there are some very effective teachers who I would say, in my view, do too much for the student. The student must be given some of the stuff to do.

Q: When did you begin writing poetry?

M.M.: I wrote light verse when I was a boy at Munro, and I continued at UCWI. By the time I graduated I had tried to write some more serious things, but the earliest poems that made it into any of my books were written in England, perhaps in 1960.

Q: Does the fact that you're a poet make your teaching of poetry more interesting, easier, the preparation work less, perhaps, extensive?

M.M.: No, it wouldn't make it less extensive. And a lot depends on the nature of the poetry. You may enjoy Milton, or you may love John Donne, but there is so much scholarship involved in understanding what they are actually doing. It may be helpful to be a poet in terms of the extent of the pleasure that poetry may give you and which pleasure you may be able to communicate, but literature, especially literature of the kind that people think may be good to have as an exam text, nearly always has a burden of knowledge. In other words, there's stuff to enjoy, but there's also a lot of stuff to know; and if you don't know [it], then there are things that you're going to get horribly wrong.

Q: Because you are a poet, though, do you come to poetry with greater insight and understanding of the way it all hangs together, the way it comes together? And, therefore, knowing it from the inside out, do you teach it better?

M.M.: I really don't know. But what I know is that – it's not a matter of being a published poet. John Lennard, who taught literature here at Mona, had his first-year poetry students doing creative writing in their introductory poetry course. That's one of the ways to foster understanding. Even if people aren't writing well, there are certain kinds of insight they may gain from the attempt, which people who are trying to write poetry on a regular basis probably would have and take for granted. I'm often surprised when I hear a misquotation from poetry which is not only a misquotation but is rhythmically bizarre in relation to what has been misremembered. Most poets wouldn't do that. They would probably get the rhythm right.

Q: So, the rhythm is a key element for you, then, in the teaching of poetry?

M.M.: One of the elements that matter. Ambiguity is another. Sometimes it's clear that the poet wants an image to point in multiple directions, making the language do more than it would do as an ordinary work-a-day thing. Controlling multiple meanings may be one of the ways of enriching poetry. But rhythm is at the heart of the enjoyment of poetry.

Q: And it's also important to pay attention to verbal play and manipulation.

M.M.: When I came to Mona as a student, one of the required courses was on the metaphysical poets – Donne, Herbert, Marvell. It was taught by Professor Croston. One of the key critics at that time would have been Cleanth Brooks, who was showing how words were being so carefully chosen that they were carrying several different meanings. Remember that all of this came out of the Cambridge thing of practical criticism with I.A. Richards and so on, who felt that there had been too many people talking in a general way about the lives of poets and not paying enough attention to the text, and it was amazing the things they could get wrong if you put a text in front of them. Also Croston knew that you can hold people's interest by going in detail through a poem and isolating particular effects, and getting people to realize that although they had read the text several times, there was more there than they had seen, and what a pleasure it was. So my interest is very often in verbal richness.

Q: You tell me that you like teaching creative writing best. Could you share a little bit about how you approach that and why it is you like it? Is it because you are a creative writer?

M.M.: Yes, it may be partly because I'm a creative writer. I wonder whether a creative writing workshop could be a success without people thinking that they were having fun. One of the things that I enjoy doing is helping people make what they have done better by developing a skill that helps them to see what is the best thing in what they have drafted, and to either allow that to direct them towards how they are going to continue the poem or to realize what is the kernel. You write something that you really felt, for maybe twenty-five or thirty lines, and somewhere in that draft there may be four or five lines where something happens that you didn't even know was happening, and where somebody else in the workshop might say *I especially like that* or whatever, and you come to realize that's where the heart of the poem is.

One of the key things which is very hard to teach, but sometimes you can help people recognize it, is that if you are all the time in intellectual control, you're probably not going to be very good. There's a Jamaican poet who, years later, thanked me for a mysterious comment I made. I'd said to her, "You know, you need to write more foolishness." In other words, a lot of the good stuff in the poems will not be what you are consciously monitoring but what you've allowed to emerge from levels that you are not fully in control of at the time when you drafted them, and if you're lucky you can look at a thing and see that maybe this is where the poem really is and develop that or cut away other things and so on.

A lot of people write repetitively and don't even know it. It can be useful to have somebody say to you, "You've said this in line 3, so why are you going on and on? Do you think that that is important?" That, in a sense, is why sometimes if you keep hacking away at the poem, it ends up very short – though this is not something to be recommended all the time. You can't cut and cut and cut forever, because very short poems only work if there's a certain tension that has been retained in what remains. So in a sense – and you asked about rhythm much earlier – rhythm is fundamental, and rhythm is controlled in part by the way you break the line. A fundamental difference between verse and prose is that in prose you write until the space runs out and then you go to the next line. In verse, you choose where the line should break, and it can be broken for several different reasons.

Q: What has it been like teaching drama, and what is your approach to teaching it? Were you in acting as well?

M.M.: Yes, but not for long. I acted in school. At Munro we had a very good drama teacher – the headmaster's wife, Mrs Daphne Ward, who had had some drama training – and when I came here to Mona I acted in my first year, but not after that. I acted in *The Lady's Not for Burning* by Christopher Fry. But because of the extent of my interest in sport, I didn't have the time for that, as I was doing academic work as well.

Q: But you paid a lot of attention to theatre.

M.M.: I love theatre.

Q: How did that affect your teaching of drama in your lectures? Did you prepare differently?

M.M.: No, the main thing I tried to do in teaching drama was to make the drama present. Not so much by trying to do it on stage, as more often by introducing videos, especially when I was lucky enough to be able to find two contrasting productions available. Watching *Othello* as played by Laurence Olivier and by Willard White can get people interested in differences of approach. Much too often you are teaching drama to a class where 50 per cent or more in the class have never seen a play, and it is hard to persuade them that they really ought to. One of the things that you do is try to enliven things by giving them a sense of what the body language might do, especially when you've been lucky enough, for example, to see a really fine production of that play that does not happen to be available to them, and then you can remind them of how a particular moment could be.

For example, in one production of Trevor Rhone's *Old Story Time*, a memorable moment for me was when Charles Hyatt as Pa Ben responds to Len claiming not to care what happens to his mother ("she must bear the consequences"). Pa Ben, who as you know is the soul of kindness and all that, raises his arm as if he will strike Len, and then the arm comes down slowly in a gesture of blessing. It was wonderful.

Something I do remember doing again, and it's very often based on the things I've enjoyed in productions I happen to have seen – I remember teaching *Dream on Monkey Mountain*, and I thought Errol Jones's Makak was really extraordinary. When Makak, transforming himself, moves from monkey into King, it's all in the upper body, really. "Saddle my horse!" he says. It's important, I think, to show students that theatre is more than words.

Q: In general, what have you found most satisfying about teaching literature, and drama in particular?

M.M.: Bright people: when you find them, you applaud. Another satisfaction is the kind of student who is attentive enough to learn from almost every hint you offer, and you can see them growing before your eyes.

Respect is absolutely crucial. The good students, the mediocre students and the weak students, they all know who respects them, and maybe even likes them; and when you get a student who has felt validated, you know that something good is going to continue to happen, because, without sounding pompous, teaching is not about subjects as much as it is about people and the way you are lucky enough to get them to interact. And, of course, more satisfying than almost anything, is to be teaching creative writing and to recognize real talent and to encourage it and then to see it bloom. People keep thanking you one way or another, but often you haven't done very much except say, "Wow!"

Q: The next question is closely aligned to the previous: Why teach literature? I mean, obviously it matters – you've been teaching it for so long. Why does it matter, or what makes it matter?

M.M.: Well, it matters because it nearly always embodies and examines values, and it gives pleasure. The old Horace: "To instruct and to delight."

Q: Yes. Any advice for beginning teachers of literature? What do they need to have?

M.M.: Well, keep rereading the books. Another thing is, listen and encourage listening, which relates, I guess, to what I said about people and respect. Respect sounds a little pompous almost – it's not exactly what I mean. You should try to like the people you're dealing with – it helps.

Velma Pollard

"Teaching literature is about bringing the text up close."

"Every line that a writer puts down has 'stuff' behind it."

Dr Velma Pollard has been teaching literature since 1959. Having just completed her degree and diploma in education that year, she began teaching English at Kingston College, a high school for boys in Jamaica. Thereafter she taught both Spanish and English at St George's College, a government high school in Trinidad, for five years, followed by high school Latin and English in Montreal for a year. Returning home to Jamaica, she taught English for a year at Knox College, a co-ed high school in Jamaica. This was a short stint, as she soon left for New York, where she worked four years, first at Consolidated Edison, Inc. (Con Edison), the light and power company, where she taught English to minority employees in a high school equivalency programme, then for two years at Hunter College in New York. On her return to the Caribbean, she taught at the University of Guyana, where she prepared teachers to teach English at both elementary and secondary levels. In 1975, she joined the staff of the University of the West Indies at Mona, where she taught both English literature and language education.

Pollard is the author of several collections of poetry, novels and critical literary texts. Her novel *Karl and other Stories* won the Casa de las Américas Prize in 1992. Other works include *And Caret Bay Again: New and Selected Poems* (2013) and *Considering Woman 1 & 2: Short Stories* (2010).

Q: Dr Pollard, what do you like about teaching literature?

Velma Pollard: What do I like about teaching literature? I like to teach literature because I was very well taught literature, and I feel that I have a duty to make some other people enjoy it as much as I was made to enjoy it, certainly in high school. I feel I am giving back. Many people don't like literature, and I believe that it is because they have not been well taught – though that may not be true.

Q: In light of that, tell us about how you prepare for your literature classes.

V.P.: First, one of the things I find is that literature is out there, a sort of isolated thing in a sense. When you pick up a text of any sort, it is in a void, really. So you have to give people some kind of context. Background information is important – and I don't mean background information about the particular poem or the particular book, but about the time it was being written. For example, one of my favourite poems outside of Caribbean literature is Matthew Arnold's "Dover Beach". If you don't know what the clash of arms at night is about, you will still enjoy the poem, you know, but the more you know, the more you can enjoy it. I'll also give you an example of teaching a poem called "The Cherry Tree" – at KC [Kingston College], before I had travelled to North America or anywhere cold – and teaching it in Montreal. There is a line: *to see the cherry hung with snow*. I could give the KC boys a good enough idea – and if you happen to have a lot of imagination you would give the students a good idea. But there in Canada, where the snow literally clings to the cherry tree, you understand *the cherry hung* – the choice of that verb, all that becomes graphic when you know what you're talking about. And I can do that now for a child who has not seen snow, because I have had the experience. I can explain exactly how it is and, in a sense, validate the use of that verb. I can give the class the context of its use.

Look at all those British novels that we're teaching where you talk about somebody hiding on the downs. People have no idea what the downs look like, and yet it's not difficult to get a film from the British Council, or something – all schools have those now – that kind of visual material is available, and the farther away you are from the location where the piece is set, the more important it is.

I had been trying to teach Caribbean literature in Richmond, Virginia, some years ago. It meant that I had to have visual and audio help. To teach Walcott's poem "Spoiler's Return", for example, I had to help students figure out who Spoiler is and where he stands among the calypsonians, as well as what his particular style is. So that when Walcott tries to reproduce Spoiler's style, they can recognize it. If they didn't, they wouldn't get it, wouldn't get what the poem is saying, and it's such a magnificent poem. I used calypso music and told them about carnival and the calypso tents as background in order for it all to make sense.

Q: I think that teachers today sometimes think, if it's a Caribbean poem . . .

V.P.: . . . everybody knows.

Q: Yes, everybody knows.

V.P.: It's not true. The Caribbean is large, and everybody picks out a particular little thing to write about. When Walcott writes about theatre in Trinidad, I know what he is talking about – I lived in Trinidad for five of the years when he was working in theatre there. I think it behoves the teacher to do the research to see what he is talking about. Every line that a Caribbean poet or a Caribbean writer, indeed any writer, puts down has "stuff" behind it that the writer is aware of or may have experienced. Another person may not have experienced just that – that thing. I am very aware of how much can get lost.

Q: How do you get students involved?

V.P.: I really try to select material that relates to their lives when I can. I remember for example that on Valentine's Day, I used to have a set of poems – Louise Bennett's "Love Letter" was one, and one by John Betjeman beginning "Miss Joan Hunter Dunn . . .", which was one of my favourite poems. Actually, it is called "A Subaltern's Love Song". Love poems, I would just share them with the class and have them bring their own choices to share with us.

I say Valentine's Day, but I also might take National Heroes' Day or something like that. I would always have some Claude McKay poems or some poems that really touch us in a more personal way, and I find that the poem is not so far removed. Nothing that we have to teach needs to be far removed, if we find a way to bring it up close. This means that teachers have to read widely.

Q: Can you recall any lesson or lessons that were particularly memorable?

V.P.: Well done?

Q: Yes.

V.P.: I'm thinking of a lesson that Peter Maxwell taught. It was Papine Secondary School, and he was teaching metaphors and similes to a grade 9 class, I think. He started with having the class go outside and write down some things they saw. It might look simple, but everybody wrote down something. Then inside the classroom he could move on to, for example, "Grass that looks like so and so . . ." One thing is that he got them out of the classroom. The other thing is that he got them to understand what a simile is. Then he showed them what a metaphor is – a kind of reality: you push the simile until it becomes the thing. Then he would teach them how to use these in their own writing. And I just thought that was such a novel way of teaching figurative language.

Q: Yes. What about in your own teaching experience? Is there anything that was particularly memorable?

V.P.: No, if I remember something it would be because it was bizarre – like an experience in a workshop in Trinidad, using Walcott's "The Light of the World". It starts with an invocation from Bob Marley's "Kaya": "Kaya now, got to have Kaya now / Got to have Kaya now / For the rain is falling." Well, of course, before I could teach that poem, I would have to find out why Kaya. I was explaining to the teachers that if you go to Bob Marley's record "Kaya", it is about Bob going back to his neighbourhood. Two of the lines strongly indicate this: "I feel so good / In my neighbourhood." Walcott is writing about going back to St Lucia, being there and getting on a minibus, coming from Gros Islet, going into town [Castries] and hearing that poem – that song on the minibus stereo. The whole thing comes together because Bob is writing about feeling good in his neighbourhood, and Walcott is trying to feel good in his neighbourhood. In fact, the poem is really about how good he was trying to feel – and it didn't work, for many reasons. In fact, when he comes off the minibus, he doesn't come off at a home, he comes off at a hotel. He is a guest, not a resident.

Come question time, a teacher stood up and asked me if I didn't feel that I was encouraging the students to smoke ganja. They really lost me that time.

Q: Yes, I can see why you would call that bizarre.

V.P.: Another thing that I remember is trying to teach an English novel, I can't remember which one, in Trinidad. I was teaching in a school where I would say 75 per cent of the students were Indian – mostly Hindu – and one of the lines in the novel is something about every heathen who ever prayed to Juggernaut. Juggernaut is a senior Hindu god – and I had to apologize to the class for the arrogance of the British empire, you know. You just can't let stuff like that pass. So those things I remember.

Q: In talking about the matter of challenges and memorable sessions, you identify how important it is to share background information with your students. That is clearly one strategy. Another strategy you mention is the idea of ensuring that you're relating the poem to what's happening in the students' lives.

V.P.: Well, in a way, yes. All of which is about bringing it up close. Now it is also true that you can read many texts and not understand much of what they are saying. But, you know, you really need to get it at different levels. I taught a course once, and one of the things I was doing was showing the teachers how it was possible for an author to write and leave out the landscape and the people in it.

Q: Could you please elaborate?

V.P.: When I was teaching that course, it was in a foreign country, Italy, and one of the things I was looking at was how a writer can write people *out* of the text. I used a piece from a text written from a colony; it's a British colonial experience, and there's this female character who is writing home to England about how bored she is. She looks out, and she sees a canoe on the river. Now the only thing she identifies in that landscape is a bird that sounds like the English nightingale. The only reason she picks it out is that it sounds like something from home. You would read that piece and have no idea of what is on the ground there, but when I put a microscope to it, I could show them that there is somebody in that canoe – who is he? This is a native, but as far as she's concerned, the native does not exist except as maybe the boy to sweep her house. So you can pick up all kinds of things by what is said, and by what is not said in many of the texts. It was important for me to help a class of European teachers discover what is really in that text.

So the whole business of looking at text becomes a different exercise from just reading it and seeing what's there. I think that this kind of engagement with the text can be more interesting to the students than a lot of other material that we bring to them, like constantly telling them to look for similes and metaphors. If you don't say what the simile or the metaphor is doing, you are wasting your time. What is it *doing*?

Okay, so this thing sounds to her like the English nightingale. What is that telling you about her? I don't think people put in those figures of speech just so; they are put there to enrich the text.

The other thing is that people who write take a lot of time and trouble to choose the right word, and I think you have to respect it. I mean, students will tell me, "It don't mean nothing, Miss, it's just poetic licence." Who ever invented that phrase? What is taken for granted is that a poet can write anything, [but] I know that sometimes you don't get the right word for years. Sometimes a poem cannot move from your desk for a very long time until you get it right. For somebody else to look at it and say it is poetic licence – because they don't want to take the trouble to try to figure out what it means or what it might mean – is a bit of an insult.

Q: Would you say that you have a particular teaching style – when you're teaching literature?

V.P.: No, I think I teach everything the same way. What I mean is, whatever I do for literature, I think I do for language too, but I do a lot of teaching language through literature.

Q: Would you like to talk a little bit about that, then?

V.P.: Well, because, you see, I think that literature is language in use, and one of the problems we have in teaching people to write is that they are not writing useful things. For example, "Write about yourself as a dog." You know, if you think of the things you ask children to write! So I like to use – I think I always use – pieces of literature to identify how you use the language. Nearly everything is literature, history, home economics. You can use the text of other disciplines. To me, using the text is an obvious thing to do, because you're helping the person who teaches that text, and you're helping yourself teach English. Students are getting a kind of double exposure to the content.

Q: So, did you pull material, for example, from home economics texts when you were teaching language or teaching literature?

V.P.: Yes, it depends on the class. You can use chemistry and you can use baking. In chemistry, for example, you never *throw* anything away unless you are getting rid of it, because you are finished with it, and then you throw it away. You *pour* liquid into a container. If you look in the textbooks, you get a lot of information about how language works in each. There's so much that students can get from us. I think that a lot of what has helped me is just watching people teach, noticing what's not happening and what students are not picking up. Then you think about it and get more ideas.

Q: Do you make a distinction between teaching poetry, prose, drama?

V.P.: Yes. We have to see that poetry, prose and drama are all very different. Poetry is so economical. You know, prose explains more things. Drama – you really need to be able to visualize it.

Q: What advice would you give young teachers about teaching poetry, for example?

V.P.: Teach poems that you like. And one of the first things that they have to be able to do is to try to identify what is a good poem, what is a well-written poem. A student once told me that she was writing a lesson plan but would be late, because she was rushing to finish a poem she wanted to use in it. I said, "Bake me a cake, make me a cake – don't make me a poem. I don't want any poem that you just made –I don't want it. I want a cake that you just made, I don't want a poem [you just made]. A poem needs far more time than that. You have to look it over several times till you are happy with it."

I'd say, if you're going to teach a poem to a class, please don't just wake up one morning and open the book and go to the class. I would say to teachers, and I say it all the time, whenever you see a class going well, believe me, it has been well prepared. Nothing happens by chance, and the better you prepare, the more likely it is that the class will go well.

Maybe none of those strategies that you write down will work for that class. What you have to learn to do is to think – think on your feet, almost. Allow yourself to look to see what is necessary, what you have to do, what might have good results, and you try it out – and if it works, then fine. If it doesn't work, then it doesn't.

Q: You said earlier that a good lesson is a well-prepared lesson. How does the teacher prepare?

V.P.: The first thing the teacher has to do is read the poem. She has to read it a number of times, for one thing, and I don't think this is just a strategy, it is a *sine qua non* – you can't [teach] without doing that. And make sure that there's nothing in there that you don't really get. Or if there's anything that you don't get, you're going to have to be up front with the students and let them know that you're really not sure what that part of the poem is about – and nothing is wrong with that. You know how many teachers wake up in the morning and open the book and say, "This is what I'm going to teach today"? Don't do that.

I really think that taking care and working hard is a strategy. And, you know, it doesn't really mean you have to be totally focused on it. You could be hushing your baby and looking at the poem. You could be ironing and thinking about it. You then can go into the class feeling confident.

Q: That is true. The teacher needs to read the poem several times.

V.P.: You need to understand and get a feeling for it. How else are you going to get somebody else to get into it if you can't get into it? It's just not possible.

Q: What are some of the things that you've noticed that young teachers need?

V.P.: They need to read more widely, and I really believe that they have to know English. You know, there's the whole business of the careless pronunciations, for example. You can understand how many of the rhymes they miss, because they're not pronouncing the words right; how many relationships between words they miss, because they don't know the meanings and don't take the trouble to check them out.

I have an example, but it is from a translation exercise. There's a Brathwaite poem that talks about a Jack Spaniard. Do you know what a Jack Spaniard is? It's a kind of wasp. I don't know if we don't have them or that is not what we call them – it's a wasp in the eastern Caribbean. Somebody translated it as *jaca español* – Spanish donkey. Now, if in the poem what you're to visualize is a wasp and what you're visualizing is a donkey, that's lost, you know! It's gone. So, I'm just saying that familiarity with words and with language is necessary for understanding a poem.

I've had some sort of frightening experiences here, for example, in teaching "As John to Patmos", another Walcott poem. It begins with those words, part of a simile, a comparison. I remember one lady taking me all through Revelations and losing Walcott completely. She went straight for the Bible in a very narrow way. She didn't see anything else, not the "As" at the beginning, nor the "So am I" later. I mean, that poem is about love for his native land and commitment to it.

I keep saying that people have to read beyond the Bible, and that is a danger in our very religious society. The Bible is a great book, but if that's the only book you are reading, you're in big trouble. I think one of the things we have to do is get the students away from this narrowness.

Q: Elaine Showalter talks about teacher anxieties in a book called *Teaching Literature*. One is "teacher isolation".

V.P.: We don't have to operate in isolation. Even within the same school people don't know what their neighbours, who are teaching the same book, are doing. We could get together and talk about it.

Q: Any last comment you want to make about teaching literature?

V.P.: Yes, it's a pity that more people are not given the chance to love literature. I know a young man who got the text on Monday and by Tuesday he was doing a test on it, and I know the teacher would not have read it yet. I remember too when my daughter was a child, they would give her all of twenty questions on one chapter of the novel they were reading, and do the same with each chapter. How you get the sense of a story that way I don't know. I think teaching literature has become like having a set of comprehension tests, and that is not right – that's just not right.

Q: So, in a sense, I suppose you're reminding us how important it is to try to create the literature experience and the love of literature?

V.P.: Right, they have to love it.

Maureen Warner-Lewis

"Literature develops your awareness of patterns of
human actions and behaviours."

Professor Maureen Warner-Lewis has been involved in teaching literature for more than thirty-five years. She began teaching in 1970, and for thirty-three years taught literature at the University of the West Indies at Mona, Jamaica. Before that, from about 1968, she taught literature at the secondary school level in Trinidad for a year. She also taught language and literature at the secondary school level in Nigeria for approximately two years.

A professor of African Caribbean language and orature, Warner-Lewis has received a number of book awards. Her publications include *Central Africa in the Caribbean: Transcending Time, Transforming Cultures* (2003) and *Guinea's Other Suns: The African Dynamic in Trinidad Culture* (1991).

Q: Professor Warner-Lewis, how did you generally prepare for your literature classes?

Maureen Warner-Lewis: Well, my main focus has always been the text itself, and my preparation depended on what particular aspect of literature I was going to teach, whether it was literary appreciation or genre, you know, whether it was a novel, drama, poetry, whatever. Or, when I moved into orature, I moved into somewhat more theoretical approaches, moved away from text-based literary analysis to discourse analysis, and then performance strategies. And then graduate work also involved a different level of preparation. But the preparation would involve the reading of the text for myself at least twice. The best thing is to read twice and to underline or highlight the important conversations, the important words, repeated ideas and things like that, as you're trying to grasp certain aspects of the structure, the themes of the work. So this would apply whether one was preparing a genre text or a poem, or a literary appreciation.

Then I would go on to read up something on the background of the author, which helps you to understand the concerns of the writer, the landscape, or anything which might influence the work in some way. Of course, along with the physical landscape there's also the social landscape, the social and personal concerns of the writer. Then you would define the major and minor themes based on your highlighting of various things and what you have read about the author. And you would also examine the relationship of characterization to themes: how did the characterization help to bring across, convey the thematic concerns of the writer? The relationship of the language to the theme(s) is also important, and so too is the examination of metaphorical language. I would also identify passages containing significant information on themes and on structure.

I am particularly fascinated with structure, and when I talk about challenges, this is one. To identify the themes is easy, but to understand what in the structure highlights, emphasizes, underlines the themes, that is harder and generally students don't want to take the trouble to look at that. They would go at the theme but want to say nothing about how language or choice of verbs/words creates mood – the *why* and the *how*. They want to remain with the *what*.

Q: Your fascination with structure – was that because of your linguistic interest and background?

M.W-L.: I don't necessarily think so. It may have been reinforced by the linguistic interest, but I think that the way that I was taught literature focused me on structure. I think we were always made to relate the theme to the structure, to say where the structure was in some way dissonant with the theme; if there was a dissonance, why? Was this the vehicle for sarcasm or satire? What I've noticed about myself in recent years is that I'm interested in patterns. It's something I have never explored artistically, but I am interested in patterns. There's something in me that responds to structure. I suspect that that may be why I am interested in how a work or piece of embroidery or anything is patterned: what are the shapes and repeated motifs that emerge? That probably accounts for my fascination with geometry at secondary school.

Q: Yes, I can see how that works with literature. Is attending to the structure of the work very important for you?

M.W-L.: Yes. The structure could also be responsible for the failure of the work. A work may fail because its patterning is not compatible with what the writer wanted to say. There's a deliberate dissonance, disagreement between the mood and what the writer wants to say. But certain patterns may make the work better, that is, more aesthetically satisfying.

Yes, so to my mind, understanding the text for myself was important, and on several occasions I had to point out to classes that they repeated opinions that critics had which were not supported or which were undercut by what was in the text, because either [students] hadn't taken the time to read the text or they didn't want to examine it. I don't know what it is, perhaps some shortcut method of theirs. They want to use the critics' opinions as the first line of approach; they shouldn't want to rely on other people's opinions so heavily that they don't feel themselves capable of even finding their own examples to support a particular viewpoint.

Something that puzzled me – one year, a past student of ours was sent to find out what we had on such and such a book. Even though she was familiar with the author, she was not able to transfer, or did not feel confident enough to transfer what she knew about one book to the other. One needs to be brave enough to see authors changing their opinions on a particular subject. One text is not going to be exactly like the other text, but if it's by the same author, then there are going to be some basic similarities somewhere that can guide you in approaching a new text. So that was my preparation – some background work, as well as my own work.

Q: How would you describe your teaching style? I just wondered if you worked by bringing in music, bringing in pictures, using film, talking about the writer. Or, given your interest in the structure of the work, did you introduce the work by having your students look at the structure? How would you introduce the work?

M.W-L.: I would start usually with the author and something about the social or historical background, and then I would go to the theme or themes, then eventually I would work around to structure. So I didn't use structure first. In terms of getting the students involved, particularly in the 1970s, I used film as much as possible, because in those days we didn't have video.

But I was disappointed that some students felt that when they knew there was going to be a film, they would absent themselves – and instead of looking at the glass as half full, I would become deflated by the glass half empty. You see, it was so difficult to use reels, and then you would have to get some technician to come to help show the film. You know, it was so much trouble, but I would feel that it was worth the effort when the students, particularly, say, with African literature, got a feel of the environment that they were dealing with, where they could actually see African people and hear them speak and realize that they didn't speak to each other always in English. The context of the work I always felt was important, but some students just wanted to get straight to what the exam was going to be about. If it's not for the exam [they thought], then it's not useful. That used to put me off so much, especially because [showing reels] took so much effort.

I also used to use recordings where possible and readings of poems.

And the problem with me, I think, is that I too often tended to take over the discussion. By the time we reached the 1980s, they couldn't buy the books, so they weren't reading. They were just depending on whatever you said. Then they would write it down. So sometimes I think I erred by not allowing the students enough space to express their ideas.

Of course, it worked better at the graduate level where the classes were smaller, and I think people were a bit more serious; they didn't think they could hide behind a larger crowd. Probably my best participation came in orature, which is where I really felt that the students were teaching me some things, and I was also teaching them to appreciate or to understand, in a more intellectual way, the living and speaking that they did, whether it was verbal abuse, whether it was proverbs, whether it was riddles or narratives.

Q: People talked a lot about this course. Could you please tell us more about it and your approach to teaching it?

M.W-L.: Yes, it spoke to our daily living, and I learned a lot. I think it was the most intense period of my learning about Jamaican life, and one felt that one was making a contribution to the life that the students lived on an everyday basis, whether in the present or in [exploring] the past, and, you see, we had few textbooks as such for that course.

I would go to the literature, to the creative writing in literature to see how particularly West Indian or African writers had used the speech culture in segments of their book, and I would have the students examine that structurally to see how they used the patterns of orature in their society. What we used for that course was Walter Ong's book *Orality and Literacy* and also books by Ruth Finnegan, including *Oral Literature in Africa*, and we also used articles on sociolinguistics, the use of formal speech in traditional Chinese folk tales, as well as folk tales from other parts of the world. We also deduced the philosophical purpose of folk tales, behind the overt excitement or comedy they presented. I would use anything that I could read; for example, verbal abuse in Turkey. So we went all over the world, and I loved that, you know, just showing how cultures are more similar than dissimilar in a sense. So that was exciting for me, and I think too for the students.

Q: You made the point earlier that students liked the course because it was so much about their lives. Is this correct?

M.W-L.: Yes, they discovered that the things that they did naturally or normally in their growing up actually had a greater, shall I say, universal significance, because those practices might have been done in other places in slightly different ways. And also, that one could subject these ways of speaking and these ways of behaving to intellectual analysis. We looked at the function of speech in establishing social or religious or political status, and in contributing to community awareness, and in affirming personal or communal relationships. It wasn't that casual – these may have been casual acts, but maybe looking again at the African origin of some of these things, you realize that they came out of a certain sense of formality. You know, if you were leaving the village to go to town or something, you would come and address your parents, and you would say certain words to begin with, and you would give up a gift, and you would make a pronouncement.

What is the significance of that pronouncement? Is that pronouncement doing something? Is it asking something? You know – all these are different aspects of this course.

Q: What about memorable lessons? Can you recall any?

M.W-L.: Those were memorable classes for me. I remember several classes very well, and the high level of student participation. I could also remember saying a prayer every time I was going, seeking enlightenment as to how to proceed.

Q: This is so interesting, because you're the first woman, first person I'm interviewing who has spoken about any kind of teacher anxiety. I recall too that I would sometimes pray and say, "Oh God, help me with this class." When you look back, what were the major challenges that you had to deal with?

M.W-L.: I would say, students' regurgitation of critics' views, as I mentioned to you before. Also, there was their failure to dissect a text on their own steam, and there was too little appreciation of structure. On the other hand, I remember listening to students, in a creative writing course, read their short stories, and they were so good. I was pleased. It is always so refreshing and heartening to get good student work.

The other challenge that I think students had was a lack of discrimination regarding [answering] the questions that they were asked. By that, I mean some of them had the tendency not to answer the question asked. They did not seem to understand that you did not want just any and every piece of information thrown at you. They were asked a specific question to which there was a specific answer. I consider the teaching of literature to be merely one way of training students at the tertiary level to analyse. It doesn't matter whether it is chemistry or whatever; you are being taught in a particular discipline the ways of analysing material, and if you are asked, "How does metaphor contribute to Walcott's whatever?", don't bother to tell me about Walcott's bedroom. I want a particular line of argumentation, and some of the students can be quite undiscriminating about what they answer. In my later years I realized that it doesn't matter if they know what the questions are going to be about, because to a great extent it is that individual's intelligence and the ability to discriminate and to focus their answers that is going to make the difference between the A and the F.

Q: What works best for you and your students?

M.W-L.: Okay, what works best for me and my students? It was when the student was willing and able! Some students arrive in front of you with a good background, a solid background in writing analytical stuff. They knew what personification was; they knew what a metaphor was; they knew what style was, and so on. So you didn't have to teach basics; you could work on the other things. This is a new text for the student – how is the student going to cut through this?

Q: I also have a key question for you about your being a writer. Did it influence you in any way in terms of how you taught?

M.W-L.: Unfortunately, I tended not to write about things that I was teaching, apart from the African post-grad course.

Q: What I was wondering, really, is whether you raised the bar for your students given the fact that you wrote and published extensively? For example, did it make you expect more of them?

M.W-L.: No, no, I don't think so, because my own writing was not perfect. I try as much as I can naturally. Every time you approach a piece of writing, you try to make it as tight as possible, and you try to be accurate. After a time, you realize that not everyone is as finicky. I could not expect the students to write with such care, though some students write extremely well. But, you see, so much depends on the foundations that you are working with. What used to get me increasingly angry towards the end was that there were too many students who were indifferent to attending to and learning the process.

Q: Any final word about teaching literature? When you look back, was it very rewarding? Do you think through teaching literature you made a significant contribution to students' lives?

M.W-L.: I hope so. I think literature should make people more sensitive to expression, to how to say things. One of the good things about literature for me is that it helps you to understand people in the world. You become aware of people having tragic flaws. You see that being played out – people who keep making the same error over and over. Certain situations you know are likely to go a particular way, because something in your literary background has prepared you for that. There is a certain trajectory – it's almost as if you are watching a play or something. There is a certain trajectory that X is on that must eventually lead to success or to failure. And also, as I said, literature develops your awareness of patterns in human actions, patterns of behaviour, patterns of expectation and patterns of self-deceit. Hopefully, it helps you to understand yourself too.

SECTION 2.

PEOPLE, PLACE AND CULTURE
The Second Generation of Caribbean Teachers

Thelma Baker, Victor Chang, Carolyn Cooper, Lorna Down, Brian Heap, Mark McWatt and David Williams are treated here as representative of the second wave of Caribbean Teachers. They are seen as continuing to develop a pedagogy of connectivity – students connected to text and to context; students connected to teacher and each other, and emphasized here, to a growing community of readers. This generation of teachers offers a distinctive approach even as there are similarities with that of the foundation teachers. Here, too, there is the passion to engender a love and valuing of literature in the next generation, a passion that had been nurtured by the teachers in the first group.

The pedagogy that emerges strongly is that the study of literary texts is a study of people and place as well as people in place, and not merely that of a "study of books". The insistence on validating students, which lay at the heart of the pedagogy of the former generation, remains at varying levels. Baker, for example, speaks to the parallel between students' self-development and literature. She explains further how through the teaching of literature, students are helped to develop their own philosophy of life. Her vision is similar to that of the first generation; she acknowledges her visioning of creative possibilities for students and lays the groundwork for them to experience the sheer pleasure of the "aha moments". Therefore, we begin with her interview, as she bridges both groups of teachers.

More strongly evinced, however, is teaching literature through the validation of place and culture. The use of traditional culture is shown as a means of connecting to students and their context as well as connecting them to the text. In cultures where there is still a strong oral tradition, such as the Caribbean, people value storytelling. A storytelling approach, then, to the teaching of literature can be very effective. Stories, like Chang's "personal"/family stories, evoking not only humour much of the time but also pathos at times, are used to introduce, annotate, reflect on, speak back to texts being taught. Students' interest is immediately captured by these personal stories, and through them they are transported into the heart of the text. Questions provoked by these stories, asked or unasked aloud, create a space for the text being studied.

Students' culture, popular culture, is also acknowledged and forms part of the teaching and learning. "Texts" such as reggae and deejay songs, usually excluded from the conventional academic curricula, are studied. Popular songs and music, with its general appeal, and often considered subculture, are shown, then, as "worthy" of serious study, and its followers (the category in which many students may be found), therefore, as having knowledge that academia considers useful and valuable. Students' knowledge and choices are thus affirmed. Students have been shown "respect" for what they know and value, and so are "open" to what else the academy may offer. In other words, student validation is foundational to effective teaching and learning, and can be easily accommodated in a subject that relies less on "content knowledge" and more on analysis, interpretation and a critical response. Cooper's interview details this approach.

In a similar way, a focus on place, on local and regional landscape in literature texts, can provide a comfortable launch pad for the exploration and study of literature. Making the familiar unfamiliar and the unfamiliar familiar has long been recognized as one of the benefits of the study of literature. It is often as a result of this that the discovery of insights, which Dennis Sumara emphasizes as a key goal of reading literature, emerges. Combining a study of the landscape with the study of literature texts can, in fact, lead to the development of particular literature strategies. Employing students' knowledge of their local landscape can also open up a text for them. Williams notes how encouraging students to "see" the landscape, to appreciate, for example, "the difference between the shoreline and the mountains and the hills", has been an interesting way of helping students interpret a text. He further points out that helping students see the connection between "the artefact that the imagination makes" and the physical landscape deepens their appreciation of the text. In this way students learn to re-value the landscape as well as themselves.

McWatt speaks to this also, as he discusses using photo narratives and photo poems. Citing Wilson Harris, whose novels vividly reconstruct the "wild" interior of a Guyana landscape, McWatt makes us consider how "reading" parallel versions of the same landscape – that through the lens of a camera and that of a literary text – can lead us to discover the truths of both the text and the landscape. Most students today, easy with and having ready access to technology (for example, cameras and cell phones with video capability), can, therefore, be encouraged to study literature through such parallel readings.

Still, there is another aspect to connecting students to the landscape as a medium of helping them connect with the text. The current earth crisis has impelled a re-visioning of all education. Orr (2004), in fact, makes the point that all education is environmental education and that learning spaces, pedagogical approaches and disciplinary boundaries as well as the curricula need to be shaped by the attention to place. We are now called, therefore, as Down explains in her interview, to reorient our teaching practices towards sustainability, to help our students understand and take critical action for the protection and conservation of our physical environment and to ensure a peaceful and just society. Understanding this pedagogy, framed in terms of eco-criticism/education for sustainable development, teachers emphasize the importance of place, of representations of the environment in literature texts and the need to have students critically examine these in terms of the concept of sustainability and their material existence. It is an understanding of a new approach to the teaching of literature which takes into account, as Garrard (2004, 14), in his text on eco-criticism, asserts, that "environmental problems require analysis in cultural as well as scientific terms because they are the outcome of an interaction between ecological knowledge of nature and its cultural inflection".

Underpinning all this is the quality of the literary experience that such a pedagogy offers to the students. Interestingly, it is the quality of the literary experience that Rosenblatt (1960) advocates for in one of her seminal essays on the reader's role in literature.

Most important, connecting students to their regional landscape, their traditional culture as well as popular culture enables a discovery of their uniqueness and what their regional literature can contribute to world literature. Williams shares with us how he facilitates students' recognition of the unique contribution of Caribbean literature to English. He speaks of how the rhythms of Caribbean prose, for example, have inserted "into English something that is unrepeatable elsewhere". Students' understanding of this, of possessing a literature that influences an already established form, frees them to explore the various expressions and styles of all literature.

This, of course, also affirms the value of teaching literature everywhere through airing the distinct voice of each region and each writer.

The general objective is, of course, to have students connect with the literary text – the novel, the poem, the play. The art and practice of teaching literature includes, therefore, students actually reading the primary text, having that literary experience. Reading the text is foundational to a rich literary experience and is a practice that is too often marginalized, as Kravis (1995) has pointed out. It is a practice that has to be planned for and encouraged. In this fast-paced, technologically driven world, the creation of a community of readers has to be a deliberate and focused undertaking. "Slow reading", reflective reading, is one that runs counter to the quick reads of WhatsApp, Twitter and other forms of social media. Williams shares how he "nudges" students to engage in this through piquing their curiosity about a new and unique element in the text. Relating signature music to cultural icons to text, and so offering students a different way into the text, he further encourages them to engage with the literature.

Creatively structured reading sessions also allow students to be caught up in the flow of the story. Creating a "nice" reading space, free from any heavy critical and theoretical work for them, teachers set the stage for students to simply enjoy the text. And having that space of pleasure, students become motivated to read and delve further into the text, as Baker attests.

The reading of the text including also "read alouds" can quietly guide students into the process of reading and interpretation. With planned brief "disruptions" of the reading by the use of probing questions, by statements countering standard interpretations of the text, by teasers, by introducing extra-textual material (for example, media headlines), and teacher "thinking aloud", these readings can help engender in students a love of literature.

Connections are made over time. They are part of a process. Immersing students in the literary experience, connecting them to the text will not always happen instantaneously. There will be the "aha moments" of sudden insight. Most often they will be part of an ongoing process. Process drama is perhaps the teaching strategy with the most potential for accomplishing this, for fully immersing students in the literary experience. Here the teacher is teaching from "the edge", as Heap notes. It is the students who occupy centre stage, who, guided into reading, discover insights into the text. Through using pre-text and pretext, through connecting with their emotions, through being in role and then not in role, students get to the heart of the matter.

Most important is Heap's assertion that drama frees students to be and allows teachers to see their possibilities or potential. In considering each of their students, teachers learn to "set no ceiling / on what he could be doctor / earth healer, pilot take wings" (Goodison, "The Woman Speaks to the Man Who Has Employed Her Son").

Using this pedagogical approach, teachers come to understand that there is a parallel between students' self-development and their involvement in literature. They show how connecting literature to traditional and popular culture and to landscape as core methodology hones their students' interpretive skills, enables them to develop deep relationships with texts and from such grounding learn to shape their communal identities. In addition, these teachers highlight how foregrounding the text and keeping secondary texts secondary encourage students to discover its pleasure and construct meaning. From such connections, therefore, students are immersed in rich literary experiences which flow out and into their lives.

Thelma Baker

"There is, in fact, a parallel between students' self-development and their involvement in literature."

Miss Thelma Baker has been teaching literature for more than thirty years. She began teaching literature as "Reading" in a preparatory school, which provided her with opportunities to introduce young children to the pleasure of listening to and reading stories and poems. She spent most of her teaching years, however, teaching literature at Merl Grove High School, a girls' school in Jamaica, to students in grades 7 to 13. She has also taught literature at the University of the West Indies at Mona. Complementing her teaching of literature are her published poems in a variety of texts. Baker has also co-authored a number of language and literature textbooks, including *What a Fright and other Stories* (a reader in the First Aid in English for the Caribbean series) (2007, with A. Maciver, K. Down and L. Down) and *English Alive*, Book 4 (2004, with A. Etherton, J. Jona and J. Pereira).

Q: Miss Baker, what do you particularly like about teaching literature?

Thelma Baker: I find that teaching literature gives an insight into the way students see themselves and others, and the way in which personal issues can be inserted and discussed without invading personal space. In fact, when I think of favourite teachers, the teachers of literature come to mind, as they seem to have helped me more than other teachers to shape a philosophy of life. I remember the quotes, lines of poetry, proverbs and indirect advice that have helped to shape my thinking. And much later I realized how much of themselves they have given; how much more than just teaching a subject. Now I too have come to realize this connection I have with my students long after they have left my classes. The impressions left especially by my first-, fifth- and sixth-form literature teachers remain to this day.

Q: Yes, teaching literature is among other things helping students shape their philosophy of life. How to teach in this way is an art in itself, and you have clearly enjoyed it. Would you like to comment?

T.B.: Yes. I enjoyed teaching literature even before I put a name to it. As a pre-trained teacher, I taught grades 1 to 4 at the preparatory level. As the emphasis was on reading and comprehension, I ended up reading stories and poems outside of prescribed texts. We, the students and I, discussed characters and setting in stories, and "word pictures" and rhyming words in poems. I had a special interest in drama, and we made up skits which were performed sometimes using costumes. Children that age are usually excited and willing to participate. Now, looking back, I realize that we were actually engaged in teaching and learning literature. Also satisfying is helping older students understand that literature is an important subject, and that through reading and discussing issues, they come up with original ideas; they arrive at aha moments. It is also equally satisfying when some students want to read books outside of set texts.

Q: Students' creativity being nourished, their experiencing "aha moments", and their desiring to read more – all these indicate students' emerging appreciation for literature as well as literature's enduring value. In what other ways was literature's importance revealed?

T.B.: Students found it pleasurable, and it became something they looked forward to. But there was a link among the stories, poetry and dramatic presentations and their writing. Even more important than a greatly improved vocabulary was the way my younger students began to use descriptive language, including similes and metaphors, terms which they did not yet know or define. It is important to maintain the link between reading and writing, especially at that level where students are not afraid to express themselves, where they are not afraid to enter the imaginary world of animals and fairy tales. I have seen too the way in which [literature] helps students to grow in confidence in expressing their own thoughts, ideas and opinions. They also learn to relate to each other in a civil way, to listen and value what others have to say. There is, in fact, a parallel between students' self-development and their involvement in literature, which the observant teacher cannot miss.

Q: How, then, do you generally prepare for your classes so that students benefit in the many ways you have found?

T.B.: In general, I prepare by reading all the time. A teacher must be an avid reader – must enjoy reading. Some teachers feel that in order to teach literature, you get away with reading only the books to be taught, which is a grave mistake. I often take a book I am reading to class, and invariably a student will ask a question about it and sometimes will ask to borrow it. Students would also often lend me books that they found interesting.

For my first class, I begin by establishing our expectations for each other; this is important as it sets the tone for the year or semester, and once that is out of the way, the real work can begin. Then I go over "rules" for myself, the way in which I address and respond to students, how I listen to what they offer, avoiding tense situations and maintaining a sense of fun and humour.

I go on to choose the books. In some cases, there is freedom of choice within the syllabus provided in the lower grades, but as the students pre-pare for the CSEC and CAPE examinations, choice is more restrictive and sometimes depends on cost and availability. So the teacher sometimes is faced with teaching what she considers an unsuitable book in which she needs to work out carefully the appropriate approach. I begin by reading the text, reading about the writer, reading about the period and reading any other books written by the author. I do this in no particular order. Even if I am familiar with the text or taught it the year before, I still reread it. I also find it useful in my own development to read books by other writers in this period, not only novels but drama and poetry.

I also try to work out ideas and interesting exercises with which to intro-duce each text. This may come in the form of possible questions for each chapter/scene/poem which can be used as a lead-in or review exercise. I also try to have a visual introduction, especially for novels or plays.

Q: How do you usually plan on getting students involved and participating in classes?

T.B.: Sometimes I begin a class by asking a question that provokes discussion. This may or may not be directly related to the lesson under consideration. At other times I might use a relevant quote or proverb from the Bible, a Shakespeare play, or from Jamaican folklore. The discussion must be guided in the direction that the teacher wants.

Q: What was a memorable experience for you, and why?

T.B.: My most memorable class was a one of forty students who I taught for a period of about two years. In the first year I focused on getting them to read just about anything they were interested in. In addition to attending a play, they watched films on various classics. We discussed themes, debated on aspects of texts, wrote reviews, did projects and presentations. I encouraged them to go through the requirements and the list of books recommended for the external examinations, although this was some years ahead.

My most memorable lesson took place when, at their request, I took a set of papers of the external examination in literature to class. The response and the level of discussion of questions shocked me. I realized that there were students who had read many of the texts and could actually answer some questions set. There were even a few who could have sat and passed the examination without further preparation. My students grew in confidence, and the lessons I learned have served me well. Know your students, develop trust and respect on both sides, take risks, and never ever just teach students to pass examinations.

Q: What works best for you, for example, what methods? What setting? What teaching aids or instructional materials?

T.B.: Setting, especially in a high school situation, is not always ideal. I have had to teach where classes are separated by chalkboards, where furniture is in short supply, and in extreme circumstances have had to teach under a tree. The one thing I have learned is to be flexible; to be able to adjust to any situation without fuss. Charts and other teaching aids sometimes fail to work, and the teacher must be ready to change plans at a moment's notice.

Even so, I like charts and artwork, and usually identify groups of students who will prepare these ahead of class and, depending on the situation, will make a short, prepared introductory presentation.

Q: Are these the same approaches that you use with all the genres? Or do you find that a particular approach will work best with prose and not with poetry and drama?

T.B.: I approach poetry as condensed language, which needs to be unravelled, drama as present-tense action, and the novel as extended narrative. There are a number of specifics for poetry – for one, it is exploring the need for poetry to make use of figurative language more than the other genres and the reasons for this. It is also, for me, getting students to understand the necessity for poets to say more in fewer words and use words which are emotionally loaded. I look at the ways too in which poetry reflects some of our unexpressed feelings, unlocks our undiscovered self. And I play a lot with language. For example, I will quote a line from a poem and ask students to identify the poem and explain the meaning of the line, the figure of speech used or the way a particular word is used. Encouraging students to talk about poems they like or do not like and the reasons for this are also key aspects of my poetry teaching. So too is having students focus on and discuss poems that are not on the syllabus, as these are often overused.

What has also worked very well in developing students' love and appreciation for poetry is the use of journals – journals in which they can write poems, stories or comments on poems and of course are given the platform to share these periodically. Sometimes with the younger classes I begin with nursery rhymes, a good way to discuss rhyme, rhythm and economy of language.

In high school, you usually teach language and literature, so in the language class you can introduce a lot of the technical terms through teaching writing. In teaching "descriptive writing", for example, you are able to introduce similes and metaphors. So in the literature classes I can focus on the poem's mood, meaning and the effect of the devices. I may ask if they recognize the metaphor and how the poet uses it.

I also have the students create their own glossary of terms, and they learn them through their writing. Moreover, I don't teach them a lot of technical terms which they won't remember anyway, as it will simply make poetry seem a difficult thing. The essential thing is to link what I teach in the language classes with the literature classes.

One of the problems with teaching poetry is that language texts treat poems simply as material for comprehension exercises. Some of the questions asked are also odd. What this does is to rob poetry of its delight, mystery and meaning.

What has worked well with some classes is my introduction of haiku poetry, but this requires careful preparation.

Q: Could you please give us some highlights of a poetry lesson?

T.B.: I am likely to introduce the poem by talking about the poet and his work, especially if we are doing a number of poems by him or her. I may also say before the reading something like, "We are going to look at the poet's concern about . . ." as a way to establish focus. After the poem is read a number of times by the class and by me, I will often have students respond to the mood of the poem. I ask my students what feeling they get when they read the poem, how the persona feels, and questions along that line. The structure of a poem is usually very important in relating its meaning, so I also have students look at the structure on the page, how the poet punctuates it, where the spaces come, whether it's formally structured in distinct stanzas. I ask them to note how the poem begins and how it ends, and we discuss the movement between both. I find as well that having students "categorize" poems – that is, find patterns that are similar [among poems] – is also a way to engage them.

Q: Do you use different strategies for teaching poetry to younger students?

T.B.: To some extent I do. I've found that older students like discussion and relating the poems to how they feel in comparison to the poet's perspective. We have had interesting discussions on this, and I've had to remind them that in the same way they insist on their perspective – "That's the way I see it" – the poet is entitled to his or her perspective. I find as well that students of all ages like the sound of words. The young students in particular like nonsense poems, for example, "The Walrus and the Carpenter". Here the sound and the rhythm provide its meaning. Poems like "Sensemayá" and "Do You Remember an Inn, Miranda" illustrate the sound quality of poems that appeal to students. The sensuality of the poems makes them feel good, and they enjoy just reading the poem. It is a good idea to spend time just reading the poem and leaving the "academic" stuff sometimes. We too often force children into analysing poems, when they do not really know what a poem is.

Q: What about the teaching of drama and prose?

T.B.: Drama is action, and at any level students must read aloud in order to get the feel of the action, of relationships and attitudes of the actors towards each other, and the feel of movement, time and place. So performing the play is part of my methodology. At one stage I used to teach drama, so I would have them engage with the play in drama classes as well.

With Shakespeare's plays, students have found it interesting working with the model of a stage. Students also find the language of Shakespeare difficult. So what I do is expose students to common phrases that have been drawn from Shakespeare's plays; additionally, I have students translate the language into teenage talk, into Creole, and explore the language differences. It becomes an exercise in "unlocking language", as much of their language, like Shakespeare's for them, is not readily accessible to us. The use of the King James Version of the Bible has also been helpful. Most of them are familiar with this, and so it lays the foundation for reading Shakespeare.

To help students understand plot and character, I find working with an outline of the play as well as a chart of the characters and their relationships extremely useful. Plays are meant to be performed, and though that may not always be possible, we can have dramatic readings of the plays. I have my class choose the readers and, as a result, have had really good class performances.

I have found as well that activities such as creating news items based on the play, producing programmes for a performance and doing research on specific aspects have helped to maintain interest.

Moreover, they find the work interesting when I have them discover that Shakespeare is writing about life experiences relevant and familiar to them. Older students like to explore themes of love. The use of a writer's biography can also make their work more accessible to students, so learning about

Shakespeare's own life and his involvement in the production of his plays make a major difference in engaging students' attention.

Prose [involves] a more leisurely exploration of the text, allowing students to consciously or subconsciously draw parallels to real life situations. I often had the texts read in class. Students would select the readers, and I would also read. Having good readers, especially for the dialogue, is essential for an effective reading. I would usually begin by giving a brief context and a focus for the reading. As in the poetry lessons, I would give them some information about the writer, his period and his contemporaries. I would position him in some context. Then we would have the reading in various forms; students would be free to ask questions, but there wouldn't be any lengthy discussion. The reading would be largely uninterrupted. After the reading we would have focused discussions and activities. I would set the stage so that students had a clear sense of characters, their relationships and the plot. They would be guided to the central conflict. Setting would be explored too, in terms of its relation to character's action, plot and theme, so the setting of a village may be seen as forcing people into closeness or apartness. The reading here is focused, as you direct it into the area that you want the students to examine.

It's important to state here as well that though I have a lesson plan, my lesson isn't controlled by it; sometimes I have to abandon the plan.

Regardless of the genres, however, what is particularly useful in encouraging reading in a non-threatening way, especially in the lower grades, is the establishment of an informal library. It is fairly easy to get a small collection going, and soon students will add to it. I have had classes which have taken over the library and established their own system, complete with librarian and fines for late returns, plus a drive to add more books to the collection.

Q: Does the type or structure of a text affect the way you teach it?

T.B.: I usually pay close attention to novels and plays which use the flashback technique, as students at all levels seem to have difficulty separating the past from the present. I deal with this in a separate class so that when we come to the text it is with some knowledge of the technique. I use examples found outside the text and from the students' own experience.

Q: How would you describe your teaching style?

T.B.: I do not think I have a fixed style. What I work most at is to have students enjoy as they learn. I try to make it fun, to maintain always a sense of humour and to accept the contribution of all students and to encourage participation.

Q: What are some of the challenges of teaching literature?

T.B.: There are a number of challenges. One includes the lack of texts, which cuts across all disciplines, but this can often be dealt with at a departmental level. The real problem with the teaching of literature is a lack of interest on the part of students and some teachers. In many high schools the focus is on English language and the reading of a few novels. I have observed teachers who are confident in teaching prose fiction but are uncomfortable with poetry and drama. This is a challenge that can be addressed at the teacher-training level. The teacher's challenge is to sell, or promote, literature in a positive way; to look at the pleasure and the skills gained from the study of literature. There is also the matter of teachers becoming comfortable with the old way of doing things and using strategies that have outlived their time. Teachers have to be risk-takers. In addition to this, there is the challenge of having to deal with large classes and inadequate resources. This is particular challenging for beginning teachers, who are also often discouraged by older, frustrated teachers. Teachers have to find strategies to address large classes, and grouping is one way. Yet more than anything else, teachers have to find ways to renew their joy and interest in the subject.

There is also the challenge of teaching Shakespeare, which I've addressed in the question about teaching drama.

Q: Elaine Showalter writes about seven teacher anxieties: training, isolation, teaching versus research, and coverage among others. What, if any, teacher anxieties do you experience?

T.B.: Yes, I sometimes suffer from teacher anxiety. This happens when I approach a new group, and especially so when this group consists of pre-university students who have been "forced" to do literature because of examination results. Many times literature has been seen as a "make-up" subject. I am also anxious or nervous when trying out new strategies or taking risks. However, my training in drama has taught me that some anxiety is necessary and can be used to power performance. Sometimes anxiety is tied to expected outcomes, but I quickly learned to accept and deal with unexpected results, which were sometimes surprisingly good. So, a little anxiety is useful!

Q: Yes – something we all need to remember. My final question is, what do you think is foundational to teaching Caribbean literature?

T.B.: My problem with this "foundation" question is that there is no clear starting point, no "basics" to teaching Caribbean literature. There is no guide as to what to teach in Caribbean literature from the primary level up. Students come to high school knowing "We have neither autumn nor winter . . ." and a few other poems, plus at preparatory level they may have read *Sprat Morrison*. High school gives us a few books with a few notes primarily with tips on how to have our students pass exams and a syllabus with demands that teachers cannot meet.

Much has been published on Caribbean literature, but how much of this is easily accessible, and how widely known is this? Something apart from CXC needs to be in the schools' curriculum. We all teach at isolational levels, and there is no connecting thing.

Q: This is clearly a situation that needs further discussion and action. Given that and other limitations which teachers work with, what advice would you give to teachers just entering the field?

T.B.: I would tell them that it is not enough to read the required texts at teachers' college, at university, and on the syllabus that they teach. It is expected that they would have read the writer's biography as well as other books written by him or her. They should read widely also on a personal level. Students are impressed when they realize that a teacher is an avid reader.

The teacher of literature must be an excellent reader, as reading aloud is part of the package, especially when teaching younger students. Many Caribbean writers use Creole, so the teacher should learn to read this well too. In addition, the teacher should foster a respect for this form of language, which is used to express a range of emotions. The teacher should also identify and correct oral language problems during training.

Effective teachers cannot rely on old notes, essays and lesson plans. They need to revise, review and follow new approaches. They need to be creative in their approach, to research to find out new developments in education. They need to talk to teachers outside their discipline; this can provide interesting and unexpected results. They should also attend plays, poetry readings and workshops/seminars in order to enhance their own development.

Victor Chang

"Literature crosses over into our lives."

D r Victor Chang taught literature at the University of the West Indies for thirty-one years. He began his university teaching career in 1978 at the UWI, Mona, where he taught a range of courses from year one through to year three. Prior to this he taught for four years at Kingston College, a boys' high school in Jamaica, two years at the State University of New York in Albany and one year at the College of the Bahamas.

Chang has published short stories and published articles and book chapters on Caribbean literature. He was also the editor for the *Journal of West Indian Literature* for over twenty years and contributed greatly to maintaining the quality of the journal. His interest in developing the arts was also seen in his editorship of *Pathways*, a journal of creative writing, and in his ongoing encouragement of his students to publish their creative pieces in *Pathways*.

Q: Dr Chang, how did you prepare for your classes?

Victor Chang: The first thing I would do is start preparing the set texts and then make a list of recommended and highly recommended secondary texts. I would then do a brief bibliography of the most pertinent books and articles that would relate to the course that I was teaching. And then, of course, I would read around in the area myself, as well as reread the texts.

In the later years, I asked the students to make up a bibliography themselves, not only to give them the practice of doing it, but also to find out really what it was like to go to the library and find relevant material. It helped me, too, because then I could do a selection or collation from all the different students and be able to say, "Everybody says this is a good book, so I can recommend it."

So generally then, it was reading around the areas, reading over the text myself, and then working up a schedule of lectures – and as I warned them at the very beginning, the lectures were merely jumping-off spots. I don't believe that if you go to the lecture, you don't have to go to the library again, like some people believe. I always stressed that literature is a matter of interpretation, of liking and taste. Some things would appeal to me more than others, but there were infinite possibilities which students were free to explore and develop on their own.

Q: You mentioned earlier students composing bibliographies as one way of getting them involved in the classes. How else did you get them to participate?

V.C.: Sometimes they had particular questions to answer, but I also made it very flexible, so when I was teaching modern drama, for instance, I would say, "If four of you want to get together and do a scene from a play and make it your presentation, then I would accept that", and give them all whatever the mark was for the overall group. That was useful. They also had to do tutorial presentations, so each student was given a particular topic, and again, they had some input in this, because I would select the topics and would say to them, "If there is anything else you wish to present on, then you are free to do this, or if you want to swap with somebody else." So from that point of view, they could also do what they particularly cared for, or particularly wanted to do.

Q: Tell me about your lectures. Actually, I've heard lots of stories about how dramatic they were!

V.C.: I always thought that lecturing should be something that would stimulate and entertain the students – so that is a combination of two things. I found out very early that if I tied a particular point I wanted to make to an anecdote or a memory from my own life, then they would be very amused and interested. You know, it is so funny. Years afterwards [a student] would say, "I remember the story when you did so and so and then tied it to a general point."

Also, in the early years when I was young and foolish and more experimental, I would use colours. For example, when I was lecturing on *The Scarlet Letter,* for the very first lecture, I dressed myself all in red! You know, it was the visual impact. So years afterwards, I would meet students who said they would never forget when I first walked in class dressed all in red! In later years, if it was on St Patrick's Day, I would wear green, or if it was near to Valentine's Day I would again wear red. So it was a visual thing, not necessarily related to the topic itself. I remember one time when I was teaching modern drama, and I wanted to make the point about costuming, I came in wearing dark glasses and a black leather jacket. Costuming changes your perception of the person, because by putting on the costume you change your response and theirs.

Q: I find that very interesting – the use of colours, of costumes to stimulate their interest in the text. What other approaches did you use?

V.C.: I would draw a lot on my own personal memories of different things and also, of course, tie it to the business of their own lives to show that the text was not something that was out there and not related to their lives. When I was teaching *A Streetcar Named Desire,* the question about rape came up, what constituted rape and how far a man should go. This led to one of the most memorable class conflicts, because there was one half of the class that said, "Yes, Blanche was begging for it", while the other half said, "Stanley was a real brute." The question of male–female relations and male–female rights became a heated discussion.

Then when I was teaching *King Lear,* the question arose of how much you owe your children and how much your children owe you in return. I was constantly trying to make the point that literature raises questions about life which were still valid, and questions which had to be confronted now in their own lives. Whether it worked or not I don't know, but the point is that, certainly in tutorials, it would bring [up] a lot of active discussion about responsibility and what you owe and how much is owed to you.

When we were doing *Antigone,* I raised the question of whether you obey the state before you obey your personal dictates. Can you on your own decide that you're not going to obey the state, because it conflicts with what you really believe? If a society decides on certain rules, how far can you go in questioning those rules and in breaking them? I also introduced the question of apartheid, segregation and the official rules of South Africa at the time. So if you as an individual say, "I refuse to accept this as a human being", can you then break that law and not face the consequences? I was hoping that all these classes would relate back to their own lives and to their own existence, so that way it should become not just something in the book to be studied but something that could make them think about, question and examine their own lives. Of course, it is a teacher's hope. A number of them would say that this aim was accomplished.

In one memorable case, we were doing Ibsen's *A Doll's House*, where Nora walks out on her husband in the end, leaving her children and husband, because she realizes that he didn't love her and she didn't really love him. Two weeks later, an army man came to my office, very threatening and carrying a gun. He said that I had told his wife to leave him. Apparently she had been in a similar situation, and she got up and left him, and he thought it was because of what I was teaching in class! I was kind of frightened, but I didn't show it. I just said to him, "Let me call Security, because I don't know you. I don't know what your wife told you, but I was just teaching a class and made a point about women having the right not to put up with certain situations." Literature crosses over into our lives.

I would also bring in audiovisual items and DVDs, and get films of different versions of the play so that the students were exposed to different perspectives. In [teaching] *King Lear*, for instance, there would be four versions, including one with James Earl Jones as a black Lear, so that we crossed over racial boundaries as well as saw different actors bringing different interpretations to the role. So looking at the scene with Nora in *A Doll's House* where she takes off her wedding ring and puts it down on the table, walks out and slams the door, you're not just reading about it, you're actually seeing it. And, of course, it provoked a lot of class discussion, because the women were commenting that she was stupid, she was giving up all this financial support and had no training and no job – how was she going to live? Where was she going to go? They also pointed out that she would be ostracized, because she had left her husband and children – worst of all. So they were very aware of the dramatic situation, and the play raised not only a lot of questions but also asked questions without providing answers, as there are no easy answers, just as in real life.

Q: Yes, that's true. Were there other memorable lectures?

V.C.: There have been so many over the years. I remember *A Streetcar Named Desire*, where, during a tutorial, the men and the women were really at loggerheads over the question of Stanley and Blanche, and a girl got to the stage where she was weeping, and we thought it was just passion! But looking back it seemed that she might have had a similar experience.

Q: What were some of the challenges that you had?

V.C.: Oh, so many! First of all, having students who either didn't have the money to buy the books, or so they said, or didn't buy the books. So they would come to classes without the text, and when you are doing close textual reading, especially in something like Shakespeare where language itself is already ancient and difficult, it became very difficult. And I was torn between letting them stay in the class without the text and just listening and hoping they would pick up something, or being very tough and saying, "No text, no class, just get out." Frequently, I would lend them texts, because I had multiple copies.

Secondly, I found over the years that the quality of the writing got worse and worse. I would give them a chance to give me a draft to correct it and come back and re-submit, but again, only a minority of them took advantage of the offer. And then, of course, the biggest worry of all was about plagiarism. The other problem was absenteeism by students who had other jobs. So there was the economics of teaching literature both in terms of some students not being able or not willing to buy a text and of some of them not being able to come to classes because they were forced to keep on working full-time to survive.

You asked what was particularly challenging and how I dealt with it. I found that the students were very homophobic. One year when I was teaching Auden, I made the mistake of saying that Auden had dedicated the poem (that the class loved so much in the beginning) to his lover, who was a man. Immediately I heard all the books closing. Not a single person chose Auden that semester! Nobody did a tutorial or an essay or exam question on Auden. So that was a clear case where the fact that somebody was gay affected them. So from then on I steered away from saying anything. The question came up with Shakespeare with the sonnets, where half were dedicated to a young man and half to a woman, and one of the students said, "Well, him was just experimenting, but him really wasn't . . . . You know what I mean?" [They] were willing to allow that, but you must not be a homosexual or committed to a homosexual lifestyle. So I never ever said Tennessee Williams was gay, in case the same response would take place. But that was definitely a drawback, because I was never brave enough to teach Auden again, and he went off the list altogether. In all the modern plays as well, I stayed away from plays that would raise the question of homosexuality on stage. Looking back, I should have been braver and forced them to examine their beliefs, as I did with the question of rape.

Q: Let's talk about your teaching style. How would you describe it?

V.C.: I would say a mixture of textual analysis and exploration, mixed in with anecdotes to clinch the point. It was analysis, plus relevance. I always encouraged them to explore the values being articulated or being questioned. So hopefully they would come away thinking about what we had discussed and want to go on and read other stuff. I always had a very informal approach. I never read the lectures. I would have a card with points to make. I would move about the stage. I would sit on the desk, I would go by the door, to break up the monotony of being in one position.

Although lectures are not usually interrupted, at certain points I would ask, "Is that clear? Do you have any questions?" to encourage immediate feedback, to keep them on track. And in fact, frequently I was very pleased to see they weren't writing; they were actually listening as opposed to constantly writing. And if [not], I would say, "Listen, this is not a stenography school!" The problem there again was related to the earlier problem of many of them not reading the texts, so that when you're making a point about a particular play and you're saying, "Did you see this?" half of them did not know, because they had not read the play. I would also encourage them to question and to query and to say, "No, I don't agree with you on that" and I would say, "Okay, that's fine."

Q: Students always said that Dr Chang's lectures were so humorous. In terms of the actual studying of the texts, in what areas did your students require a lot of help?

V.C.: They had problems with language, especially when I was teaching Chaucer and Shakespeare, because both wrote forms of older English – medieval and seventeenth century. So it meant that we spent a lot more time going through the text, to show them that Shakespeare's and Chaucer's language, with the help of the glossary, is "decipherable".

Q: The final question: Is there anything you would like to have done differently?

V.C.: Yes, I think I would. I would have used more audiovisual material.

Q: When you look back, if you had to do it again, what would you definitely keep?

V.C.: Oh, I would keep all of it – it's just that I would add more to it.

Q: But clearly, I think, for you, the interactive nature of teaching . . .

V.C.: Yes, the interactive nature of the teaching is what I liked. It wasn't just a one-way thing. It's a wonderful thing to hear the students say that they enjoy the classes.

Carolyn Cooper

"Making the connection between the literary text and the student's own experience turns reading into a process of personal enrichment."

Professor Carolyn Cooper taught literature full-time for forty-one years. From 1975 to 1980, she was an assistant professor of English at Atlantic Union College, a small private college in New England. From 1980 to 2016 she taught at the University of the West Indies at Mona. As a graduate student at the University of Toronto, she taught undergraduate literature courses part-time. She also taught for six weeks at St Hugh's High School, her alma mater, a girls' school in Jamaica. She enjoyed interacting with first-, fourth- and fifth-formers. The fourth-formers, she says, were the most challenging.

Cooper's publications include *Sound Clash: Jamaican Dancehall Culture at Large* (2004) and *Noises in the Blood: Orality, Gender and the "Vulgar" Body of Jamaican Popular Culture* (1993). Teacher, writer, literary critic, newspaper columnist, advocate of popular culture in the literary canon, Cooper provides us with a new perspective on the teaching of literature.

Q: Professor Cooper, how do you actually prepare for your lessons?

Carolyn Cooper: I didn't do teacher training, so I don't have formal "objectives" and "lesson plans". The main preparation I make is being enthusiastic about the subject, selecting books I enjoy, which I hope the students will enjoy as well. Of course, I also read the prescribed texts several times, so I know them intimately. And I generate a bibliography of readings which the students should find helpful. I also encourage them to go to the library and to go online to look for additional materials. Students don't always like the books you choose, so you have to motivate them to do research. I think it's essential to introduce books that will stretch and challenge students to move outside their so-called comfort zone. You have to engage them. And on that score, I must say that my lectures are interactive. Instead of standing up and talking for fifty minutes, I stop when I see the students' eyes getting glazed and allow them a short break to chat to each other. So it's not just one long period of listening. And especially these young people now, who are into the Internet and modern modes of gaining knowledge, I don't think they are too keen on sitting down and listening for even fifteen minutes.

In fact, one of my most memorable teaching experiences came right here at this university, where I was teaching a large first-year course – Introduction to Prose Fiction – with about 150 students. I looked out and realized that most of the class was not paying any attention to me. So I stopped immediately. And because I teach in both English and Jamaican, I asked, "So why unno look like dem tie unno and bring unno? Unno don't want to be here?" A big chorus replied, "No, Miss!" As it turned out, they wanted to be doing law or mass communication, but because they were qualified – they had A levels or CAPE English literature – they were allowed to take the course. So they were doing it with a "might as well" attitude. I told them that since they were here, they might as well do the best they could, because if they did well in literature, they might be able to transfer to the programmes they really wanted to do.

I was then head of the department, and I initiated a seminar series in which graduates who were doing all kinds of interesting jobs came back and talked to the students about how their degree in literature helped them in their current work. These included professionals in banking, advertising, public relations, editing, and explicitly literature-related disciplines like publishing. So that was one thing I did to try to help the students see the value of the degree in literature. They were learning analytical skills as they analysed character, and they were learning how to write well. These are skills that can be transferred to a variety of disciplines and fields of work, like law, for example. A first degree in literature is a good preparation for law. I also proposed an internship in the creative industries that would allow students in literature to go into a publishing house or to work with a literary festival, or a PR firm, where they could use their writing skills and gain some experience which might be marketable when they were job hunting. So far, that hasn't happened.

Q: Yes. I see the value in that. Let us return to your lectures. One of the things I remembered when sitting in on some of your lectures was not only your wide-ranging approach to the text, but you were always relating it to what was current, or to its historical context and making connections. Would you like to tell us about this?

C.C.: Yes, I feel that trying to bring in current issues helps the student to see the relevance of the text, and it is a way of engaging them. They begin to see the broader implications of the specific literary text they are studying, so it is not just about *Jane Eyre* or *Wide Sargasso Sea*. It's also about how the issues in the texts relate to contemporary notions of identity and gender politics. When, for example, Christophine says, "A man don't treat you good, pick up your skirt and walk out", students can relate to that. It makes them think about how women negotiate a space for themselves in patriarchal societies that attempt to constrain them. Students begin to see that the text is not just about the past; it affects their own lives. African and diaspora women writers have been very influential in getting predominantly black students, especially women, to look at how female identity is being represented. Reading literature is not just an academic exercise. Making the connection between the literary text and the student's own experience turns reading into a process of personal enrichment.

Q: In light of what you have just said about connecting the text to students' experience, what are your views about teaching "popular" literature?

C.C.: I developed a course called Reggae Poetry, which analyses the literary qualities of song lyrics. It's very popular. One semester, when the department was struggling to fill courses, I had more than forty students in a relatively new course. And I would always tell students that the course was not going to be easy, because it's reggae poetry. They would be studying orature, which is different from the more familiar forms of literature they knew. And I would also add that I knew that if I called the course Reggae Orature, nobody would be interested in it. But I assured them that they would have fun exploring reggae poetry. I also warned them that students who underperformed always failed.

Q: One of the things I've noticed that you have done for the Department of Literatures in English is you forced us all again to look at popular culture and to see the value of popular culture. How important do you think this should be at the teachers' colleges and at high schools? Do you think that we should be including more popular culture at those levels and developing a critical approach towards these?

C.C.: I think so, because one of the theoretical issues in literary studies has been the question of value, of judgement, of who decides what is canonical and what is not. And the notion of the canon itself has been contested – this list of "great" books which comes to us in an authoritative, biblical-like way, may not represent all that is valuable for us to explore about our experience. So the oral text, the popular text and popular literature have become important. I also developed a course called The Romance, which I never taught.

It starts with traditional English romance novels like *Pamela* as early as the eighteenth century and goes right up to Colin Channer's *Waiting in Vain*. So it's a wide spectrum. The course looks at how the genre developed in England and how it has evolved. The department is also teaching film, another area of popular culture. The curriculum is really expanding beyond the purely scribal and traditional literary text.

Q: Why do you think there is such a struggle to get students interested in literature?

C.C.: Well, I think one of the issues is that students don't like to read. I had an interesting experience at Hellshire Beach, which I wrote about in a column. I was talking to some young men to see how far they had gone in school and so on. One of them who was doing plumbing said he got interested in the computer, and when he went on it, he discovered that "a bare reading dis!" At school, he hadn't been interested in reading. But now that he wanted to access the world of the Internet, he had to take on the reading business. He said he was embarrassed when his friends would email him and ask, "How you tek so long fi answer?" His response took a long time, because he could not spell some of the words he wanted to write. University students will complain about studying four books in a course, because they don't really like reading, and so if literature is all about reading, then they are not going to like literature. And sometimes, the books that are selected seem very distant from their own experiences, although one of the values, traditionally of literature, is that it exposes you to worlds other than your own. For some of us, that's the joy of literature. I've just been reading Maeve Binchy from Ireland, and you know, you just enter a whole new world; it is also similar to your world but not identical to it, and you are engaged in the story as well. Some of the students are basically not really interested in the university at all; they are just here because they want a piece of paper which they think will get them a good job. That's about it!

Q: How do you manage, then, to get your students to read?

C.C.: Well, who don't read – fail! For the first-year course I taught, students had to answer on only two of the four books in the exam. So I used a sensational analogy to motivate: If you're the kind of risk-taker who would have sex with a stranger without using a condom, then you can read only two books. You can just make a gamble that you'll be able to answer the questions on "your books". If not, *yu salt*! So I would encourage them to read all four books, so that they could go confidently into the exam.

Q: Are there other challenges that you have had to face over your forty-one years of teaching?

C.C.: The big challenge is how to get students interested in literature, so they can invest themselves in it. Another basic challenge is economic. A lot of the students cannot afford to buy the books, and many times it's difficult to get [books] in the library. These days, they can sometimes access free downloads, so that makes things easier.

Q: You mentioned one very memorable session. Can you share another one?

C.C.: A beautiful one was a tutorial in the Reggae Poetry course. Believe it or not, one of the young men, Sheldon Reid, discovered Peter Tosh in the course. But it's not his fault; it's ours. All he knows is dancehall. How many radio stations in Jamaica consistently playing reggae? So Sheldon did a tutorial presentation on Tosh, and when he finished, he said, "But, Miss, da man ya bad!" It was such a wonderful moment of illumination. He had discovered that incendiary lyrics did not begin with Sizzla, Capleton or Anthony B. The presentation was so good, he gave it again at the Peter Tosh Symposium, and it was published in the *Gleaner*. Reid also wrote a poem in tribute to Tosh as part of his paper. It reflected his understanding of the way in which Tosh chanted down "peace" because of its complicity with the status quo: "Everyone is crying out for peace, yes, / no one is crying out for justice. / I don't want no peace, / I want equal rights and justice." Introducing students to a new world and firing up their imagination is exciting and emphasizes the value of teaching literature. There are these moments when teaching produces extraordinary results.

Q: Speaking of other popular forms – for example, dancehall – do you think that the students in teachers' colleges, or pre-service teachers, need to be exposed to the poetry of dancehall? I think many of them relate more to reggae artists and are reluctant to move into dancehall.

C.C.: I think they should be exposed, and they will discover that there are different types of dancehall lyrics. Of course, there are slack lyrics, but there's also conscious dancehall. There's a whole range for students to explore.

Q: There appears to be a strong relationship between your research, writing and teaching. Is this so?

C.C.: What has happened is that my individual research interests have now impacted my teaching. When I returned from teaching in the United States, I decided I was going to focus on black people's writing. There were enough white people writing about their own literature. Then I realized that most of my colleagues who were lecturing on Caribbean literature were focusing on the conventional scribal texts. So I decided to focus on the oral end of the continuum. Mervyn Morris had led the way with his excellent research and teaching on the work of Louise Bennett. I was assigned to teach the course on West Indian literature with him. One of the lectures I did was on representations of female sexuality in the poetry of Louise Bennett, which evolved into one of the chapters of my first book, *Noises in the Blood*. So there has been a symbiotic relationship between the teaching and the writing. The innovations in the curriculum that I've been able to introduce have come out of my own research interests. It was my friend and colleague Kathryn Brodber who suggested that I design a black women writers course. I called it African/Diaspora Women's Narratives instead. I wanted to focus not just on race but also on ethnicity and cultural diversity.

Q: You have done a lot of work on the popular speech form of Jamaican Creole, so have you focused on poetry in Jamaican?

C.C.: Some of the poets I've studied, Louise Bennett and Mikey Smith, for example, write in Jamaican.

Q: Do you find that it makes a difference teaching poetry that is written in Jamaican as against standard English? How do the students respond? Is it a kind of drawing card?

C.C.: In general, students do not like studying poetry, because they feel that its meaning is elusive. Instead of analysing, they end up paraphrasing. But I think a course like Reggae Poetry is popular because it deals with accessible texts. In that course, students feel less afraid of saying the wrong thing.

Q: In light of all that you have said, what are some of the changes you would like made in the teaching of literature? You have mentioned some of this already, but I just want to pursue it a little more.

C.C.: The main change I would like to see is that we give our students much clearer explanations about why a particular text is "great" and therefore deserves critical attention. Let me give you an amusing example of the problem. I was reading an *Essence* magazine and saw a poem dedicated to black hair. I read the poem and decided that it was facile. And then I noticed that it was written by Gwendolyn Brooks! A great poet! So I read it again, looking for subtleties I might have missed. And I had a good laugh at my expense. This doesn't mean that great poets can't write bad poems; it's just that my knowledge that this was a poem by a great person forced me to consider revising my earlier opinion. This is one of the problems with literary studies. We cannot always give our students precise explanations for why one text is canonical and the other is not. We need to be able to come up with clear explanations. "Greatness" is, at times, contingent.

Q: So what is your view about the dancehall artiste Macka Diamond's books? Would you take such books into a classroom. Would you consider teaching them?

C.C.: I wouldn't necessarily teach them, but I would write about them, as I did in a 2010 paper "Dancehall Fictions: Macka Diamond's 'Roots' Novels", which I presented at the annual conference on West Indian literature. There is now a body of texts that suggests that dancehall is getting a literary profile. So maybe, in another few years, some good dancehall novels will emerge. I think it's important to pay attention to this development. I've designed a Reggae Narratives course, which has been approved but not yet taught.

Q: One of the things we who teach literature say is that literature is for pleasure. But very often there is a real gap between this belief in literature giving pleasure and the actual practice of teaching. What has been your experience?

C.C.: Well, one of the questions I've always asked my first-year class as part of a formal assignment is, "What's the difference between the books you read for pleasure and the ones you study at university?" Their answer [books they read for pleasure]: romance novels, detective fiction, science fiction, thrillers, inspirational/motivational books – most of which are not canonical texts.

Q: So how do you think teachers can make the books that their students have to study appealing? How can they help their students get pleasure from reading?

C.C.: Well, it may not be possible, you know. They may just have to suffer through the course, because if they're not really interested in literature, then they are not going to be willing to stretch themselves. I'm not optimistic that we can always get everybody interested. A lot of students are taking the course because they need a first-year course, and they need this and they need that. They are very pragmatic, and they do not expect to enjoy it.

Q: What about the use of technology in classes as a way to engage students?

C.C.: What type of technology?

Q: Well, I notice, for example, that even in your presentations at conferences and in your public lectures, you usually bring in some video clips or something.

C.C.: Yes, the old-time visual aids meet the new technologies. Visuals disrupt the monotony of the voice. I wish I were more organized; then I would have my lectures on PowerPoint and drop in the visuals.

Q: Did you find that it made a huge difference – or it didn't after a while?

C.C.: It does make a difference, as the old adage asserts: A picture is worth a thousand words!

Q: My last question is, what advice would you give to teachers preparing to teach literature? What do you think they really need to be doing now in this twenty-first century?

C.C.: Well, first of all, they need to select texts that cover a wide range of interests. And they need to help students appreciate the relevance of these texts. The formidable Dr Victor Chang was very good at that. When he taught Chaucer's *Canterbury Tales*, students could see that the fourteenth-century Wife of Bath would be completely at home in the world of Jamaican dancehall culture.

David Williams

"The text is something to be savoured."

Mr David Williams has taught literature, including both undergraduate and graduate courses at the University of the West Indies for over thirty years. His research interests have included "the city" in British, American and postcolonial fiction, as well as feminist criticism. He has published poetry and critical pieces in the areas of African American and Caribbean women's writing and cultural studies. *A World of Prose*, an anthology that he co-edited with Hazel Simmonds-McDonald, is a popular text in Caribbean secondary schools.

Q: Mr Williams, what has been your overall experience with the teaching of literature?

David Williams: I want to address this by looking at the nature of literature, which in a way either allows a teacher or compels somebody who might be uncertain of his method to follow a particular direction. That is, the nature of literature encourages teacher qualities such as being able to listen, being able to give students the assurance that they can say valuable things without at the same time burdening them with the belief that they should have all of the greatest theories and background materials at their fingertips all the time. In short, I wonder if certain subject areas make for better teachers than other subject areas. And is literature one such subject area? Maybe teachers often perform better precisely because they are working in a certain subject area which makes for a certain set of behaviours in the process of teaching.

Q: But haven't you had some pretty "bad" teachers of literature? Have you never experienced bad teachers of literature who have not opened up a text for you or allowed you to express your views but instead simply gave the critics' views?

D.W.: Yes, I have had a few like that, and I know that there are teachers like that even now. But at the same time, it may be that those people are not themselves responding to the precise nature of the field that they have entered. Because if you begin with the premise that literature is the product of a creative act that is supposed to give to the reader the sense of a text whose meanings he can complete, then I don't see how you can't also accept that in teaching, you should open up a text to allow all of its possibilities to come to the forefront. In other words, for those teachers who are "bad", it may be that they are simply resistant to the very quality of the discipline that they have entered.

Q: I think that you are right to say that. Let us talk about you and your approach. For example, how do you prepare to teach a novel or a poem? Where do you begin?

D.W.: Well, for me, it has to involve a renewal of the text. It is a text I would have known and would have certainly read, but for me when I bring that into the act of teaching, I first of all have to reconfigure the text so it becomes, as it were, new for me again, and that often works for me in terms of taking a text and putting it into relationships with other texts or other discourses that I believe will enrich it. One of the things I try to do is to use music – song lyrics, obviously, but also references to other creative arts – to try to enrich a particular text, and I find that if you can choose your material carefully enough, what it does is illuminate that text so freshly for you that in turn you communicate some of that freshness with the student. I'll give you an example. I am teaching classic American prose fiction currently with all of the canonical texts: Hemingway, Twain, Fitzgerald, Cooper and others. I found Paul Simon lyrics, "American Tune", which address the equivocal sense of being American, of both having a heritage of terrorism but also having a creeping sense of doubt. I found that when I played that in class and used that as an excerpt, it really pulled out of students a set of responses that I believe makes the books, the literary text much fresher than they otherwise might have been. I also find that excerpts from journalism can help in that way. So it's a matter of making the text fresher for myself first, finding material that illuminates it all over again and in turn makes the process of talking about it more creative.

Q: May we go back to the Paul Simon lyrics? Could you tell us a little more specifically about how you worked that? Was it a tutorial, or was it a lecture?

D.W.: A lecture to begin with – for instance, I was talking about the background to American literature and the relationship between American literature, American culture and American history, and, of course, I began talking about some of those visual icons which define America in the general eye. The Paul Simon lyrics have a reference to the Statue of Liberty sailing away to sea, so I talked about that, and I set it against the actual symbolic resonance of the Statue of Liberty sitting in New York harbour and next to Ellis Island, and how for many migrants arriving in America, that was the first thing that they saw; that was the gateway to the American experience. So when I set that against Simon's lyrics about the Statute of Liberty sailing to sea, I think it enabled them to see how American literature replicates other things in the popular culture that speak to the duality of being American. Paul Simon's lyrics again have these two lovely lines: "We come on the ship they call the *Mayflower*. / We come on a ship that sailed the moon." With those two lines, he bracketed American history from the Puritan fathers to that of the moon landing. So that reference in the lyrics gave me a chance to talk about the American journey. So that's the kind of thing that I find very useful in making a text an open territory for students.

Q: Thank you, that sounds very interesting and very creative. What about how you prepare for poetry? Does the fact that you are a poet influence in any way how you teach poetry? We have spoken about prose and I guess this holds true for the other two genres?

D.W.: Yes, I would also try to find useful material. Material that can throw an interesting light on the text, whatever genre it is – whether it's prose fiction, poetry or drama.

Q: Maybe I should tease that out a little bit more. You spoke about music references, but you also said that you would use material from journalism.

D.W.: Okay, I'll give an example. In the 1960s, this American author called Studs Terkel published a book of journalism called *The Working*. It comprises interviews with a hundred working Americans from different fields, and he basically transcribed the interviews, of course beginning with an introduction and concluding with an epilogue. What that kind of journalism did was to give the voices of actual Americans reacting to their sense of what being American meant for them, and I found that it was very useful to use excerpts from Terkel's book to talk about how the Americans are experiencing these values that I was concerned with. Students, I think, I hope, got a sense of how actual Americans speaking off the cuff, as it were, understood and represented their lives, and how that could be stacked up against the way in which the American sense, the American personality, the American identity was shaped in the text. So this is how I try to supplement the literary text by using excerpts from journalism.

Q: What about the fact that you are a poet? Does that in any way affect your preparation for teaching poetry or any of the other genres?

D.W.: Yes and no, because I have to say that when I am teaching prose and poetry, I think to some extent the authors that I choose to focus on will in some way be aligned with my own sense of how poetry does work.

Q: So are you saying you actually select poets based too on how . . .

D.W.: No, not just based on what my own taste or direction of writing poetry is, but I do acknowledge, as it were, that *I* am a better teacher when I am teaching material that seems to me to work according to certain basic qualities that I also try to practise. That is not the only fact, but I have to be honest – it does enter into my choice. Another thing that enters in, I think, and equally important, is my sense of poetry that leaves students feeling for the genre as something that is not a coded, hidden territory that is not related to their own life. So I try to select poetry that I think gives them a sense of being in dialogue with discourses that they hear around them all the time and the discourses that they see functioning in the world around them, because I want to emphasize the relationship between poetry and all of the other competing discourses that we take for granted. I want them to see poetry in terms of a continuum with existing, somewhat ordinary discourse that they use all the time. That for me is a very important door that has to be opened if students are to respond to poetry without some of the dread that they are often burdened with.

Q: Yes. Could you please explain more fully what you mean when you say that you want your students to see the relationship between poetry and other competing discourses so that they see poetry as part of a continuum of discourses?

D.W.: Yes. This involves my trying to do away with the notion of poetry as belonging to high culture, and other everyday discourses that they hear belonging to low culture. So I try to point out or demonstrate to them the relationship between basic rhythms which are devoted to communicating a sense of the lyrical and a rhythm that constitutes a line of poetry. This is whether [the rhythms] work in terms of the line of a popular song or a particular sentence. So when the line of poetry is given a name such as iambic pentameter, they see that there is a relationship between the movement of a line in a poem and the movement in the line used in the environment all around them; for instance, when a man expresses his pleasure in watching a good stroke played in cricket or something like that. I try to talk about the commonality of the rhythm, whether that rhythm moves within the structures of a poem or occurs within some statement in which someone is expressing their emotions strongly. I find that that connection often allows them to see that whatever rhythms that may acquire certain labels of poetry, what those labels do is merely designate something that they are already familiar with.

Q: Are there aspects of poetry, though, for which they may not have a ready parallel?

D.W.: I don't believe that, because I think that though poetry, made more intensely and more economically, addresses certain things, all of those things are found in most of the other discourses that they deal with. So it's a matter of trying to show them how poetry's methodology may sometimes concentratedly intensify something that they are already familiar with. Hence, I don't think it's different in kind, [but] maybe different in terms of levels or intensity. Although many persons have the impression that poetic language is something high-flown, I try to show them that it is a matter of the poet selecting a word or a phrase that is likely to leave a groove in the reader's mind. And that in itself is similar to somebody engaged in a cursing match with somebody else, finding a particular swear word or a particularly vivid phrase to communicate how he feels about a certain occasion. The poetic act of finding that memorable phrase is equivalent to the person in that situation finding that memorable phrase.

Q: This is certainly a novel way of looking at the language and rhythm of poetry. How did your students respond? Can you recall any particularly engaging teaching session?

D.W.: I remember one moment – teaching a Walcott poem – where the poetic voice behind the poem remembers a moment of pleasure or intense feeling and produces an image which evokes a woman's breast "in my cupped palm". I remember when we were talking about that poem in that tutorial, the line in the Walcott poem did not evoke what I thought [and feared] it might evoke in the students: a sense of distaste for that erotic touch. In fact, what it did was to evoke from two of the male students there in the class at the time a memory of an equivalent moment when a sensual experience left a strong impression on them, and the basic response was, "Boy, I can appreciate that line." It wasn't a response based on any kind of salacious understanding. Walcott had found an image, a memorable core for these male students.

Q: Was there any particular teaching experience that you can recall that was very disappointing or challenging?

D.W.: Yes, I remember a Dylan Thomas poem which I loved, "Fern Hill"; it is a lovely poem about childhood and the exhilaration of the physical experiences of being a child; it's about remembering sensations of being young and responding to landscape. I remember that I was more than a little disappointed, because when I brought that to the class, there seemed to be so little appreciation among the students for something I thought as young people they would all be able to remember very well – that kind of exhilaration of being young and responding to all of the sensuous images in the world. Even when I attempted a reading of the poem in which I tried to communicate that sense of joy, it didn't seem to move them very much. I was disappointed, even though they did eventually undertake a reasonable analysis of the poem. That analysis was almost too rational; that analysis reflected a too limited emotional engagement with the poem, and the analysis was mainly a kind of reasoned taking-apart of the images of the poem. For me I would have wanted them, as it were, to respond [to the poem] just at the level of the sensuous. That taught me that it isn't always the case that my personal pleasure in a poem will find an echo in students who may have a different kind of relationship with the world than I have, or may simply have a different response to the rhythm. I think I learned there that there is a limit to the reach and effectiveness of any of the universal languages that we associate with poetry. In the end, individual students are people coming from a varied range of backgrounds and coming from a varied range of vocabularies, and these vocabularies will include different rhythms which perhaps make it slightly more difficult for them to respond to things that I have had a different exposure to.

Q: I would like to return to something you said about reading the poem in class. Do you always do this as a lecturer, and why?

D.W.: Yes. I found that reading the poem always first of all translates the poem from being an artefact on a page to being something in the air. I try to read it in total, so they get a sense of how the poem evolves and how the poem arrives at some kind of destination. In reading the poem what I do is re-experience the poem. In hearing the poem read, [students] are provided with an opportunity to perceive the differences in emphasis with the way in which they would have read it. They therefore begin to see the poem as an individual artefact that can be shaped by a voice. It becomes something that is now associated with a voice, with accents, and they can perhaps imaginatively hear their own voices and accents taking hold of that artefacts. So I always try to read the poem. Of course, this works much better if you are working with poems that are really short, because if it's a matter of a lecture or a tutorial, it's simply not always practical to read the long poems.

Q: Are there other approaches that you find work particularly well?

D.W.: I find that an attempt at historicizing a text can be very useful. If you can connect the production of a particular work, whether it's a poem, a novel or play, with an event, a historical personality or a set of historical circumstances, it gives the poem a context which goes beyond simply putting it in the frame. It gives the poem a connection with events which themselves have a certain grammar. So if you can connect a work like Stephen Crane's *The Red Badge of Courage* with the American Civil War – not just as a statement about something dramatic that happened from 1861 to 1865 but with an experience [as a result of] which so much American blood was shed and so many allegiances were split – then that contextualization gives the whole text a more immediate resonance, I think, for students. In a way they can connect the text with human cost, with human sacrifices and human endeavours.

Q: So is it, then, a matter of the lecturer just coming in and talking about the historical period?

D.W.: No, I think the lecturer would try more specifically to pick out human choices, events which were determined by human choices and events that therefore led to some kind of outcome. They can pick these out of a period and talk about these events as being emblematic of that period and then connect the text via these events to the historical moment. I think that's much more effective in terms of just talking about those dark periods themselves.

Q: Yes, perhaps that's the mistake some teachers make in just giving a general sense of the time period in which the text was written or the historical time frame, instead of stating that the piece of literature is inspired by something representative or emblematic, as you said, of the historical time. Have I understood what you said correctly?

D.W.: Yes, it is about individual human choice.

Q: What has been particularly interesting for you in teaching Caribbean literature?

D.W.: What I try to do, and I found this is quite effective at times, is I try to communicate to my students what we already know, like the specific qualities of the Caribbean landscape. I mean, we are dealing with islands here, and we are dealing with a fairly intimate sense of living in places where one is always aware of the horizon. One is always aware as well of the difference between the shoreline and the mountains and the hills, and I have found that using their knowledge of the Caribbean landscape, physical landscape, and asking them to bring that awareness into their response to the Caribbean text has often been a very effective way of opening up a text for them. I suppose it's trying to translate geography away from being just spatial concepts into being something that is connected with the artefact that the imagination makes, so they see a relationship between the Caribbean beach and the monarch and the figure of "the castaway", which is such a recurring image in Caribbean literature. So that is one of the things that I have found to be very effective when teaching Caribbean literature.

Q: This is a unique way of bringing across the literature.

D.W.: Yes. I have found another approach also very useful, although I haven't used it as often as the one I stated previously. I have tried at times to use the particular rhythms of the Caribbean voice and even the regional differences in accents to talk about the way in which Caribbean literature has found a very specific way of handling prose. I think that's a valid claim, so that when we read, for instance, a section of a Lamming novel or a Naipaul novel or a Lovelace novel, what we are getting is – and of course [it's] more sophisticated than this, but to some extent – a transcription of Caribbean accents and Caribbean rhythms which have made the English language something different and specific. I found that that approach can often make the business of reading a novel a little bit more attractive to the students. I try to convince them from the very beginning that these novels are using the common language, the English language, in ways that are fundamentally different from the way in which a James Baldwin novel would use the language, or a Patrick White novel would use the language or a Muriel Spark novel would use the language, and I often find that that lowers the resistance that some of them may have to reading prose fiction. It's not just a matter of identifying the echo of Caribbean accents there. It's also a matter of them believing finally that the Caribbean experience inserts into English something that is unrepeatable, something that they won't find elsewhere, and consequently it gives them a sense of exploring the novel in ways that are perhaps more reassuring to them.

It doesn't always work perfectly, but it generally does create what at the beginning you always need: a relaxation and a sense of literature as something that doesn't demand from them a tension. And that lowering of tension is often the first step in making the experience of reading a little bit more entertaining and a little bit more enlightening.

Q: You mentioned the matter of having to lower the resistance of students to reading. Do you find that to be a major challenge?

D.W.: Yes, even now and even at the level of final-year students, I encounter an attitude that says a text is something to be gone through, and where possible a text is something to be gone through utilizing as many shortcuts as one can possibly find. I don't often enough encounter an attitude that says that a text is something to be savoured. So very often, and I am sure other teachers have this experience too, your first task must involve persuading them in some way to lessen their resistance and to bring to the text the same kind of attention that they bring to other moments when they consume cultural artefacts, like, for instance, when they are on the Internet, or they are listening to a song on the radio. The resistance is sometimes lowered if you make an explicit connection to something that they take pleasure in. However, there are times as well when you have to remind them that reading is a very personal thing, and what they can begin to discover in these texts that they are studying for these courses is precisely the sense or the pleasure that they would take in a text which they read without any expectation or fear that they would be examined on it. I try to ask them to put away the thought that this is something that they will be tested on and simply enter the text as something that they would begin to be curious about.

Mark McWatt

"The real context of any work of literature is literature itself . . ."

Professor Mark McWatt has been teaching literature for forty years, since 1976, at the University of the West Indies' Cave Hill campus in Barbados. He began teaching at Cave Hill as an assistant lecturer. However, he has been teaching informally for much longer – since he was in sixth form – as he taught fellow students, discussing literature, writing literary essays and assignments with them. He was also a literature teacher to his friends, who were science students at university and had to understand and respond to compulsory questions on literature and writing. His experience in teaching literature has also no doubt been informed by his writing, which has won him a number of awards including the Guyana Prize for Poetry, the Commonwealth Writers' Prize, the Guyana Prize for Literature for best first book of fiction, and the Casa de Las Américas Prize.

His publications include *The Journey to Le Repentir* (2009) and *Suspended Sentences* (2005), which was the winner of a Commonwealth Writers' Prize in 2006, as well as the Casa de las Américas Prize for best book of Caribbean literature in English or Creole.

Q: Professor McWatt, what is your interest in literature?

Mark McWatt: What I like is literature itself – reading and rereading the literary texts we teach. I like discussing these with students, discovering any original ideas they might have about the texts we study; reading new work and trying to include some of these in the courses I teach. I like the way literature stimulates my own writing and keeps me focused on the wonder and the infinite possibilities of language. I like the way literature recreates and renews the familiar world I live in. I also enjoy the more mundane aspects of teaching – such as observing students grasp and enjoy the meaning of a poem or other literary text and grow in their understanding of the subject, I enjoy some students' own satisfaction or wonder at what they have learned and their consequent ability to discuss and analyse important or difficult texts.

[Literature] has always been very important to me – it sometimes amazes me to think that I have been paid all my working life for reading novels, poems and plays, talking to others about these and trying my own hand at writing literature. There has never been anything else that I'd rather be doing. Literature – writing – contains all other disciplines and subjects; a novel, poem or play can be about *anything*. For this reason literature will always be important to me – and teaching it is probably the best way to learn and experience it.

Q: Given such interest in literature, how, then, do you actually prepare for your literature lectures and classes?

M.M.: I prepare for lectures by renewing my familiarity with the text(s) to be taught, rewriting or revising or just rereading my teaching notes, and often checking for the latest critical writing on the text. For tutorials I think of questions that will prompt discussion among the students and topics that relate the literary text being studied to contemporary problems and concerns – in an effort to stimulate debate and make tutorial sessions lively.

Quite often the students are assigned tutorial topics upon which to make presentations or stimulate discussions. I never give a lecture to students without asking questions and eliciting responses. Students, like all of us, vary in their readiness to participate in discussions – and often those most eager to participate are not the ones with the most important or interesting contributions to make. Hence, it is necessary to assign topics and questions for discussion and to draw the less-talkative students into participating.

Q: What has been a memorable literature session for you?

M.M.: There have been many – it's hard to think of one. I enjoy lectures to first-year students (introductory courses in lit) where students have fun with definitions and examples – figures of speech, rhythm and metre, character, point of view, dramatic irony and so on. Also, I will always remember with pleasure some classes in a small specialist course I taught on Milton's *Paradise Lost*, where students were assigned small parts of the text for performance. They had fun, particularly with the debate in Hell, where they enjoyed playing such characters as Satan, Moloch, Belial, Beelzebub and so on. It was memorable because the students understood the concept of improvisation and of getting into the various characters, in terms of voice, tone and attitude.

The ones that I'd rather forget are those where the students assigned to make presentations did not show up or else obviously had not prepared. I also remember a few lectures, usually late in the evening, where the students appeared tired and uninterested and were dying to get home, some leaving before the class ended – and this despite my efforts to spice up the proceedings with questions, anecdotes and so on.

Q: In reflecting on the positive and not-so-positive experiences of teaching literature, can you recall teaching methods that worked particularly well for you?

M.M.: I believe that most methods can be made to work and that it is necessary to vary the teaching methods from time to time. By the same token almost any method can be ineffectual if it is overused or if it marginalizes student input and lively discussion. For example, PowerPoint presentations: to me these work best if the slides projected are visually interesting, short on wordiness and permitted to prompt discussions which the students will remember much more than simply copying down lots of words from the screen. I think classes work best when both lecturer and students are prepared – and it is therefore necessary to assign specific readings topics and tasks. In this way lecturer and students will be sharing and improving work already done and opinions already tentatively worked out, rather than blundering through material confronted for the first time. I also think it is appropriate to provide students at once with positive feedback for their efforts – that is, to commend good performances and presentations and to explain what made them worthwhile.

I think that I have already mentioned some of these. I would say, though, that it's probably a mistake to be too prescriptive in terms of strategies. The best strategies will evolve from the dynamics of the classes and the knowledge, experience and personalities of the students. Groups with different abilities and commitment will require different strategies.

For me, poetry requires voice: poems have to be read aloud with the required emphases and sound effects. In this way poetry comes alive and is understood, instead of remaining on the page.

For drama, I always find it less than effective to simply read or talk about scenes. I always encourage students to enact and dramatize bits of the plays they study – or to see performances or videos thereof. Enacting even bits of scenes enables a sharper understanding and appreciation and helps communicate the emotional impact of the play and the importance of performance.

For prose fiction, I always find it worthwhile to get into the intricacies of plot and character and to discuss such areas as irony and point of view. I would even encourage disagreements among students about the apparatus and the techniques of fiction – as I feel that this enables the class to understand more clearly what is involved in the writing of fiction, and to appreciate that there's no single "correct" way of interpreting a novel or short story. For this reason, I tend to quote the comments of critics and scholars and ask students whether they agree or not with those views – and why?

I also emphasize the connection between poetry and music, and the fact that it needs to be voiced or read aloud, rather than silently – thus the importance of sound and rhythm. I get the students to read poems aloud, and I often encourage them to try writing a poem or two of their own.

Of course, the type or structure of a work will determine the way you teach it. You cannot approach Jane Austen's *Pride and Prejudice* in the same way as you would Joyce's *Ulysses*, or Robert Antoni's *Divina Trace*, or Wilson Harris's *Palace of the Peacock*. I always try to elicit the students' own response to the type of novel and then work from there, explaining that the real context of any work of literature is literature itself, rather than the "real" world and, therefore, the necessity of finding literary precedents and comparisons.

Q: Overall, what works best for you in the literature class? What methods? What setting? What teaching aids or instructional materials?

M.M.: Again, there's need to vary these according to the teacher's perception of the abilities and grasp of the students. Perhaps one develops an instinct for what would work with each particular group of students. The important thing to realize is that the students' needs, in terms of understanding and involvement, should be fulfilled, rather than the teacher's.

Q: You recently stated that you were now writing "picture poems". Will you please explain what these are, and how you moved into doing those?

M.M.: My writing of picture poems emerged from my interest in taking photographs of interesting scenery. The photos became a stimulus for my writing. I don't want to suggest that the photos created the poems or that the poems created the photos. Neither one is subordinate to the other. It is more a matter of the photos interfacing with the text.

Q: Is that in a kind of intertextuality way?

M.M.: Yes. The photos and the text exist in a kind of dialogue with each other; the photos are linked with the poems.

Q: In the Teaching Caribbean Poetry workshops, you introduced teachers to using photos as a stimulus for teaching poetry. How has that strategy been working?

M.M.: It has worked well. It is not for everybody; it just depends on how it moves you. I usually work with six interesting photographs and ask the teachers, as an overnight exercise, to select one and use it as a stimulus for writing a poem.

Q: Yes, I've seen how well it works. I was actually surprised at some of the very sharp lines and images that emerged. What would be the next step with such a poetry writing exercise?

M.M.: The poems were really very good. Some of the lines were sharp. They have a draft of a poem that they could go on to refine. Instead of a photo, you could also use a favourite song.

Q: I hadn't thought of that, but I can see that working really well. I guess we could extend that to a favourite line of a poem or a startling/disturbing/creative/cryptic line from a prose piece, newspaper and any other media.

Q:You often focus on landscape in your work, both in your writing and in your critical work, and of course in your teaching. Why that focus?

M.M.: It's the influence of the landscape of Guyana – its rivers, forests. I lived in the interior, and it has had a tremendous influence on me, mostly positive. When I moved to the city, I actually felt cut off.

Q: How have you used that as a strategy for teaching literature?

M.M.: I ask students to pay attention to place. For example, in teaching Derek Walcott's "A City's Death by Fire", I ask students to think about and research, the importance of the actual situation to which the poem is linked. In teaching Kamau Brathwaite's "Mother Poem", based on mother, motherland, home, I emphasize the matter of landscape and home. I'm interested, too, in the fiction of Wilson Harris and note the way landscape drives a writer to a startling revolutionary way of expression. I've asked students to focus on the words in the text and to see how landscapes affect people. In fact, I developed a set of PowerPoint slides about landscape and show how landscapes can be inverted. Wilson Harris talks about sunlight coming up. And, of course, in dense foliage where you cannot even see the sky, you can see sunlight reflected in a river, sunlight coming up.

Q: What specific help do your students generally need? How do you provide it?

M.M.: It is difficult to talk about "specific" help that is "generally" needed. The kind of help that a class of students needs is largely provided in the classes themselves through information, questioning and discussion. More difficult is providing the help needed by individuals who have special problems of understanding: these I encourage to see me outside of class, where they can ask specific questions without the embarrassment of having the whole class listen, and where student and teacher can try to understand each other and solve specific problems.

Q: What have been interesting assignments for them and for you?

M.M.: Students have responded well to assignments involving group work, such as enacting small portions of text and submitting a written account of the experience and the difficulties encountered; debating both sides of questions that arise in literary texts; for example, "Does the narrating voice in 'The Schooner Flight' represent views and attitudes that are typical of the ordinary Caribbean man?" Better students sometimes enjoy being given the task of refuting a published critical opinion of a text, and some have responded well to the idea of "writing back" to the poem or to a particular argument within a text.

Q: Yet even with our best methods, we still face challenges of teaching literature. How have you been addressing them?

M.M.: I'm afraid I never think formally about this. I just twist and adapt and improvise, as the class or the occasion appears to require. I guess I feel that the need to "address" problems or challenges can lead to attempts to impose solutions – whereas I prefer to have solutions work themselves out through the interaction of students and teacher and literary text.

Q: That is certainly a creative approach to facing challenges. Yet that may in turn generate some anxieties. Elaine Showalter, in fact, writes about seven teacher anxieties: training, isolation, teaching versus research, coverage of the material among others. What, if any, teacher anxieties do you experience?

M.M.: Again, I tend not to think in these terms, perhaps because I have had no formal teacher-training. My main anxiety or concern is being able to communicate an enthusiasm for literature to the students.

Q: In hearing you speak about your use of landscape as a teaching strategy, I've detected a particular teaching style. How would you describe it?

M.M.: I would say relaxed, informal, questioning – at times histrionic.

Q: Your students have been mainly Caribbean. Given that experience, what do you think is essential for teaching Caribbean literature effectively?

M.M.: I think anyone who can teach literature effectively can teach Caribbean literature. For me Caribbean literature is related much more to literature in general than it is to the Caribbean as a special place or experience.

Lorna Down

"Literature can help us connect the 'scattered pieces' of ourselves."

Dr Lorna Down has been teaching for over thirty-four years. She began her career teaching Spanish, though she had graduated from Shortwood Teachers' College in Kingston, Jamaica, with a teachers' certificate in both English and Spanish. This changed, however, after she completed her first degree at the University of the West Indies at Mona, where she focused on English literature. Further studies at drama school (now the Edna Manley College of the Visual and Performing Arts) grounded her love of literature and the teaching of literature. She taught literature and drama in education at Mico Teachers' College (now Mico University College), and literature, and literature education for sustainable development at the UWI.

Down has also researched and published widely on literature and education for sustainable development. In addition she has co-authored a series of language textbooks.

Q: Dr Down, what do you particularly like about teaching literature?

Lorna Down: I love literature. It gives me a great deal of pleasure, helps me understand myself and life in general. I want my students to experience this pleasure; I want them to have insights into their own lives and others. For me, literature helps to develop our critical thinking skills; it helps us to read people and life very carefully.

Q: Why is teaching literature still important?

L.D.: I think more than ever people need to have pleasure, and to "escape" from their lives occasionally. Reading gives pleasure, introduces us to beauty in the broadest of senses. The beauty of a book enriches our lives. People need to be able to have different perspectives on the same subject. One of the things literature does for all of us is that it helps us to realize that our perspective is not the only one and that there are different and many ways of interpreting a particular situation. I want my students to understand this. Equally important, I want them to know that literature provides insights into their lives and others' lives. Good books, good literature helps to see us through life, helps us to see ourselves and our situation, clarifies situations. In fact, literature can help us connect the "scattered pieces of ourselves". I've returned home after a long trip; I'm in that twilight zone where I'm not fully home, some of me is still over there – and reading poetry or a novel can help pull it all together.

I think literature is also important as our world is forced to focus on sustainability. Based on my experience, literature can be employed to develop emotional and spiritual responses to sustainability. There is also, of course, the values dimension, which can be explored very well through literature. I've also found eco-criticism a useful approach, as students learn to "see" more clearly the environment and understand issues of place. I've actually designed a course called Literature and Education for Sustainable Development, which allows for these dimensions to be brought into play.

Q: How do you generally prepare for your lectures and tutorials?

L.D.: I read the text itself or the poems several times; I make notes on it and add as well other related material; it could be a newspaper article or material from a nonfiction text. I also like to read the author's biography and other works by the same writer. After this I read critical material on the text. I try to get a sense of what others have to say about it, the historical context, and the theoretical contexts. I usually return to the text then, having engaged in a kind of dialogue with other materials. I know how you teach the text is very important, so I also explore different ways to do so, and because I am very interested in the concept, in the theory of sustainability, I read the texts from a sustainable development or eco-critical perspective. I think about ways in which I can get my students to explore the representation of the physical environment, especially in relation to the social, cultural and economic environment.

Like many other teachers, I prepare by finding my own connections to the text. I have to be interested in what I'm going to teach.

Equally important, I try to get into the mind of the student, imagine myself as the student. So I ask myself the following questions: What knowledge are they likely to bring to this? What may they not understand? What would make this meaningful and relevant to them?

By the time I enter the class, I have a good sense of the text and most times a clear shape of the lesson format. One of the things I try to do, however, is to remain open to my students' interpretation of the texts, which a well-prepared entry may inhibit.

Q: How do you usually get students participating in classes?

L.D.: What has worked very well is to have students do presentations based on their research; I organize for group discussions, and these can take different forms. I have them write responses on sheets of paper, Post-its, and display these. I've tried pre- or post-class online discussions. One of the most engaging things is when I've been doing a particular text and looking at particular themes, and I ask them to take photographs of things around them that suggest that theme, and they come and present, or they post these to the class. Useful too has been the creation of theme boards – in which students in groups create a collage of pictures, or phrases from newspapers or magazines around a central theme.

Q: What was a memorable session for you, and why?

L.D.: I remember this class, very expressive, very articulate, and noisy. One day I took in a John Donne poem, one of my favourites. I read the poem, and there was a kind of magic that happened, and I'm not quite sure precisely what the strategy was. Somehow the poem's words caught them, and all of us were caught up in the poem. I don't know if I read it in a way that revealed my strong sense of connection with the poem, or if it was just the magic of the words. They were caught up and silent while I was reading this poem. There was just this big connection between us, and so we moved to some initial responses, in particular to the very moving last three lines. Then I read the poem again, and there was that still quality in the classroom. There was just this real connection between students, me, the poem. Something like that can happen in a literature class. It was a really heightened emotional experience.

Q: There are also those sessions you wish to forget. Can you recall a session you wish to forget?

L.D.: I recall a session where the students hadn't read the text, were blasé about the text; they came to class unprepared, and they were just sitting there waiting for me to "expound". I remember feeling very frustrated in that session.

Q: What works best for you? What methods? What setting? What teaching aids or instructional materials?

L.D.: I like to have the actual reading aloud of a section of a text in the class. If it's a poem, it has to be read aloud, and more than once. If it's a novel, I have to read aloud a page or two. I try to find strategies that would have the text itself central in the class. I like to have the texts; the words do its work. A major loss in many literature classes is the "disappearance" of the text. Somehow we've gotten it into our heads that the text is to be discussed, not read. Reading is a personal matter, not to be done on class time. I even feel some anxiety about reading the text in class – what if a colleague walked in? What would they think? Would the students consider it childish? So I've never read an entire prose text or most of a text in class. I too have bought into the fallacy that the meaning of the text lies "outside" the text, in arguing with and critically examining the literature on the text. The text, in effect, gets replaced by discussion, by examining critical material, critical theories. Of course, there is a place for these activities, these activities are necessary – but not at the expense of marginalizing the actual text.

So how do I ensure the reading of the text, of keeping the text in class?

I must confess that I am still in the learning process; I haven't fully figured this out. Usually I begin reading, sometimes the opening pages of the text or key sections, to stir interest, to develop students' appreciation for the beauty of the words, the craft, among other things. I have students read aloud, and silently, sections they select. Discussion is kept to a minimum in this kind of session.

I have also experimented with readers' theatre. I have the text read "on stage", with parts assigned. This has worked with a short story. I guess I could have taken this further by assigning a director, and a costume manager, for example. I'd have the director explain their perspective – feminist, postcolonial, eco-critical – and so also set the stage for the analysis of the text. The problem I've found with trying to do this in three hours per week is that the time is too limited. A lecture is so much easier. Yet ways have to be found to keep the text central.

Another way I've found to help students read the text is by selecting sections for close reading. I have students identify the relation between that section and others. I explore with them whether or not that section extends the story, repeats an earlier point, uncovers, clarifies . . . .

The use of video clips is also another method for encouraging discussion on the text. Used to introduce the text, they can stimulate interest in theme, character and structure of the texts being studied. I have found in fact that listening to poets read their poetry – which is often available on DVDs or videos – is a good way to engage students' interest.

I don't know if I can express this clearly: for me, really special times in a literature class are when we just suddenly get an insight into the text. I tell my students that we need to listen to each other, and that each person has an important role to play in class, and we need to know when we are to come in and play our part. And sometimes – not often – when people come in on cue, when they listen, when they respond, there is this mental and spiritual connection, and ideas just keep coming and coming, the text opens up – and exactly how that happens I'm not sure.

Q: That is so interesting. What other strategies have you tried?

L.D.: Very often I do wall work, where they all have to do some responding, going to the wall to write; they move around, get a sense of what others are saying. I'm concerned about the students who are shy. I often find the shy student is one who knows a lot about the text. I try to create a space for them to feel comfortable enough to offer what they have to say, so for some students, writing on the wall works better for them. Small groups work. I also have students do individual presentations – they choose how they are going to present. The use of video clips and interesting PowerPoints also works. Students have also responded very well to guest lecturers, and the forms of their presentations vary. Sometimes it's a brief presentation; other times I engage them in an informal conversation. The latter seems to work very well.

One of the things I tried which was really nice was to ask them to move around the campus and share a poem with someone. I suggest that they ask the person to read the poem and share their response to it. This may be the security guard, a student from another faculty. Students enjoyed going around and hearing a "non-literature" person respond to the text. The responses have been insightful.

My students also like leaving the classroom and seeing how they can connect some aspect of campus life with the text. Campus tours where we imagine the campus in previous decades, or we envision the future of the campus have worked well with some students.

It is also about finding the hook – what will hook them into the story, as with Michael in the movie *The Blind Side*. What in their makeup, their life experience can be employed to hook them to the story, to provide the necessary line, the necessary understanding. In *The Blind Side*, Michael's father is able to get Michael emotionally connected to the poem "The Charge of the Light Brigade" by speaking to him about authority figures not always getting it right, not always knowing what is right – something Michael is presently dealing with. Michael is asked what he thinks about the people in authority over him and whether they always know what's right or get it right, and to compare that with the situation in the poem. The father helps his son connect emotionally with the poem.

Q: How do teachers help students connect with the text?

L.D.: First, I believe that the teacher has to connect emotionally with the text, with some aspect of it. I recall teaching Donne's poem "For Whom the Bell Tolls". I'd actually got to this poem through reading Hemingway's *For Whom the Bell Tolls*; and wanting to know more about the source of the title, I "found" Donne. So Hemingway, in a reverse kind of way, prepared me for Donne. Derek Walcott's poem "Ruins of a Great House" has in its last stanza an elliptical reference to Donne, and this also made another connection for me. The line "And therefore never send to know for whom the bell tolls; it tolls for thee" is still enigmatic. Each time I think I understand it, I realize that I don't fully. So that other quality of literature – the enigma, the discovery and then the enigma again, the not ever quite getting it "right", is also another pull factor. A good poem for me teases, flirts with me. So a good poem is always new and yet deeply felt. That's how I connect with the work. Each teacher has to find their own way of connecting.

One of my teachers, Dennis Scott, also taught me in a very dramatic way that to get this emotional connection, one has to build trust. I recall one particular lesson in which he engaged us students in a trust exercise. He asked us to form a net by holding our hands to catch him, and then he, a tall and muscular man, climbed up onto a raised platform; we below, nervously yet with determination, held hands. With ease, he simply allowed himself to fall into our "net of hands". The thrill and fear of this activity are unforgettable. The result was that he gained for all times our trust. There are, of course, less dramatic and less "threatening" trust exercises. I certainly never tried this with any set of students, nor do I recommend it. I am pointing, however, to the need for establishing trust.

Q: That was certainly part of Scott's distinctive style. You have described interesting strategies. Do you find these vary according to the genre? How do you differentiate your teaching of poetry, prose and drama?

L.D.: I remember a friend who taught poetry at a high school, and one of the things she told me was how important it was for her to create a particular mood when she taught poetry. I've always taken that to heart.

I also believe that students have to "live a little" with the poem before going on to the discussion of it. So I try to encourage them to see the poem, identify what's happening, who's talking, how the poem is making them feel, what is standing out for them. Students are asked to have a "quiet time" with the poem.

I have also used a video clip of a dramatic reading and staging of a poem to help students experience the power of a poem when rhythm, rhyme, diction, image, form and theme are "perfectly" matched. There is little doubt that the film, the visual, made a tremendous difference to students' response to the poem.

The big task, however, is how you encourage students to explore the poem after they connect with the poem, have spent some time "dwelling" in the poem and have some sense of the poem as a whole. I believe that one way to do this is to decide on a focus, a particular entry point. The lesson will then move to the "opening up" of the poem, as students and teacher focus on the selected aspect – for example, style, imagery, relation to other texts. The aim is to deepen the poetry experience for them, to help them understand, in the broadest of senses, the themes, the ideas the poet presents and the ones we discover or construct.

Let me give an example. In Goodison's poem "The Woman Speaks to the Man Who Has Employed Her Son", I may choose to focus on the poem's imagery. To begin the lesson, I ask my students to jot down comments on dominant images in the poem, including noting their relation to the poem as a whole or the poem's theme. I then share my perspective on the contrasting images, on images of betrayal and so on. Or I may approach it from the point of view of commenting on images depicting social, economic and spiritual environments. This would then be followed by students sharing their earlier written comments and responding to my presentation as well as each other's. Introducing selected critics' perspectives would be the next step. Further discussion would include an examination of what had been changed by hearing others' perspectives, what hadn't and why. The class would end by having students write questions posed by poems raised. I've also tried giving them a statement about what the poem is about, what the theme is, and having them consider it by close reading of the poem. They are then asked to respond to the idea – refuting it, agreeing with it or modifying it.

What I've found particularly useful is to have students engage in an analysis of their interpretation of a poem – that is, to examine how they are interpreting the work. This usually helps them to understand the process of interpretation.

Seems to me as well that we shouldn't try to "finish" the reading of the poem, sew it up pat and give the students the impression that any interpretation is the final interpretation. It may even be useful to return towards the end of the course to a poem studied earlier and see what other insights emerge.

In general, what I have found is that different poets, different poems evoke different responses, and so the teaching style will vary depending on the poem.

For drama there has to be some performance. Brian Heap's workshops on how to make the play come alive have been most helpful. I became aware of the importance of having students pay attention to costumes, staging, directing, lighting and other performance elements. Classes too with Denis Scott, Honor Ford-Smith and Leonie Forbes have trained me to attend to these elements. I've often found it useful on a number of levels, therefore, to take my students to the theatre so that they get a clear sense of a stage, of movement, of performance, even though the play seen may not be the play being studied.

Q: How would you describe your teaching style?

L.D.: I would say eclectic. Generally, I aim for student-centred lessons using a workshop and seminar approach. I will usually have a brief lecture, but I plan for many group activities and student presentations. I want students to understand that their interpretation of the text is important and that the text's "meaning" [will] emerge through their interaction with it. So classes are planned with that in mind. I also use a lot of audiovisual materials, as they really engage students' interest as well as mine. At my best, I'm enthusiastic and passionate about my teaching and student learning.

Q: What have been some of the challenges of teaching literature? How have you been addressing them?

L.D.: I think that the challenge most teachers face is students not reading the text. Getting them to buy the text, to read the text, to read what others have to say about the text and writing about literature are the major challenges. I find that getting them really interested in the text helps to address this. Another challenge is how to keep the text central. It's easy to use the text simply as a way to elaborate on literary theory or as a stimulus for discussion on a particular theme. In these ways, however, we miss the richness of the text. So reading a section of the text in class and referencing it a lot are some of the ways I try to keep our focus on the text.

Q: Elaine Showalter writes about seven teacher anxieties: training, isolation, teaching versus research, coverage among others. What, if any, teacher anxieties do you experience?

L.D.: Syllabus coverage. I am usually anxious about covering the syllabus, because it's easy for me to pursue different though related aspects. I am sometimes anxious about engaging students, about ensuring that the lecture or lesson is at their level of understanding, readiness or interest.

Q: What do you think is foundational for teaching Caribbean literature effectively?

L.D.: I think it's easy to assume that the students know Caribbean history and our current realities in relation to global realities. Yet they do not necessarily come with that knowledge, and so we have to ensure that they are introduced to this. I also think that it's important to teach Caribbean literature in relation to other literatures. A too-narrow focus will likely cause students to miss its richness. Knowledge of the development of Caribbean literature also needs to be there. The literature is relatively new, and today's students need to appreciate that there wasn't always something called Caribbean literature. Classic West Indian texts, therefore, need to be included in any course in Caribbean literature.

Brian Heap

"The reason drama has such an enormous impact is because it liberates the classroom; it is emancipatory in the way it uses time and space."

D r Brian Heap, drama teacher extraordinaire, actor, producer of many award-winning plays and the Jamaican national pantomime for many years, began teaching in Jamaica as a teacher of economics and history. (His first degree was in these subjects.) Yet a love for the arts, and in particular drama, had been nurtured by teachers who took him as a student on theatre, concert and gallery visits. His involvement in theatre and his talent as actor and producer soon led to his teaching drama in a teachers' college and further studies with world-renowned teacher of drama Dorothy Heathcote. Heap recalls how those studies changed his life. Heap went on to teach drama at the Edna Manley College of the Visual and Performing Arts in Kingston, Jamaica, and became director of studies there. He taught there for approximately twenty-five years. After this, Heap became staff tutor and later head of the Philip Sherlock Creative Arts Centre at the University of the West Indies at Mona. He was also artistic director of the University Players, the outstanding theatre group of the UWI. Heap taught at the UWI for twenty-five years, fifteen of those full time.

Heap has also published a number of books and articles on drama and Caribbean. These include *Planning Process Drama* (with Pamela Bowell, 2013) and *Putting Process Drama into Action* (with Pamela Bowell, 2017).

Q: Dr Heap, thank you very much for agreeing to do this interview. When did you get involved in teaching drama? How did you manage to move into this direction?

Brian Heap: Well, I have to go back a bit, because I was recruited as a high school teacher to teach economics and history at Campion College [in Kingston, Jamaica]. My first degree was in economics and history, though I had always been interested in the arts. I was very fortunate in that I had teachers at high school, in particular, who encouraged us in the arts, you know. They took us to concerts, to theatre; we had trips to London, to galleries and shows and that sort of thing. So I was very much a consumer of the arts, and my years at university doing my first degree were very much taken up by my engagement in the arts. I think what was happening during those undergrad years was that I was getting a kind of arts education through appreciation.

So when I taught at Campion, I eventually took charge of the drama group and had the group enter the Secondary Schools Drama Festival. But also, being a white Englishman in Jamaica, I got involved in theatre, as very often people do plays where a white person is required. My first stage experience in Jamaica was replacing Bob Kerr in Trevor Rhone's *School's Out*. *School's Out* had been running for six months, and Bob had something else to do and wanted me to just finish off the last six weeks of the run, but in actual fact it ran for another six months. And then Bob Kerr, Natalie Thompson – who was the managing director of Cinecom Productions, but who was a very fine actress – and I started the Children's Theatre Trust in the 1970s. We did three major productions, and adaptations of *Goody Two Shoes* and *Cinderella* called *Goody and Cindy*. They were basically adaptations of traditional pantomime stories. By this time, of course, you know, Jamaican pantomime was doing *Johnny Reggae*, and they were well and truly Jamaican.

It was during this time that I was invited to teach drama at St Joseph's [Teachers' College, Kingston, Jamaica]. So, armed with Peter Slade's book *Child Drama*, that's what I did. A lot of my teaching in those days for primary school teachers was about playing games, doing different exercises, adapting Jamaican ring games and having small-group improvisations. It was very limited in a way. Yet we brought a lot of play and joy into learning, which is still a very valuable thing. We did poetry; we did things that could motivate the children in the classroom. I had a small Theatre in Education group one year, where we did a play. It was called *Puss Boots – Puss in Boots*, really – and we took it out to schools. We performed in primary schools. It was very creative.

And the opportunity came in the early 1980s for me to go and do further studies. So I went off to do a post-grad degree at the University of Newcastle upon Tyne (now Newcastle University), which is where Dorothy Heathcote was based.

Dorothy was the staff tutor in drama at Newcastle and was world-renowned for her approach to drama in education. And I went there on Dennis Scott's recommendation – and it changed my life. It just changed everything. Dorothy took you to a whole different level. I mean, I think I floundered around for the first two or three months with Dorothy, not knowing what on earth I was doing, because it's like she just totally turned everything that I had been doing upside down, and what she began to impress on us was the care you take with preparing a drama lesson. She showed us how much of an impact drama could have in the classroom with the teacher actually taking on a role and driving the drama from within the role. And the thing is that the whole curriculum could be accommodated, so you could be using a dramatic situation to teach science, to teach maths, to teach just about anything. There were wonderful projects, and it might involve, for example, going to Edinburgh to work with nurses or something like that, or you were working with town planners or family therapists and things like that. There was just a whole range of applications of the drama.

Q: Were you able to replicate anything like that here?

B.H.: We have done. I remember one amazing occasion where I walked twenty soldiers from Up-Park Camp to the Drama School, and basically the drama was about people's perceptions of uniform.

The soldiers were amazing. They got involved, and even though they were in uniform, they demonstrated how their behaviour changed when they were out of uniform and how the perception of other people of them changed. We sort of reconstructed all sorts of things, like soldiers rescuing old ladies in clubs and stuff like that.

I've worked with different groups apart from teachers, and later on I did a lot of work here on the campus with the nurse trainers at the School of Advanced Nursing Education, and it was on one of those occasions that a colleague of mine – we were at school together, Dr Anthony Simpson, who is an anthropologist and lecturer at Manchester University – watched me do this. We were actually looking at HIV education and how HIV might affect relationships within a family. At the end of the session he said to me, "You have to come and do this in Zambia", and he got some funding – Save the Children, in Sweden and South Africa – for me to go for three weeks and do work with teacher-training colleges – about three colleges. There I concentrated on behaviour change, because what I realized was that the kids knew all the messages – they knew everything about abstinence, how to use a condom, being faithful – they knew all of those messages, but it didn't translate into behaviour change. And so I did work where I concentrated on the sociological aspects of HIV.

I created a situation where there was a child who had been orphaned as a baby and was HIV positive. The child's sibling was not HIV positive, but the sibling was fourteen years. The fourteen-year-old had to take care of this newborn and make decisions about what should be done. Eventually the child had to be abandoned in an orphanage, because the fourteen-year-old changed as a result of circumstances. He had to go and look after himself on the street, kind of thing, and make a life. But I refused to let the students just abandon the baby. They had to write notes to pin to the child.

Q: Could you walk me through a little bit of how you actually set up that drama? Did you, for example, take a role?

B.H.: I started with the jacket. The driver who drove us all over Zambia had this lovely windbreaker, and it became a big joke that every time we got to a school, they had to take his jacket off and lend it to me. Or if the fourteen-year-old was female, I had a *chitenge*. I draped it around the chair and asked them to imagine a fourteen-year-old boy or a fourteen-year-old girl who was HIV positive, and then I said, "How do you think that child" – he or she, depending on what we had selected – "how did they come to be HIV positive?" And they would say – they really don't get dramatic – rape or prostitution or abuse. It was always something sexual. And I said, "She was born with it", and then the difficult thing was that they couldn't believe that anybody who was born HIV positive could survive to be fourteen. That was the big thing, because this was before anti-retrovirals became widely

121

available in Zambia, and I said, "No, she was taken care of." We then flashed back. It was amazing, really. If it was the *chitenge* cloth, I took the cloth off the chair and turned it into a baby, so that this child now became a baby, and I didn't want anybody to play the role, because I didn't want to put the burden of being HIV positive on any of the kids who were participating. So we then turned it into a baby, and then I asked if somebody would become the older brother or the older sister and take the baby. So now we got to the next stage, which was, "I'm not HIV positive, but the baby is. What am I going to do with it?" And they wrote a lot of stuff about the situation, because I asked them, "What's this brother feeling right now? What's he thinking?" And they wrote a lot; for example, "I'm young, I need to make my own way in life, this baby won't survive", and so on and so forth. And so they wrote a lot of stuff like that, and then gradually, we began to develop the story, and used flashbacks, moving between present and past times.

The basic argument of my PhD thesis is that the reason why drama has such an enormous impact in an educational setting is that it liberates the classroom. It is emancipatory in the way it uses time and space – it liberates children to be. Even if they are still in the confines of a classroom, they are liberated from that time and space, and they move into all sorts of other experiences of time and space.

And so we flashed forward [to] where the fourteen-year-old brother was now twenty-eight years old, and he was married; he'd been successful. And the kids all chose this. I said, "What did you want him to be in life?" And so everything that they wanted for themselves was what that fourteen-year-old became. So the baby is now twenty-eight, he's married, he's educated, he's got two children, he's got a good job. So all of those things were agreed on. And I said, "But he's guilty", and they said, "Yes, he feels guilty that he abandoned his sister [or he abandoned his brother]", and I said, "So what do we do about that?" And so there's a whole drama in, should he go to the orphanage now or try to bring the sibling into the family? And there were terrible repercussions, because the wife said no she didn't want an infected person in her family and all that sort of thing. So it was all this sociology and psychology and relationships and things like that which began to develop. And at the end of each session, I eventually would say, "Who is willing to represent the infected sister or brother?" And so what they had to do then was to put on the jacket, and I said, "It's such an act of courage to do that, because you are putting on a mantle of HIV." And they did it – they were willing to do it at that point, because the lesson had been taught that they weren't going to get sick.

I think there were all sorts of little things that I did with them in between, because when we first had the baby, I asked them to sing a lullaby in the vernacular, their vernacular, and that was contentious, because in one school that I went to, they had class rules, and one of the class rules was no speaking of vernacular languages. Zambia has seventy-five languages, and my driver spoke Bemba, his wife spoke Tanga, and the two kids – they had two boys – spoke Nyanga. So there were three different African languages in one family. I said, "How do you communicate?" And he said, "In English." And it's a shame, really, because I haven't really had the opportunity to do that kind of work in the Caribbean.

Q: When I read about Dorothy Heathcote myself, I tried to do it a little like that. I tried to move away from the usual small group performing a skit. But I didn't have much success, because I wasn't trained in that way of doing it.

B.H.: It can be difficult. I note that students that I've had have tried to follow Betty Jane Wagner's book on Dorothy Heathcote's *Drama as a Learning Medium*, and they simply can't make any sense of it. So I think that was one of the reasons why Pam Bowell and I wrote *Planning Process Drama*, which was a way of saying, Look, it's really not rocket science, it's very straightforward, and these are the questions that you ask yourselves – and it's been very successful. We've had a lot of good feedback from drama departments worldwide who said, We used that book because it just sets it out in a very clear way what you need to do in order to make it happen. And I think sometimes what teachers tend to do is to cling to the drama too long. One of the things that I always say is this: once you have got your point across, shift gears; go into something else; give them another perspective.

I remember doing drama with some kids about people who had bought government land. I set up the situation: "So you've all bought land from the government, and you've all bought your housing lot, and you're coming to the contractor to decide what kind of structure you're going to put on the land – and I'm going to take you over to the contractor – studios, one bedroom, two bedrooms, three bedrooms. What size you have depends on the size of the lot, so I need to go and inspect the land." So all we did was actually step outside the room, and then we came back in, and I said, "I've got some bad news for you", and they said, "What?" And I said, in the role as the contractor, "You can't build on that land," and they said, "Why not?" and I said, "Well, it used to be a burial ground, and it must not be disturbed at all; there's actually a caveat on the land title that says it can't be disturbed for 150 years – and it's still got, like, fifteen years on the title." I continued, "What I'd be willing to do is buy it cheap from you," and they said, "Why should we sell it cheap?" and I replied, "Well, I can't build for fifteen years, so I would have to be holding onto the land; therefore I can't pay the full price for it." Well, they were furious, absolutely furious that the government had sold them land that they couldn't use. But then we switched and I said, "Well, talk to the press." So then the roles changed, and one of them became a representative of the purchasers and explained everything.

What made me laugh was how nobody ever asked me what "caveat" meant, and they started using it. So the representative was talking to the press and said, "We understand that there's a caveat on the land title that says we can't build, and we're furious." Then, of course, they all went into the role as journalist and role-talked the story of this demonstration that was going on and how the government had been unfair. And in every story, the word "caveat" – spelled in endless different ways, because they had never seen it – came in. And at the end of the drama, I said to them, "What is interesting is that nobody asked what the word 'caveat' meant." And I said, "What does it mean?" And they said, "It means a condition." So I said, "Who told you?" And they said, "No, we just got it – we just understood."

And that is the other aspect of drama, which is that when you use language in context, you don't have to explain. They begin almost immediately to use it, and I think that's one of the very powerful aspects of this type of drama. It gives you that context for language and the context for learning as well. So you're learning in context, and you're learning language in context. So if the teacher is sensitive, the teacher can start using big words or unfamiliar words, but instinctively the students understand what they mean. I think we are kind of obsessed in our education system about explaining things to people. We're always telling people stuff instead of allowing them to find it out for themselves.

Another experiment that I did was I took a group of teachers from St Joseph's on a field trip to Port Royal. I gave them a questionnaire before they went, and it was questions about Port Royal – for example, the church treasure, the parish church that belonged to Henry Morgan, but lots and lots of different questions about Port Royal. When we came back to college, I said, "What you're going to do now is put together an exhibition on Port Royal, based on the questions that were asked." And so some of them had replicas of gravestones, some had pictures and drawings, others had sketches that they had done and little bits of information on charts and posters and things like that.

When the exhibition was ready, I brought in a group of children from St Francis Primary School next door, and I gave them the same questionnaire that I'd given the teachers, and I said, "Go around and see what you can find out." Within forty-five minutes they'd completed the questionnaire. They had all the information that the teachers had found out about Port Royal, even though they were now getting it second-hand. I then followed up with a drama exercise, which was about picking up survivors out of the ocean immediately after the earthquake in 1692. So we were actually pulling people onto the ship and hearing their stories about how they survived.

Later in the day, I brought in another set of students. They were designated a "B" stream – non-readers. I gave them the same questionnaire, and when the teacher said to me that they can't read, I just ignored her, and I spoke directly to the children. "These teachers are very fortunate, they've been to Port Royal and have had a lovely time, and they've come back, and they're sharing what their experience was like in Port Royal with you. So they put together this exhibition, and on this paper there are some questions to be answered about Port Royal, and I'm wondering if you're clever enough to find the answers. You know what you can do? We've got about twenty-two teachers here, and they are more than willing to help you. If you're stuck with anything, just ask a teacher." A few of the children pointed at their papers and asked, "What does this question say?" And the teacher read it for them and said, "Right, go around and see if you see any words that look like that." And that's what they did. I told them, "If you find the answer, if you can't write a full sentence, just write one word." And that's what they did; they gave me one-word answers or short phrases. It took them about two hours, but they completed the same questionnaire.

So the point that I am making is that the same questionnaire functioned for the teachers, the children who were considered bright, and the children who were streamed as non-readers. What we often do is cut out the latter group from having the same experience as the former group. And the amazing thing is, when we did the drama, they pushed the teacher into the boat with them, and she complained! I could see her attitude changing completely, because she didn't realize that these kids were so capable of doing things, of finding answers, of finding information, and she didn't see their lack of reading ability as just a kind of temporary disability. She had seen it as a permanent flaw, as something they were never going to get through. The most miraculous thing about that lesson was that she actually realized it was only temporary, and it was something they could get over. I think she probably felt overwhelmed by having thirty or forty kids who couldn't read in her charge, and she couldn't possibly listen to all of them read or give them individual attention. But what she began to realize was that through drama, through other kinds of stimulus, they were able to find information, use information and be creative.

Q: All right, listening to you and hearing about some of these fantastic experiences, it's clear that you spent a great deal of time preparing for your sessions. I think a lot of teachers who are teaching drama don't realize the importance of this. But would you like to say something about preparing for your classes?

B.H.: You have to think very carefully about all the elements that go in, and then, once the drama has got going, you have to think on your feet; you have to keep shifting gear and taking on board what the students offer you.

Pam and I wrote an article for the *Journal of Aesthetic Education* where we talk about this spiral of creative exchange, where the teacher initiates the drama and is working as a teacher, a director, a playwright and an actor in the drama. If you're in role or you're devising a play and you're directing where it's going to go – because you want the children to have the best experience – you're also teaching. And using those four roles simultaneously, you get the children started. Then suddenly they take up the drama, and they start feeding back, and they're working in four different roles as well, because they're also actors, they're students, they're learners and they're teachers as well. They're learner-teachers, and that is what I say happens to me. I'm not really a teacher, I'm a teacher-learner, because I learn from every experience. Then there's this constant feedback that you're getting where students may say, "Oh, we could do this, and we could do that."

A lot of teachers very often say to me that they could never be like me, because they don't see the world the way I see it. And Dorothy Hepworth said she felt she had this ability. She said, "If you imagine a tree, I can immediately go into about six or eight different engagements with the tree: somebody coming to cut down the tree, I'm in the tree, like a bird in the tree, or I'm sitting under the tree." She said, "I can sort of almost immediately position myself in relation to the tree and get a drama going from that." But usually, I say to the teachers, what you need is a dilemma, and the dilemma then starts that spiral going. I say "dilemma" rather than "conflict", because conflict tends to be interpreted as violence, and that's what teachers are shying away from. But a dilemma – I'll give you an example of a dilemma. So I read them *The Brothers Grimm* story about the old man and his grandson, where the family treat the old man very cruelly, because he's got old and dithery. He spills his soup on the table, and the daughter-in-law gets angry with him and puts him to sit by the stool on the floor and gives him a wooden bowl to eat his food out of, and sometimes you could hear the old man crying because of this treatment. One day the son and daughter-in-law are sitting at the table, and their four-year-old son is playing on the floor. The grandfather is by the stove, and the grandson is putting some pieces of wood together, and the grandfather says, "What are you doing?" And the grandson says, "I'm making a trough so that my parents can eat out of it when I'm big."

So then we think of ways of bringing the old man back to the table. We did a whole drama with this. It was all about repositioning ourselves. It was not about playing the members of the family. We explored different options: suppose we shift the drama to the neighbourhood, and we have a meeting of the Neighbourhood Watch where somebody reports that they've heard the old man crying, and they suspect that there's abuse going on in the house. What do we do? That's the dilemma. How do we deal with this? Do we call the police? We can't falsely accuse the people. Do we try to do an intervention some other way? Are there other ways we could sort of try to find out whether what's happening is really true – whether he's been badly treated? And the teachers had long discussions about this. One suggestion was that somebody could go to check the blood pressure of the old man, ask questions and see whether he's all right and whether we can deal with the situation.

Q: So do you go, then, with a lot of stories? You seem to have a lot of stories.

B.H.: Well, I mean, the thing is that you only need one – you only need one story. But I think what's critical, certainly in process drama, is shifting the point of view. I tell the story of Molly Woppy, which is almost like "Jack and the Beanstalk", but a feminist version with a girl as the hero who conquers the giant. However, Molly and her two older sisters are abandoned by their parents. At the beginning of the story, they're abandoned in the forest. The reason is that their parents had so many children, they could not get meat for them. This is what the story says. And I wrote a role as the father. We put the father on trial as a deadbeat dad who abandoned his girls in a dangerous forest. And because I played devil's advocate, they immediately assumed the moral high ground and raised questions like, "How dare you abandon your daughters to their fate in the forest?" And I said, "Well, I couldn't feed them. If they'd stayed home, they would starve." And they said, "Yes, yes, but you know, you're putting them at risk. Why didn't you abandon the three boys instead?" And I said, "Because people don't feel sorry for boys. They might feel sorry for girls, so that's why I did it. The girls stood a better chance of surviving than the boys would." Suddenly the point of view began to change, and they realized that nothing's black and white. Everything's shaded; everything has these grey areas that if you really look, you will see.

Q: Let's backtrack a little bit. When you actually go in to set up the drama, do you usually begin with a story, or do you move automatically into role?

B.H.: It can be anything. I mean, like in the HIV drama, it was an object. I started with an object. I could have started with a picture. We talked about this in some of the courses that I taught. I remember one of the girls doing something absolutely amazing; everybody cried when they saw it. She used the poem "Ballad of Birmingham", which was about the little girls who were blown up in the church during the civil rights era. She got a little girl's church dress, partially scorched by an iron. She laid out this dress on burnt wood with two little girls' shoes beside it. I think they were scuffed. She had burned one at the heel and one at the toe. Then she put police tape around it – the crime scene – and everybody who came and looked at it burst into tears! So it was the power of the image to evoke what the seriousness of the story was about.

You know, I've had big rows with teachers about teaching children about death. They deal with it every day. I said, if I looked at "The Pied Piper of Hamelin" as a story, it's a huge tragedy. It's a very tragic story – the people lose their children. Because they won't honour their debt, they pay the ultimate price, and they lose their children. And, of course, I'm very theatrical in the classroom. I'll get the teachers to write about this. I'll say, "Imagine yourselves as parents. It's six months since the children have disappeared. How many children did you lose? How many children went with the Pied Piper from your house? Was it your only child? Was it two? Was it more than two? How are you feeling now? Is there any hope that they're ever going to come back?" and other questions like these, and they write these wonderful things about it. And then we read them. One person will read theirs, and then we sing: "*Where have all the children gone, long time passing? / Where have all the children gone, long time ago.*"

And, of course, they start to bawl. There was one teacher who when I did that exercise made a big mistake of naming the children after her own children, and she couldn't get past the first sentence. She just burst into tears. She said, "I can't believe this."

I consider that one really, really important aspect of drama education is about emotional education. Children have to be able to put a name to the emotion that they are feeling. Too often they are frustrated because they are inarticulate. They don't know the name of the feeling that they are experiencing. They can't put a name to it, and so very often it just becomes vexing, but it's more nuanced than that. When you think the feelings that they have are nuanced and confusing, when they're hurt they will say that they've been "dissed". They can't say why they feel they've been "dissed", or what it is. So I think talking about emotions is important – and the drama can help them to experience joy in a joyless existence. A lot of children have enormous responsibilities at home: they work, their parents exploit them, send them on the road to go and beg money and sell, you know, all those sort of things. We don't know a lot of the time what our kids are experiencing. I will just say why I think this is important. There's a book by Sylvia Ashton-Warner called *Teacher*, and she taught Maori children in New Zealand.

Sylvia Ashton-Warner is a very well-known educator. She taught Maori children and she could not get these children to read, because they were using the Dick and Jane books – Spot the dog, see Spot run, see Dick chase the ball, and all of that. The children were just not interested, it was not in their experience – it was not part of what they were about. So she said, "I'm going to ask you all to give me a word that you want to read, and then I'll write it for you, and then this is the word that you will learn to read." And the first little boy said, "Frightened." Now that's not a word that you would give a child to sight-read – with the *ght* combination. So, she said, "Why do you want to read that word?" And he said, "Because my dad comes home drunk at night and beats my mum, and I'm frightened." And that to me gives you the reason why children have to be taught how to put a name to what they've experienced.

Q: You integrate so much into the lessons. There's the writing, there's the reading, there's the music, there's the art and there's the actual drama. It's a holistic approach to teaching literature.

B.H.: Yes, it is.

Q: When it comes now to the formal text, how do you get your students to read? Do you have any problems in any way with them actually reading? Let's take *A Doll's House*, or even one of our own plays, a Trevor Rhone. Do they read?

B.H.: Yes, well, of course, they don't read it, and that's what the article is about that I've just done for the *Caribbean Journal of Education* [CJE]. It is how do you get them to read and to study? If you're studying dramatic litera-ture, then you have a specific approach to that, and the thing is that children need to have a reason to read the play. Their basic reason, which is because it's on the syllabus, is not a good enough reason for them to read anything. I always say to the teachers, the first problem you're going to have is that they don't have the book, they haven't bought it – so when are you going to start teaching this text? When the entire class can prove to you that they've bought the book? No. You can't wait that long.

There are problems on both sides. There's the problem that the teacher's already taught this book so many times that she's fed up with it anyway. That could be the case. Or that it's brand new to her as well, and she doesn't really feel very confident in teaching it. Then you've got this whole thing of, "Why should we do Shakespeare?" or "Why should we even be doing Trevor Rhone?" You know – what's the point? So I think that's one of the reasons why I say, Look, cut up two copies of the book, stick them on cartridge paper, put them on the wall – and then you see the whole play as it is set out. And then it's so important to know the shape and form of the play. Is it five acts? Some acts have seven, eight, nine scenes. Some acts only have one. A Caribbean play will have two acts and maybe even five or six scenes in each; maybe one; maybe a few more. So what's the basic difference between a scene and an act?

If we set up a process drama, we can imagine that we're a company of set designers, and we've been asked to submit set designs for this play, and nobody has ever read it before. We can ask the students to go through and see what the different scenes are. Where is it set? Is it in a castle? Is it in a village? So in an oblique way, they realize that there are so many acts, so many scenes; the scenes seem to shift from Macbeth's castle to the heath, whatever that is. It's giving them permission to know it's all right to be ignorant. They don't get that in school. What they get is it's *not* all right to be ignorant – it's only all right to know things. And if you don't know things, then you're not in it.

So it's teaching from a position of "the edge". Dorothy Heathcote would sit there, then suggestions would start coming, and then she would start edging in; it's what she called "edging into the thing", instead of heads down and we all start with "Let's get with the programme first" and things like that. And of course, the thing is, if we're now seeing designers, set designers, we're actually looking at something else. I'm talking to them almost like colleagues now: "Well, if it's going to be inside the castle, what do you suggest?" "Are there some big walls?" You know, things like that. "But remember that it has to change, and it has to open up so it can't be too solid." And you're arguing about something completely different, but very gradually somebody will get up, and they will go back to the text and say, "Well, there's a banquet scene, and it says a ghost comes in", and I would say, "Oh, so we need a ghost effect as well." So you, as a teacher, are kind of processing the stuff that's coming from them.

I always remember John Fines was one of Dorothy's followers. He was a great teacher himself, he was a history man, and he always said Dorothy Heathcote had taught him that if you think you know where you're starting point is for teaching, take two steps back, because you're too far ahead. So I think my idea there of the pre-text is a double thing. It's before you engage with the text, but it's also learning about the text on the pretext of doing something else. So that I might not start with scenery, I might start with props. If I've got a load of boys, it might be how many daggers do we need for this play? For *Old Story Time* or something like that, you're dealing with this feeling of a country place. What are some of the things that give you that feel of, you know, what a *yabba* is, or a kitchen bitch? A lot of them don't know, but they learn, or somebody in the room will say, "Oh yeah, my granny has a kitchen bitch", or something like that.

Q: Will you share with us some of your teaching experiences at the UWI? What are some of the challenges with this work, and how do you deal with them?

B.H.: Tradition – breaking the yoke of tradition. It's what Ken Robinson refers to. First, you still have an education system that was designed for the industrial revolution, and second, the scientific revolution and children have more computer power in their phones than it took to send [people] maybe to the moon. It's that kind of strange situation. And knowledge is ubiquitous – it's press a button and you find something, you find some information. And so this whole thing of teachers trying to be the fountain of knowledge is a false premise.

In the article that I've sent to *CJE*, I quote Charles Dickens where he talks about the teacher who has been churned out in a factory, and how many courses, head-breaking [difficult] questions he's answered. And Dickens goes on to say that perhaps if he had learned a little bit less, he would have been able to teach much more. And that's the thing – teachers need to learn to let go of seeing themselves as the fountain of knowledge. I say in the paper that the hardest thing for a teacher to say is, "I don't know, so let's find out." Being an educated person is not about how much you know; being an educated person is about knowing where to find it when you need it. That's where it is. A lot of our people who suffer from lack of education in Jamaica suffer because they don't know where to go and look; they don't know where to go and find answers to seemingly impossible questions and problems. The solutions are there, but they just don't know where to look.

Q: So you think the tradition needs to be changed?

B.H.: I think that many teachers teach how they were taught, and so there's this paradox in a way that you "play at teaching". The real inauthentic behaviour is a teacher going in and going through the motions of being a teacher. It's like a "go in" role as a teacher – when you go into the classroom, and then the kids go into role as learners, and it's a totally inauthentic experience. What drama does is it breaks all of that, and it gives me permission to say, "Well, I don't know, this play's a complete mystery to me." Now if a teacher takes that position, then the children look at it and say, "Yeah." Where do you begin with something like this? You say, "Well, let's look at the beginning and see where this is."

Q: Dr Heap, that's just really hard to do.

B.H.: Well, it isn't. It isn't hard to do –but teachers don't trust the children. They've built up this antagonistic relationship between themselves and the children. I remember going to do a film for the Ministry of Education, a drama class – because when we were doing the ROSE [Reform of Secondary Education] curriculum, Janet Johnson said, I want some films to show the minister why we're doing drama.

So I went to a boys' high school with the film crew, which included one of my former drama students. That's why I chose him, because I thought, he's sympathetic to drama. When I got to there, I said, "I'm here to film a drama lesson with some of the boys", and a couple of teachers came and looked at one of them and said, "Oh yes, it's 8B, they're the worst class in the school!" And I looked at them and said, "Well, I'll be the judge of that." And I went across to 8B, and I said, "Good afternoon, gentlemen." The boys replied, "Good afternoon, sir." I said, "Right, let's get the hard part over with quick. You see the camera there? Wave to your mother, pull faces; do everything that you'd do when you stand in front of a camera; pose hard." And things like that. So they all exhibited all of that, and I said, "Now he's invisible, forget him, he's not even here, so just ignore him for the rest of the class."

And I did a lesson on how it was possible in drama to play an inanimate object. You could act, you could be a person, but you could also be a thing if the play required it. And we decided that we would all become kitchen appliances – and it was fantastic. They had such a good time. They were so creative. So, it was, like, this guy was a two-burner stove, and when somebody came and struck a match. . . . You know, it was wonderful. They had a good time; we had a good time; the cameraman was filming everything – and when we came out, we see these teachers. They kind of can't believe that all these boys are around saying, "Sir, when are you coming back?" But then, of course, what they're going to do is they're going to turn around and say, "It's because you're white or because you're a stranger or because you're exotic or because you beguiled them", or things like that. And I say, "The problem is that you allowed familiarity to breed contempt. You breed contempt for them, and they will respond with contempt for you."

So, anytime there is school, school must have a chalkboard and desks all facing the same way, and, you know, it's a ritual. Schools have become ritualized and not authentic places for learning, and it's hard to break that. Plus given the stigma associated with the aesthetic objects like dance and drama, it's not serious work.

I always say, a lot of teachers when they're in the classroom spend half of the class time trying to attract the attention of students: "Would you look over here?" "Excuse me!" They're bored – they're absolutely bored stiff! And then if you look at what drama does, if you put the play on the wall when you're sitting there and say, "Well, we're supposed to design the scenery for this, and I don't know where to start. Anybody got any good ideas?" then suddenly, people are doing stuff and don't want to leave it when the bell rings, because what they've done is they've gone through so many levels of engagement, they've got to it very quickly. You're not sort of attracting their attention; their attention is already attracted. So they move very quickly through attraction, attention, involvement, when somebody gets up and does something, commitment, interest, passion – and when the bell goes, nobody wants to leave until we've finished this. How do you get them to that point instead of skirting along the surface of trying to attract attention and never getting to levels of passion?

Q: Dr Heap, my final question, although I think you have answered it throughout, really, is do you think that all the grand claims for drama can actually be realized?

B.H.: If people take it seriously and encourage training, people can be trained. I mean, teachers have said to me up here when they have finished the Story Drama course, why did I not do this in college, because it would have saved twenty years of grief.

SECTION 3.

MILLENNIALS, THE GLOBAL
AND NEW TECHNOLOGY

The Third Generation of Caribbean Teachers

The third generation of teachers, represented by Kelly Baker Josephs, Norval Edwards, Sharon Phillips, Sandra Robinson, Samuel Soyer, Aisha Spencer and Ann-Marie Wilmot, also speak to a pedagogy of connectivity. Teaching the new millennials, the twenty-first-century learner, they are faced with students who are dealing with different challenges. Attached to their smart phones, linked in to tablets and computers, these "digital natives", as they have also been called, are living in an ever-increasing complex, ambiguous and fast-paced world. There is also their deep involvement in social media: Instagram, Facebook, Twitter. Technology is central to their lives. Very focused on the present and on the "immediate", for them the future is "open", uncertain. They appear to be at ease with the future. The anxiety of planning for the future, so much a part of other generations, is absent. And their penchant for futuristic films suggests more than anything else their view of the future as intriguing and filled with possibilities.

Yet it is a future edged by threats of planetary extinction. Globally they are all confronted by the question of the sustainability of the environment, of climate change and its impacts, for example. Social and economic relationships raise questions of justice, of equity, inclusivity and peace. This is the era in which they live and the context of their lives. With information so readily accessible, even in bite size, they cannot escape the beauty and ugliness of this age. In today's classroom, teachers, therefore, have to possess knowledge not only of their subject area and its pedagogy but also of global issues and the technology in which their students are immersed and what this portends.

The immediacy and fast-paced living of these millennials contrasts greatly with the slow-paced act of reading literature texts. Deep reading, with its making of space and time for reflection and contemplation, can thus be a challenge at best, or at the least an inconvenience for them. How this impacts the teaching of literature is revealed as these teachers discuss the methods and teaching approaches they found best suited for these learners.

With this generation of teachers, the element of connections that dominates is that of first connecting to students and their global context and then connecting them to the text. In addition to this, they, like the teachers in previous generations who have taught them or with whom they have worked, continue to acknowledge the importance of valuing the students. Interestingly, each generation emphasizes and elaborates on the specific elements of connections.

Millennials live within the paradox of an extended world and at the same time a contained world; they possess a technology that both puts them in immediate contact with people all over the world and at the same time limits their social interactions on a face-to-face basis. Many are, therefore, known for poor social skills and the accompanying longing for emotionally satisfying connections with others. Literature can provide a site for such longings to be met, as students connect deeply with the text, with each other and their teacher. They link together, making for a community conscious of the global space they inhabit and need to conserve.

This generation of teachers, then, addresses specific ways to connect to millennials as they create, re-create or co-create methodologies for engaging them in literature.

Essential for connecting to the millennials is researching how they learn, how they construct their own modes of knowledge and what knowledge they possess, value and want to discover. Edwards discusses this in depth as he explains how he researches the way students construct their own modes of knowledge. Visiting their popular social media sites, noting what they comment on and reading their comments, he gains insight into their particular ways at arriving at and building knowledge. Employing these insights, he is able to craft strategies for engaging students in literature and so create a community of readers relating to each other, the teacher and the text.

Being mindful about their context does not mean, however, abandoning old methodologies that worked in the past. It will mean revising them. Such "old time things", as Soyer asserts, can be revisited and redesigned to meet the needs of this generation. He shares details of these strategies that led students to connect to and enjoy the texts. Most important, he tells us, it is not a single strategy but a variety that will lead students to learn to appreciate the texts being studied and discover the many truths they offer.

Mindful also of students' love of and "dependence" on technology, Wilmot speaks to how she encourages them to set aside their tech tools for a while and connect with their inner selves, and to draw from within, to discover how much they know. Employing strategies that allow for the creation of a community of readers, for finding the "personal" response to the literature material, they come to a new appreciation of literature. And though there will always be the challenge of students who wish to short-circuit the process by settling for the ready summaries on the Internet, Wilmot's consciousness of the changing landscape of her students prepares her to experiment with different strategies for reaching them.

On the other hand is Joseph's approach to technology. Her work on the Digital Caribbean focusing currently on *As Flies to Whatless Boys* is a fine example of how technology can be used to deepen learning and have students critically reflect on the how, what and why of the literature text. Her use, too, of online discussions, of smart classrooms also help her to relate to them, to connect to their world and engender a love of literature.

This generation of teachers in connecting students to text also deliberately addresses the global context. The previous generation showed this mainly as they attended to traditional as well popular culture and historical place. Here it is the wider, global context that is considered. It is a context that demands knowledge as well as action. Literature learning, therefore, also means "engaging students in issues of concern to them, from global warming to world hunger", so that they gain "the confidence to act" (Lombardi 2007).

This approach is exemplified in the way the teachers interviewed also approach the social, economic and cultural context of their students. So Soyer speaks of his "fascination with words which among other things help take poor people to places they can't afford to go". Here the teacher of literature positions himself in the wider context of education's purpose to transform people and place.

Josephs reflects on another aspect of this consciousness of the global context in the literature classroom. She speaks about her classroom as a space of multiples, which complexifies the Caribbean. It is a space that allows Asian students, Caribbean students and "Caribbean-identified" students who have never actually been to the Caribbean to voice ways in which a common history has shaped their lives. Local, regional and global issues are thus incorporated into the teaching of the text.

Surprisingly many of these students have to be introduced to the practice of reading – a practice foundational for the avid reader of literature that these students may not have engaged in. Spencer tells us that students do not necessarily know how to read for pleasure or how to reflect on a text so that its deep insights emerge. Living in a world of sound bytes, abbreviated text messages, of ready visuals, and quick and instant communication, some students may not have known the pleasure that the art and practice of sustained reading can bring. Spencer's unique way of addressing this through the use of "manipulatives" is a creative response.

Modelling the practice of reading, the opening up of the text – or "uncovering the text", as Robinson expresses it – is also a singularly important way of connecting the students to the text. This strategy acknowledges the assumption that the often taken-for-granted practice of reading is known by students. It realizes that in the same way that the ear has to be trained to listen to music, whose patterns and sounds may not be part of one's familiar musical landscape, so too have the "eyes" for reading. The current slow reading movement in all its various forms recognizes this. The following quote from Ottawa-based John Miedema, author of *Slow Reading* (2009), in an article by Patrick Kingsley in *The Art of Slow Reading*, is illustrative: "If you want the deep experience of a book, if you want to internalise it, to mix an author's ideas with your own and make it a more personal experience, you have to read it slowly." Quoted also in the same article is Tracy Seeley's comments that underline the idea that reading is a particular practice and, therefore, settling for the skimming and the reading of a book's summary is a limiting experience: "for the kinds of reading I want my students to do, the words matter. The physical shape of sentences matter."

Robinson is mindful of this. She knows, too, "how miraculous a process it is, this art of reading, 'this turning of scratches and dots into understanding, unease and inspiration", as discussed in Damon Young's *The Art of Reading* has declared. The strategies that Robinson has devised do just this help students learn how to read so that the words "come alive", rich in meaning and insights.

Valuing the students remains, however, central to a pedagogy attuned to students' context. Phillips notes that valuing of students occurs when their ideas and insights into texts are acknowledged, named and validated.

So having students know that the insights and discoveries they make have also been identified by established theorists and critics is important. It leads them to an appreciation of their own reading and interpretation. Moreso, it frees them to extend literary ideas and interpretations.

Moreover, as Phillips explains, her student-teachers, being made aware of the theories that have undergirded their "commonplace" (using the Sumara term) practice of teaching literature, are empowered to become more creative teachers. In addition to this, a constant "provoking them to think and respond" instead of creating a dependence on her or critics' thinking builds a self-confidence in their own capabilities.

Another way of connecting to students through valuing them is Robinson's idea of the "callaloo pot", which she explains fully in her interview. Robinson speaks to the importance of valuing difference, of celebrating her students' varied "callaloo pot" selves, and so engages in the reversal of a "colonial" narrative which has sought to erase, to diminish, to "other" people – a people whose sense of self and place has been shaped by ways that are different from the writers of that colonial narrative. Her teaching strategies, therefore, encourage to a great extent individual voices and responses even as she configures these in collaborative settings.

At the heart of teaching literature using this approach is that students are treated as co-learners with the teachers. Robinson tells us that teaching literature is about "uncovering the text for and with her students". In effect, she models what Lambert and Cuper insist as necessary for effective teaching in the twenty-first century, which is the teacher surrendering "some of her power as expert to join the students as co-learners"; the teacher expecting "students to collaborate with each other"; the teacher replacing lectures with "problem-based activities" and supporting "these with innovative technologies". Translating these general education principles into the literature class makes for the effective teaching of literature.

Emphasized also is the close reading of the texts, of a formal/formalist approach through strategies that are particularly engaging for these students. Josephs speaks, therefore, to the use of performance strategies, of employing students' love for popular films and movie stars, of re-visioning the examination in order to delve deeply into the text, of "response papers" among other methodologies.

Finally, these teachers address also teacher anxiety. As they open up, reflect on their professional identities and reveal their own anxieties as teachers, they create a space for other teachers of literature to face their strengths and weaknesses. They speak about student expectations concerning race, age, knowledge of the teacher, of their uncertainty and dealing with change, of finding the "right" methodology and of having the depth of knowledge required among others. And in facing these anxieties, they are enabled to find their way through challenging paths and so become the kind of teacher who will help to achieve the goals for literature education.

This third generation of teachers makes even clearer the impact of a pedagogical approach that deliberately embraces connections. They elaborate on the importance of considering context – students' context as well as the text's context. They highlight the importance of connecting with the students and ways of doing so. Furthermore, they bring another dimension to engaging students in literature through student validation. And most important, theirs is a vision of literature being employed to help students see themselves more fully and more completely.

Norval Edwards

"Make the text human by humanizing the writer."

D r Norval (Nadi) Edwards has been teaching at the Mona campus of the University of the West Indies since September 1991. He has taught primarily at the UWI except for brief teaching stints elsewhere. These included a teaching assistantship at York University in Toronto, Canada, for two years (1989/1990–91), an online teaching stint at Fairleigh Dickinson University, New Jersey, in 1999, and a year teaching part-time at Church Teachers' College in Jamaica from 2012 to 2013. He has always taught literature at the UWI, but in the few years away from the UWI, he taught an American history course at York and an interdisciplinary global studies course at Fairleigh Dickinson.

Known for his work in literary theories, Edwards has published extensively in this area as well as on a number of Caribbean writers including Wilson Harris, Jamaica Kincaid, George Lamming and Derek Walcott.

Q: Dr Edwards, could you please share with us your ideas about the teaching of literature in general, and how you prepare for your lectures?

Norval Edwards: I teach a West Indian novel course, for example, and so, based on the books, I might choose a theme or attitude which runs throughout the books, and I use that as a handle for introducing the course. I try to get the students interested by relating the ideas which they find in the text to the contexts of the writers' lives. I find that if you can bring the writers alive for them, they become very interested in the work.

There are also students who are turned off by what they see as the difficulty of writers, like, say, a George Lamming or a Wilson Harris, but when I begin to talk about the biographical details of these writers' lives, they become interested. For example, I will talk about the fact that Wilson Harris was a surveyor, and how this explains his interest in exploring the interior, in using the exploration of landscape as a way of talking about the human psyche – so cartography then becomes a trope for psychological exploration. As a result, the students begin to see the relationship between the flesh-and-blood human being who wrote the book and the seemingly abstract ideas that the course is grappling with. In fact, I found that for students who are not interested in reading, one of the best ways to get them interested is to make the text human by humanizing the writer. And I know this might sound like a paradox or a contradiction, because the writers *are* human, but many of our students have no awareness of who these writers are.

When you think about it, for example, we have students coming in who were born in 1991/92. A George Lamming born in 1927 is bemusing to them, and so you cannot assume that our students have that kind of cultural intimacy. Very often, teachers of Caribbean literature within a Caribbean institution assume that our students have the kind of cultural literacy that we have, when in fact there are numerous generational differences and disparities. There are many things you and I can relate to that they simply wouldn't, and in many ways it is finding ways to bridge the generational gap between teacher and student, and I suppose that's what I mean by humanizing the text – that is, making it relevant to their contemporary concerns.

Q: I like that idea – humanizing the text, and you also said humanizing the author.

N.E.: Yes, because, as I said, the author for them is a very abstract concept. They think of the author as some kind of strange, secluded figure, locked away in some attic somewhere, writing these impenetrable discourses to afflict them with. So you have to make them aware that these are real flesh-and-blood people. They relate a lot to anecdotes, especially anecdotes about writers.

Q: So then, these are your two main ways, you would say, to get your students interested and involved. Is there anything else?

N.E.: Yes, I also use controversies. I try to find something problematic in the text, something troubling, something provocative, and I've tended in recent years to go for writers like a Jamaica Kincaid, who is always guaranteed to stir up some trouble, or a Shani Mootoo. In *Cereus Blooms at Night*, she has characters who are transgender, characters who are gay; and within the context of a homophobic society like Jamaica, these concerns allow me to "trouble" the students, to provoke them into thinking about their own understanding of sexuality, of sexual identities, of the politics of gender. These instances always provoke a very stimulating and invigorating discussion, and they become very interested in reading the text when there are these issues. So to me, I find that there has to be a certain kind of, what I call, a politics of interest that will draw the students in. And it is interesting that once they have identified a core issue that they agree or disagree with, they will take the trouble to engage with the text; and even if they find it difficult stylistically, conceptually they will still try to grapple with these questions.

Q: I really like this idea of a politics of interest.

N.E.: Yes, I think that students have to be troubled out of certain kinds of complacencies, or just plain apathy and disinterest. What happens is that when students get agitated and angry and very excited about stuff, so very often I find I have to step back as a lecturer and allow them to talk and debate and quarrel among themselves, and I will step in if I think things are getting out of hand, or I will intervene to correct an error. Because very often when the students find the text provocative, they take it from there, and so in those situations, I don't have a lot of work to do within a tutorial setting. A lecture setting, as you know, is a bit different, because the onus is on me as the lecturer to frame the discussion from beginning to end. But we do have a substantive amount of intervention, because I allow students to interrupt me, and if I have material that I need to deliver in that space of time, I will say to them, "Stop me fifteen minutes before the hour so that we can ask questions." But sometimes there are no questions.

Q: What do you do then?

N.E.: Well, I would berate them, and they would laugh and confess that "Sir, we never read the book, but the things that you have said about it sound so impressive, we will read it for the next lecture." But, of course, they will be delinquent again for the next lecture. Sometimes they never really catch up with the reading until the third or the final lecture. I usually give between three and four lectures on a text. So that is the situation.

Q: I want to go back to something you said earlier, that is, you have to step back sometimes. And I think, perhaps, that is something teachers and lecturers forget to do – this notion of stepping back.

N.E.: You're totally right, and it took me a while to learn to step back and see my role as a facilitator rather than as the conductor of the orchestra. I had to learn to be another player in the orchestra rather than try to conduct and direct everything. It's one of the hardest lessons to be learned, but it makes such a difference once you've learned it. I wasn't trained formally in pedagogical methods, I am not a trained teacher, so in many ways I had to learn on the job, like many of us who went through UWI and experienced the teaching of some remarkable lecturers like Professor Edward Baugh, for example, who brought a certain passion and erudition to the work. I think of the passion and the commitment of the people who taught us. I think I learned from them. I learned that there were certain basic standards that I shouldn't fall below, and I think the advent of the Internet has allowed me, in a sense, to broaden my understanding of pedagogical techniques, because I've had the chance to go to various educational sites and download materials about teaching. I've been able to visit the course sites of colleagues at other institutions to see how they construct their curricula, and I've been able to look at lesson plans. The Internet has definitely allowed me to broaden my horizon, and in many ways it has confirmed for me some of the practices which I've developed on my own. I was pleasantly surprised to recognize them in the course designs and teaching plans of colleagues elsewhere. I thought, Wow, I came up with this on my own, and I am glad to see that these methods are recognized – which makes sense, because I think there's a kind of common sense; it's almost as if water will naturally flow downhill. I think anyone who teaches will find that there are certain methods which work better than others, and for those of us who were never trained as teachers, I think all of us will arrive at these methods sooner or later.

I remember a talk I gave to people in the health profession – doctors and public health inspectors who were doing a PhD in Public Health. I was asked to give a talk about literature and medicine. So I went and spoke about the representation of AIDS in Patricia Powell's *A Small Gathering of Bones* and Jamaica Kincaid's memoir *My Brother*. The talk went very well. I kind of broke the ice by saying that I was going to talk about literature and the representation of medical practices, medical institutions and medical practitioners in literature. And then I said, as strange as it may sound, literature and medicine are not that mutually exclusive. I then gave some quotes by philosophers, writers and doctors that referred to both literature and medicine. I spoke about the differences between the imaginative text and the clinical record, that the language of the writer is charged with emotion because the writer seeks to convey meaning through feeling, but the doctor's case history seeks to convey information about physical conditions – the body. And then I listed the affinities, that is, the narrative affinities. I then called out some names and asked, "What do all of these writers have in common?" Of course, they were all medical doctors: Anton Chekhov was a medical doctor; Somerset Maugham trained as a physician; John Keats was trained as a physician – nobody would have associated Keats with medicine. I said to them that one of the most important poets of the twentieth century was William Carlos Williams, who was a general practitioner all his life. So the audience perked up as I gave a list of names. It was a very interesting talk, and they asked very interesting, pertinent questions.

It made me realize that interacting with people in another discipline is so useful. I talked about the representation of the nurse in C.L.R. James's *Minty Alley*, and Benoit and obeah – when Benoit asked Haynes if he had any books on science. Haynes had said that the books he had were science books, and Benoit thought that they were "science" in the Caribbean vernacular sense of the term. So we were talking about science and the cultural construction of healing in the Caribbean, and the fact that the nurse herself, who is a medical professional, is still a practitioner of obeah and science. And it was interesting; the questions that they asked were very, very illuminating because they were looking at the text from the point of view of a doctor. For instance, I spoke about the way in which the doctor was represented in Patricia Powell's *A Small Gathering of Bones*, because the doctor asked questions which appeared very intrusive, rude and prejudicial to the character. The doctor seemed more interested in trying to find out whether Dale was one of those "funny men" – because Ian is Dale's friend who collapsed in the park, and Ian was suffering from AIDS. So one of the doctors said that although the attitude was wrong, if Ian was unconscious, those questions being asked of Dale, since he was the only person who came into the hospital whom Ian knew, were not out of line, because knowing the sexuality of the patient constitutes part of a case history, because doctors have what they call a discovery procedure.

So the talk was very interesting, as I was just reading it from a totally literary angle, but the questions asked could be seen as a discovery procedure. Granted, the doctors in the novel were rude, but the questions themselves were necessary in order to ascertain the medical history of the patient, as the patient was unconscious and, therefore, couldn't speak for himself.

Q: I want to go back to our earlier discussion about your lecture style, because sometimes people think all you have to do is simply go up there and deliver and act.

N.E.: At the beginning of each semester in our first meeting that I have with the class, I explain my lecture style, and I tell them that they are free to ask questions. There are some lectures, however, where I need to get through a certain amount of materials, and I tell them before that, "Listen, guys, I have X amount of materials to get through today, so I'm going to ask you to save your questions for the Q and A in the final ten to fifteen minutes that we have." So, yes, I basically tell them up front from the beginning about my lecture style.

Q: You also once mentioned how you visit Internet sites and learn a lot about what is taking place on the ground in Jamaica. Doing this helped you to connect with the students, as these sites would provide you with information about, perhaps, popular artistes and so on. So I'm going to ask if you could share more about that.

N.E.: Yes, one of the things I found is that it is very easy to get a sense of youth culture by visiting the relevant sites, and these are usually entertainment sites. But calling them "entertainment" is somewhat of a misnomer, because they also aggregate links to news, and there might be articles of cultural and political interest as well on these sites. So Yard Flex, for example, is an entertainment site; and there is this other site called Jamaican Matie and Groupies, which is a kind of dancehall gossip site, because it deals a lot with the goings-on in the private lives of entertainers, who they're dating, who's seeing whom and so on. But even that site will post links to news articles and commentary on ongoing events like theDudus extradition Affairs –and not only do they post articles from news sites, but many of the comments beneath these articles are incisive and informed.

How is this relevant to teaching? In many ways, what I learned from these sites was that our students, who we sometimes tend to think of as lacking in critical and communication skills, are actually very creative, very critical and very analytical – but it depends on the particular context. They are very comfortable writing within the zone of a Jamaican Matie and Groupies. Some of the regular bloggers on that site are university students, and one of them, in fact, is writing what I can only call a dancehall novel, in serial instalments. It is called "Confessions of a Dancehall Ex-wife", and it gives you a window into the whole world of dancehall and young people and the kinds of relationships that they get into. It is all fictional, but fiction has always had a way of exposing us to reality. Therefore, in visiting these sites, I glean information that I can throw out in class. Sometimes my students will stop and say, "But sir, mi nevva know seh you know dem tings deh!" And I would say, "Yes, not only do I visit the sites, but I have nieces and nephews who are your age and who will tell me things." I think when you teach young people, in many ways I think there has to be some kind of reciprocity, and I don't think that as teachers we should refuse to immerse ourselves in youth culture. In other words, there is a certain epistemology, and we need to understand that epistemology. We need to understand what they know, how they know, and how they construct their own modes of knowledge, because I think that has helped me in teaching. Even when I disagree with certain conceptual positions that they keep, I can manoeuvre and negotiate with them, because I am aware of the epistemological stand-point that they inhabit. I just don't put them down, or I don't knock their position as being due to stupidity or laziness. Sometimes their resistance to reading a particular text or of understanding a particular concept is actually grounded in a rational position, and we have to understand where they're coming from.

Q: This is very useful. I don't think perhaps we do enough of this.

N.E.: Yes, our students are very interested in issues of, like, sexuality and citizenship. The stereotype of Jamaica being the most homophobic place on earth is exactly that – a stereotype. I've been able to introduce texts that are very pro-queer, and the students have read them without any problems whatsoever. Even students who might have a religious position have read texts that are written by queer authors, with queer characters, which take very strong pro-queer political positions, and the students have been able to read them and deal with them even where they might disagree with these political positions, without any problems whatsoever. So we have had some very vigorous debates in class, but no student has refused to read the material. So our students can be engaged even on the most controversial issues. In fact, the students love controversy. They like those seminars or tutorials where provocative and controversial topics are raised, because I think, too, young people like a certain amount of controversy, as it brings a level of excitement to the mundane boredom of a classroom. Maybe I shouldn't say boredom, but we know our students get bored; even our best students get bored every now and then.

Q: Yes. What have you found particularly challenging?

N.E.: Well, particularly challenging [to me] as a teacher of literature – and it's not unique to literature but [especially so] given the nature of our discipline, which revolves around reading – is the limited reading. We assume that our students read and have knowledge of many texts, but when you are teaching students who are for the most part from a society which does not really do a lot of reading, we run into serious problems. That is the bugbear for you, and I will break down some of this for you. It would not occur to many of our students at all to read other books by a prescribed author on the course. So if they are reading, for example, Naipaul's *Mystic Masseur*, it would not occur to them to read *Miguel Street* or *A House for Mr Biswas* or any of the almost thirty books that Naipaul wrote. They have this one-book mentality, and some of them have the nerve to say, "Sir, I really like Naipaul", and I ask if they have gone out and read others, to which they reply, "Oh, no, sir, I don't have the time!" So I think that is something teachers, and the university itself, as an institution, will have to work on – that is, try to cultivate a culture of reading for our students.

Q: How have you been trying to do this?

N.E.: Well, two ways. The way of gentle persuasion by recommending stuff, and the way of sheer hegemony, the prerogative of the teacher to set reading assignments where I will actually force people to go and read a text by saying, "Okay, John Brown, by next week I want you to read this other novel by Naipaul so that you can get a sense of how this theme recurs in Naipaul's work." There is usually a lot of resistance, but very often they will do the reading, and they will come back and say, "You know, sir, I really like the book." So, I am hopeful, although I encounter resistance whenever I do this. Those are basically the two ways – gentle persuasion or brute force. If you have any other ideas, let me know!

Q: All right. The other thing I want to know - is your approach to the teaching of poetry different from the teaching of prose? I assume you do both? Do you teach drama as well?

N.E.: No, I don't teach drama, and I haven't taught poetry in years. When I started teaching at UWI, I did tutorials for a first-year group. There are common strategies, but my approach to poetry is probably more intensive, and I tend to do a lot more recommending of extracurricular reading where I try to obtain as many audio recordings of poets as possible. I was teaching West Indian poetry online, and I would say my approach is a bit more intensive. This is so because of the strategy of close reading which I use for both poetry and prose; but poetry by its very nature, I think, demands that we do more close reading. And then there are peculiar circumstances, I think, in teaching poetry, to primarily Jamaican students coming in from our high schools, where the teaching of poetry, I find, is a kind of weak link. Many of the teachers tend to be averse to poetry, and I'm sure you've found this in your own experience with that. I find that even with the good students who come in, they tend to be strategically and tactically unprepared for poetry, and they will struggle more with poetry than they would with prose.

Q: What would you advise high school teachers to do about this? What do you see as really needed in the high schools?

N.E.: First, I think there needs to be a total transformation of the mindset which says that poetry is difficult and that poets like Walcott are difficult. Sometimes there is almost like a knee-jerk reaction when you say Derek Walcott or Kamau Brathwaite. I think there is a need for that mental transformation, and I think teachers need to recognize that poetry is not some difficult and esoteric discourse, but that poetry is part of the language of our daily negotiations around us. I think more inventive ways have to be found in the teaching of poetry. I am going to go back to my memories in high school. When I was doing A levels, I remember our teacher would bring in the lyrics of Burning Spear or Bob Marley for us to analyse so that we didn't feel culturally alienated from poetry, and from that we were able to recognize the commonalities between, for example, Burning Spear and Chaucer, or Burning Spear and, say, Percy Bysshe Shelley. So I think more inventive ways are to be found to teach poetry by maybe drawing on the poetic traditions that exist in Jamaican popular culture to make the students and teachers realize that poetry is not something alien to us. Having said that, I realize that nothing beats exposure, and I think that probably more teachers need to be exposed to a wider range of poems.

The teachers whom I've taught might be well versed in the nineteenth-century and early twentieth-century canon, but they are totally at sea when it comes to contemporary poets, and they are not exposed to non-anglophone poems. So they need to read more, both in other languages and in translation, because there are excellent poets out there – Latin American poets, European poets, African poets, Chinese poets – poets writing in other languages. So I think more exposure, especially to contemporary poets, would help.

Q: I'm just wondering if your writing shapes the way you approach your students' writing or even the way you teach them. Does it have an influence in any way?

N.E.: I think so, you know. My students will probably tell you that it makes me demand certain results from them, and they probably think that I'm overly rigorous with them – but yes, I do pay a lot of attention to writing in my teaching. I try to impart to my students the fact that writing constitutes a mode of thinking and that very often if they have ideas, these ideas can only take form in the process of writing, and so they need to write and write and keep on writing. My students don't do enough writing, and I also try to impress upon them, of course, the need to be meticulous in terms of copy editing and proofreading and in general take pride in their expression. So I pay a lot of attention to style, to syntax, to grammar, to the details of expression. My students complain all the time that I am too rigorous and that my expectations are too high, that I am too demanding. But I refuse to let go of these expectations. I think even the students who complain the most can discern improvement in their writing, because they have a sense of where I stand, and they try to meet me, not necessarily halfway, but they do try to improve their writing, because they know that is a clear-cut expectation.

Q: I think that teachers who also write and read a lot make a tremendous difference. What do you think?

N.E.: Theoretically and technically it should be, because if you read a lot, it is easier to recommend books for students. The problem we have, though, is that many of our students don't follow through on our recommendations.

Q: The fact that you are a model of this, though, does it help, do you think?

N.E.: I don't know. I think that's probably a question best directed at the students. You know, there are students who have come up to me and said that they're glad that I recommended such and such a text, but nobody has ever come and said, "Oh, I want to be like you when I grow up" and that kind of thing.

Q: But the very fact that you write and you publish, and they see that – I'm thinking that it must make a difference to them.

N.E.: Yes, there are students who have gone on to graduate school who have emulated my teaching, who have been inspired – and I am basing this on what they have said – who have expressed their appreciation for ideas that I threw out in a particular class. One of the things I've learned is that you never know what will inspire a student. Sometimes a little throwaway comment will prove inspiring for a student, whereas a detailed exposition, a learned exposition, might not. You never can tell, but I think the idea lying behind your question is a very interesting and relevant one. How do we function as models for our students? I can only hope that some students will try to emulate what I do.

Q: I'm sure you must be communicating your passion for reading and writing, and I think part of the problem you see in the high schools is that some of the teachers are not reading and writing themselves, and that perhaps . . .

N.E.: And they're not teaching with passion. What I'm going to say here now isn't anything new to you. The students experience a cognitive dissonance coming from the high school, where everything is taught to the exact syllabus and where there is a kind of model where an answer is either right or wrong, and the student's creative intelligence is not foregrounded, and then the student comes into university and is expected to produce original work. Nobody is impressed with a student who simply spouts off other people's ideas. So I find that students take a while to get accustomed to this. They are actually expected to think for themselves rather than just regurgitate conventional wisdom. One of the hardest tasks that I still have is trying to convince students not to regurgitate my lecture notes. The comments I make in the lectures, I see them replayed in essays or in tutorial presentations, and I will say, "No, you cannot do that." I don't mind if they take an idea that I've thrown out and then elaborate on it, but just merely repeating it is not good enough; and they have a hard time dealing with it, because they come out of a system where they do well by simply regurgitating what the teacher said. So creativity and originality are two of the hardest skills or attributes that any teacher of literature can encourage. You really can't teach people creativity. You can only encourage them to keep on plumbing the depths of their own analytical and creative skills.

Q: I've been reading a book by Elaine Showalter, *Teaching Literature*. I was quite surprised actually to find that she had moved into this field.

N.E.: You mean pedagogy? Is that what she's doing now?

Q: She has produced a book on that.

N.E.: You know, I did see a review of her book, and I said to myself that I needed to get this book, because it seemed very interesting, but unfortunately I haven't obtained it yet.

Q: In the book, she mentions anxieties that teachers and professors have, and I found that particularly revealing, because this is not something you see often in a book on teaching literature or even in ordinary educational texts on pedagogy. Nobody talks about anxieties in teaching, and I wondered if you would like to share just a little bit. Do you have any anxieties in terms of delivering a lecture or doing a tutorial or preparing?

N.E.: I do, you know, and after nineteen years as a teacher you would think – what is there to be anxious about? But I think that if one wants to be a good teacher, there has to be some kind of a necessary anxiety; there has to be some uncertainty which keeps you striving. It's a kind of self-correcting mechanism. I'm always anxious, because I think that I have to understand this enough to be able to express it clearly enough to my students. I would think, Am I oversimplifying? Or, Is this material too difficult? Yes, there are anxieties, which usually go after the first five minutes of the class, but they will return the next day with the next class. They are not crippling anxieties, I must say, but they are anxieties nonetheless. I am always – not nervous, but I'm always kind of wound up to an extent. But now I think I welcome those anxieties, because, as I said before, they keep me in check. The day when I can just walk into a classroom without any niggling doubt, I think is the day that I have become too complacent. But I would love to read up on what Showalter says about anxiety.

Q: She identifies seven teacher anxieties – for example, teacher isolation – but we teachers don't really discuss teaching.

N.E.: Yes. There's a lot we need to do in terms of issues of pedagogy and in terms of even advancing our discipline – the issue of teaching. How do we teach? What modes of teaching are best suited for a particular course or for a particular component of a course?

Q: Those are clearly important questions for us to consider. And now my final question: Your vision of English literature studies – where do you think it is going, and how will the teaching of literature help to achieve that kind of vision?

N.E.: Years ago, Eddie Baugh wrote an essay – I think it appeared in *Caribbean Quarterly*, on English studies at the University of the West Indies. I think it was subtitled "Retrospect and Prospect". In it he raised issues such as what happens when the canon taught in the English department shifts, what happens when there is the West Indianization of the English department. Implicit in some of the questions that he raised was what pedagogical approaches we are going to take. Can we continue with the old approaches that worked for, say, *Beowulf* and Milton? There were some very interesting questions and questions that indicate the vision for a present and future transformation of English literature studies.

Samuel Soyer

"I still find that there is value in the old-time things like recitation and choral speaking and asking students to memorize or to perform."

Mr Samuel Soyer has been teaching literature continuously from 1984 to the present, and he did some teaching in 1981 between January and April. He has taught from first form in secondary school, which would be eleven-year-olds, to the university level. His teaching at the secondary level included Queen's College, a secondary school in Barbados, and Schenectady High School, in upstate New York. His teaching at the tertiary level has been at Erdiston Teachers' Training College in Barbados and most recently the University of the West Indies at Cave Hill, Barbados. Between 2012 and 2015, he has been part of a joint project involving the University of Cambridge, the UWI and the Commonwealth Education Trust, which has involved his presenting a series of workshops in various Caribbean countries. Soyer has also co-authored a number of language arts textbooks.

In 2015/16 Soyer became the Fulbright Scholar-in-Residence at Alabama State University. Soyer has published a number of language and literature textbooks. These include *CXC Revision Guides: The Chrysalids* (1997), *Kaleidoscope Skills Book Three* (co-authored, 2004), *Kaleidoscope Teachers' Guide Three* (co-authored, 2005) and *Connect Students' Book Four* (co-authored, 2008).

Q: Mr Soyer, why do you like teaching literature?

Samuel Soyer: Well, I have been in love with literature from at least seven years old, when my father first took me to the library. I can't remember at what age I started to read, but I loved words, and I found that books stimulated my imagination; and I'm fascinated with words, which among other things help to take poor people to places they can't afford to go in literal terms and which do give lots of insight into human nature and the human condition.

Q: Tell me a little bit more about your father taking you to the library. That's not a usual, a common experience.

S.S.: Well, I can't remember lots of the details. But I do remember going with my sister; and at that time we were allowed about three books, given our age. I would typically finish reading them in two days, and when I went back, the librarian would say, "You cannot have read these books already; take them back and come back after a week or so." But then, I was a voracious reader. We didn't have electricity in the house, so I would read by lamplight, and my mother would say, "Samuel, it's two o'clock now; it's time to turn off the light, boy, before you go blind." So I would get a piece of card and put it around the lamp, you know, so it would have a slit. The light would shine so she wouldn't see it, and I would continue reading.

Q: How do we create that kind of interest in literature today? Given the variety of activities now available to young people, do you think it's still important to teach literature?

S.S.: I believe the ways of creating deep interest in literature are limited only by our imaginations. Researchers have given us several possibilities. We can match literary works to the varied topics which already absorb students. We can help students to access literature written in the styles and at the vocabulary levels with which they are comfortable rather than frustrated. We can afford students as wide a choice in literary genres as possible. Various researchers also stress that adults showing their own appreciation for reading is a powerful encouragement to students to value reading and literature. The Internet is a wonderful asset here, because students in homes, schools and community centres with limited money can now access millions of possibilities, an almost limitless library, at no extra cost. What is more, the same Internet can be used by parents and teachers of all kinds to do research on encouraging reading.

You ask if it is still important to teach literature. Decidedly! Outside of doing psychology, I believe that literature is the best way – and it may even be better than psychology – of giving people insights into the human condition. No matter what genre writers use, no matter what age they are writing in and for, ultimately they concern themselves with the human condition, and so literature gives us that opportunity to understand and appreciate people. It helps us to understand the social, political, cultural, religious and spiritual dimensions of human life without having to do formal study, which most of us can't do or won't do over the course of a lifetime. And it takes us to all sorts of places around the world. I downloaded a BBC Series sometime earlier this year called *Why Reading Matters*. I didn't know this information at the time, but it confirms, I guess, what we almost felt intuitively, that reading does a lot to stimulate the human mind in positive ways. And this program shows that when you read certain kinds of works, for example, Emily Brontë's, that there are parts of the brain which are stimulated and new connections made.

In addition to that, language is the currency by which we communicate; and one of the most powerful ways to build our vocabulary and to be able to communicate in ways that you want is through reading, because there are lots of words and sentence structures that you will encounter if you read literature that you don't find in everyday conversation. In fact, in the twenty-first century, young people seem to be adopting a style of language that is working towards being as minimal as possible, and beating basically the same few words to death. It is a reflection of a mental laziness and a limited vocabulary.

Q: Yes, I agree with you there. Let's talk now about your particular teaching style. How do you actually teach literature?

S.S.: Well, there is no one style that I would say that I have, given that I have been teaching for over twenty-five years. What I do has evolved as I have learned things and been exposed to different ways of doing things. I also know that people have different learning styles and that there are multiple intelligences. So if you want to be an effective teacher, you capitalize on all these different avenues to people's understanding. But basically what I try to do is to use as many modalities as possible to help students to appreciate literature. So, for example, if I am teaching a poem, I use audio recordings or CDs or DVDs of the poem. If not, and I can find something that's by a good reader other than the poet, I would use that too. Where there is biographical information that will help to give the students context for the particular work, whatever forms it takes, whether it's a picture, videos, whether it is a text, I would use that. An example of this is my introduction of Lorna Goodison's poem "The Woman Speaks to the Man Who Has Employed Her Son". When I was doing the workshops across the Caribbean, I used Elvis Presley's "In the Ghetto", John King's "How Many More", and Bob Marley's "Johnny Was a Good Man", all of which present a comparable situation of a mother going through the anguish of having a son who is involved in a life of crime and who is actually killed as a consequence. So I use things which help students to appreciate that poetry is being written about the human condition and that in many instances, even if it is written by somebody who's from the past, the issues are still current issues.

In addition to that, I adapt and adopt strategies or methods which I find are commonly used or intended to be used in other fields. So when I was working at Erdiston Teachers' Training College as a teacher trainer, I did some research and found some tools that people who teach literacy studies use; for example, there is a tool called a "Three-Level Reading Guide". With this you construct statements at the literal level, inferential level and the application level. I have adapted that. So you prepare a set of statements, some of which are true and some of which are false, but ultimately they all require the students to interact with the text directly and to justify with evidence from the literature why they believe the statements to be true or false.

I've also used another literacy strategy, that of DRTA, that is, directed reading thinking activity, where you read pre-selected sections of the text in class, and you have students predict what is going to happen next and also tell you what is in the text to have prompted their particular prediction. Then you have them read to see whether their prediction was accurate, and you follow up with discussing their responses.

Now, one of the most powerful things I have ever used in teaching literature, and this is based on students' feedback, is something called a reader response journal, which can be used at various grades. For instance, let's say that you are teaching *Julius Caesar*. You might create a series of probes, statements and questions, such as: "Politicians care far more about themselves than the people. Do you agree?" And there is not a right or a wrong answer that you are looking for from the students; this is to give them a springboard into addressing what you believe to be important aspects of the literary work in terms of human experience.

Alternatively, you might tell the students to write a half-page response or a five-line response or a three-sentence response to two things which they think are most important in the scene or the verse of the poem or the particular chapter of the novel. The ultimate focus is on eliciting from the students some kind of response to the text. And I remember years ago, maybe fifteen years ago, when there was a parents' meeting, one of the third-formers said in my presence to her mother that the thing that she will always remember and that drew her to my class in literature was the fact that she got to express her opinion of the books as opposed to writing back what the teacher said was the correct answer.

Q: Very interesting approaches, Sam. Tell me, to follow up on this, can you recall any particularly memorable session?

S.S.: Again, this was with the teaching of poetry, but it could have been with any genre of literature: I had given the students the opportunity to dramatize a particular work, and a group of them did work that was so impressive that I had to say to them that I didn't know that they had it in them. I find that drama is a very powerful way of helping students to be engaged with literature. People who teach literature may not be involved in drama themselves or have had any particular training in theatre, so I think we miss a wonderful opportunity to engage students with literature, because we have that limitation ourselves as teachers.

I also remember another occasion that we were doing a poem called "Atieno". I gave students the option of representing their understanding in various ways, one of which included drawing, and there was this boy in the classroom who was not particularly strong in terms of articulating responses to the literature in writing, but he did this clock, a representation of Atieno, and added twelve bars representing each hour of the day, and each one he connected to a particular aspect or to a particular verse of the poem. Half of it showed Atieno as a normal-looking human being, and the other half showed her as a skeleton. It is a poem that fundamentally makes you look at child abuse. And I still have that particular piece of art today. As you know, lots of boys might not like to write their responses to poetry, but they can still demonstrate understanding and knowledge through a different modality.

Q: You have explained that through the use of drama and working with different modalities, you are able to get your students involved in literature classes. Is there any other way that you have tried?

S.S.: Well, as you would know, one of the most effective ways, which is not a specific way in itself, is having an understanding of what is going on in the student's life; what the students are interested in. Choose, where possible, content that connects to their lives. The important thing is to start early and not wait until it gets to an examination class to try to encourage or nurture an interest in literature in students.

Q: Let's look at the other side. Is there any session you would rather forget? Is there any session where things just really went wrong, and why?

S.S.: Lots! Lots of them! As a human being you are fallible, and sometimes you make mistakes. There are times when there are limitations that you struggle under, because education is expensive, and even with the best intention in the world and the most generous funding from the government, the resources don't extend as far. Some of the sessions that I would most want to forget would have been A-level sessions where fundamentally you have a class of students, many of whom have not chosen the subject because of genuine interest, but because the school system stipulates that if you want to be in sixth form, you must do a minimum of 3 A levels. So what you often find is that students will pick one or two which they actually care about, and then they will choose a third one because they got a grade 1 or grade 2 at CXC, not because they have any interest in the subject at all. Now, as you would appreciate as a person and a teacher of literature yourself, if you are doing something like the poems of Margaret Atwood, poems which are intellectually challenging, it can't be just entertainment. Sometimes the students have to grapple with the language and the syntax, and the challenges of a sophisticated writer dealing with serious matters.

Well, to be quite honest with you, the major challenge that I have when it comes to teaching literature has nothing to do with the teaching itself. Directly, it has to do with the administrators who determine the texts we use.

Q: What works best for you, then, in terms of classroom environment and methods? You have listed a number of methods – which one actually works best for you?

S.S.: If I understand the question correctly, basically it would be a classroom environment where you have access at this point to multimedia resources. So it is not so much the environment in itself, but it's the resources. It's where you have space, where you could put things on the wall, or where you could divide students into groups; where they can have a certain amount of physical space in which they can do various things, rather than cramped classrooms where you can't really move around or where you just have a blackboard and chalk. As you would appreciate, in the twentieth century, students come to us overstimulated. Many of them have technological devices which they walk with and are being stimulated en route to school or in between classes or sometimes even in the classes themselves. So to have a fighting chance, so to speak, it helps if you have the kind of technology that would include multimedia – the projectors and DVD players and so on [you can use to] try to engage them through their different intelligences.

Q: But I am sure you have been in situations yourself where you have not had such media available. I'm thinking about teachers who don't have access to such media. Can you say what methods or strategies may work?

S.S.: Well, you have some of the things that people have been doing for generations, for better or for worse. I think perhaps the single most important starting point is that the teacher brings powerful enthusiasm to the classroom. I find sometimes that even if you don't have all the gadgetry, if you exude an interest and a keenness for the literature, and if you verbalize it, you can nurture an appreciation for or capture their interest. In contrast, if you yourself project no interest, and if what you are doing is because they are paying you and you are supposed to cover the syllabus, then your lack of enthusiasm will be diffused into the classroom. And, of course, I still find that there is value in the old-time things like recitation and choral speaking and asking students to memorize or to perform – all of these things still work.

Q: Yes. Do you differentiate in your teaching between the teaching of poetry and prose or drama?

S.S.: I would say basically no, because fundamentally we are talking about bringing as much relevant variety to the delivery of instruction no matter what the genre is. Obviously there would be different emphases, because if you are dealing with drama, you would deal with things like stage directions and so on which you don't have to deal with in poetry and prose.

Q: Is there any particular word that you would use to describe your teaching style?

S.S.: The word that most comes to mind is "eclectic".

Q: Given your varied experiences in teaching literature from first form to university level, what are some of the limitations you have observed with students of literature? What is it that students fail to bring to the table? And how can we, as teachers of literature, help to address those needs in the classroom?

S.S.: Perhaps a good place to start might be to say that what the students many times don't bring to the classroom is the *experience* of literature. We can help them by laying a proper foundation in literature. Literature in the primary school is sometimes treated in a haphazard and occasional way. If it is Christmas or something coming up for a programme; or because you are doing the theme of Water, you are supposed to find a poem about water or something like that. But there is no real structure; there is no real proper foundation. Secondly, in many instances examining boards or English departments in schools pick texts because they have many hundreds of them in the cupboard or storeroom, rather than selecting texts which deal with concerns that students can relate to. So, for example, you are teaching thirteen-, fourteen- or fifteen-year-olds – what are some of the things that are on their minds typically? Sex is one of them! So why not find a literary work like *Green Days by the River*, in which coming to terms with sexuality is a central concern of the literary work?

There is a dictum in teaching, as you know, that you move from the familiar to the unfamiliar. I don't see that represented in what goes on in schools in terms of literature. So rather than dealing first with works written in language which students can relate to, schools assign texts written by the great whoever-this-person-is, and they are part of the canon, and you could say this is a wonderful literary work, but the language is alien to the students. So rather than building up progressively from the known and accessible to the challenging, there's an unreasoned approach to the literature and very often a lack of continuity.

Furthermore, literature is often presented as something divorced from the real world. So, for example, in Barbados, there is the National Independence Festival of the Creative Arts, which is an annual opportunity for citizens to write in the various genres as part of the literary arts competition. In half of the schools, I find that participation in such things is limited to the students who are interested in a particular genre and who will volunteer to enter. Sometimes the teacher or the head of department will mandate that students should enter the competition. Instead, we could see this as an opportunity for students to have their work published and celebrated as well as to demonstrate their creativity and to feel a sense of accomplishment. We should help students see themselves as contributing to the national heritage by composing a poem, or writing a short story, an essay or a drama script. So again, there is no real holistic approach. The result is that some students don't see that literature is about life, that anybody's life can be the subject of a literary piece and can bring life to other people.

Q: What do your students really like about your classes? Is it the drama? What have they said?

S.S.: I would say essentially it is the variety, and it is the enthusiasm that I take into the classroom.

Q: Elaine Showalter has listed a number of teacher anxieties in her book on teaching literature, for example, teacher isolation. Do you have any teacher anxieties in terms of teaching literature?

S.S.: No, I don't have any. But I can understand why those anxieties are listed. Teachers don't understand that they can share their strategies; no one is the poorer for sharing. We are afraid to let people come inside our classroom and see what it is that we do. And this, of course, obtains from our teaching practice assessment. If we, however, placed value on collaboration and collegiality, a lot of these anxieties would disappear. We may not have the time to visit each other's classes, but with today's technology, your class could be recorded. I could watch it in the privacy of my home and learn from you. We could refine our techniques.

Q: My final question: what do you think is absolutely essential for teaching Caribbean literature?

S.S.: I would say I can't reduce it to one thing; I would say two things minimum – knowledge and passion. The passion has to come from within. The knowledge can be gained from all kinds of places. You can go to the public library; you can go to all sorts of places and find their resources, and there are many books written about Caribbean poetry which give a historical context, which highlight important writers and definitive pieces. There's lots of information out there. So if teachers really want to know and really want to improve and do better, there are lots of resources out there that they can use to help themselves. And then ultimately you must bring some passion into the classroom while you teach literature.

Q: Would you like to elaborate on that? What is this passion that you are talking about?

S.S.: Fundamentally, it is a genuine love and a genuine fervour for literature.

Ann-Marie Wilmot

"Literature creates a community, while it simultaneously develops the individual."

Dr Ann-Marie Wilmot has been teaching literature for eighteen years. She taught literature at the secondary level for six years and since then has taught at Church Teachers' College in Mandeville, Jamaica. She has also taught literature at the University College of the Caribbean, in Kingston, Jamaica, where she prepares students teachers to teach literature. This has led her to work closely with schools to facilitate, monitor and evaluate student teachers' performance in the field. As a result, she has also been able to observe in many schools how literature is being taught and received.

An experienced and creative teacher of literature, and a poet herself, Wilmot has been able to transform literature classrooms into places of excitement, pleasure and insights.

Q: Dr Wilmot, why do you like teaching literature?

Ann-Marie Wilmot: Actually, I love teaching literature. Literature challenges my intellect and my students'. I love the jostle and the challenge of making meaning from the text and the wide spectrum of responses that a text generates. Teaching literature also provides a great space for me to relate to my students as well. I think when I'm teaching literature, I spring to life at the, sometimes, awesome possibilities of a text, and I love teaching it because I think it's unpredictable; it allows multiple ways of seeing. Each student can make an input, and as a result, each student has a voice. Literature creates a space for inclusion and consequently the development of self-worth. I really enjoy teaching literature because there is a type of beauty, a type of satisfaction you get when a student really gets it, and you see their effort. I feel that when you're teaching literature, you're teaching, in a sense, life.

Q: This generation of young people has so much choice of activities, so do you think that it is still important to teach literature?

A-M.W.: Yes, it is still important to teach literature. It helps our students develop some of those soft skills that are easily overlooked and fast disappearing in a very fast-paced society, and where students are sometimes very isolated. Young people today appear to have less personal interaction because of technology. The literature classroom provides space for the communal, the collective, where we can learn to appreciate each other's opinion, learn something from somebody else, value what somebody else brings to the table. Literature creates a community, while it simultaneously develops the individual. Even while the individual experiences and interpretations are valued, the literature classroom provides for that communal/ collective discussion and appreciation of each other's opinion, of learning something from somebody else, of valuing what somebody else brings to the table; literature really really helps students and teachers to do that. So the literature serves to unify the particular learning community, while it simultaneously develops the individual. It also helps, of course, with developing empathy and critical thinking. I think that literature is important because it requires and encourages critical thinking, especially when the subject under scrutiny is not just a tap on a few electronic buttons away on the Internet. That way when they have that "raw text" before them, and they are confronted with making meaning from it, devoid of anything electronic, they are forced to pull on what they know. Once the brain has this experience, I believe that it will store that information and make it available for use external to the classroom. This is yet another reason why literature should not be allowed to lose its importance in the classroom.

Q: Yes, definitely. I like, particularly, the point you make about literature helping to create a community and taking people away from the isolation, the individual cubicles in which technology in some instances seems to push us. How do you get young people interested in literature?

A-M.W.: To be honest, it is not an easy task because of competing activities. So I feel that one way of getting students interested in literature is to get them to relate to the text. Students also have to feel a positive energy coming from the teacher. I was teaching a group of teenagers, mainly girls, and they kept saying that the text was boring, and so I started to have them read related material. These had to do with experiences of young girls in different cultures, and that sparked their interest in the primary text.

Q: What is your particular teaching style? Let's begin with how you prepare for your classes.

A-M.W.: I try to do several readings of the text. If I have read it before, I will always reread the text, because it helps me to guide the students well. I reflect on what I want students to learn from the particular teaching episode. If I'm, for example, teaching themes, I always want to make sure that I have a couple examples from the text and have the page numbers ready. I also consider the different ways that students could think about the text, about some of questions that they might ask and life experiences that I could link the text to. A variety of methods work for me, but best of all, I like to show the process of understanding the text; I ask them to see the literal and concrete before discussing the metaphorical levels. If, for example, I'm discussing symbolism, I begin with asking students to think about the literal, concrete object, perhaps a gate, and encourage them to reflect on why people use it, how it functions. Also, I would have students develop thematic statements, and this would stimulate further discussion. Key is modelling for my students how to *read* the text and then leaving them to do so independently.

I think that learning the process of independent meaning-making is very important. There is a lot of critical material on the texts available, and students, drawn to focus on this, can easily stifle their own understanding and insights of the text. I prefer a teaching style, therefore, that really encourages them to reckon with the text itself, to wrestle with it and to make something of it independently, even as they acknowledge the good critical and useful information out there. Sometimes, of course, you have to give them the information so that they can understand and move on.

Q: Clearly your approach is student-centred rather than teacher-centred, even as you acknowledge the importance of the teacher sharing information. To follow up on this, can you recall any particularly memorable session?

A-M.W.: Yes. I was teaching *Julius Caesar* recently and wanted students to explore the text without simply Googling the information. So, I created "cases", based on the text's themes, dramatic techniques, characterization and other elements of the play, which students had to examine and resolve. These cases were also related to problems their classmates were having with the text – for example, the soliloquies and how they function in the play. Students were really excited about doing this, as they became the experts. It was really fulfilling for me, as they were teaching themselves. The students enjoyed it and remarked how useful they found the exercise.

Q: That's an interesting and fun approach. Let's look at the other side. Is there any session you would rather forget? You know, was there a session where things just really went wrong?

A-M.W.: Yes. I think the most recent one was with a group of students I had asked to present on "themes". The first presenter just told the story of the text. I was surprised, because I had assumed she knew the difference between the story and the theme. Then the next presenter did the same. So did the others. I wondered if they were taking the class for a joke. No, they were not; they just did not know. I had expected that these students, be-cause of their years of experience in literature, would know the difference. I had made a wrong assumption and had built an entire lesson on that. I hadn't paid sufficient attention to students' context.

Q: What works best for you, then, in terms of classroom methods or class-room environment?

A-M.W.: I think that I love a classroom where the students have fun with the material and where I facilitate students' meaning-making experiences. I provide the stimulus and ask probing questions. I usually provide a set of guided questions for the students, for example, "What do you think will happen as a result of how this character thinks?" "How does what he or she thinks/believes presents a challenge based on other characters' view-points?" Sometimes you start in the middle of the text. But usually before I start teaching a text, I would ask students to do some small task with the text, like write a poem about character X in the text; write this text as a little children's story in no more than sixty or so words; create a puzzle; respond to the play using a poem; share your reaction to an insightful moment. These are some of the activities that will encourage them to read the text, and they are also activities that I know will not be readily available on the Internet. I find that once they get a start, students will really delve into the text, and I try to help them to do that. I love when everyone participates and walks away with a rich experience.

Q: Do you differentiate, then, in your teaching of poetry, prose or drama?

A-M.W.: I think in some cases I do. I differentiate as I help them understand the textual features of the genres. I feel that having this knowledge, they are able to navigate their way into a deeper understanding of the text. With poetry, for example, I help students understand the textual features of the different genres of poetry. I know that they might not always use it, but when a student is faced with a text and they do not know where to go, at least they will be able to recognize the form – for example, the sonnet. This gives them a point of entry in the text, as there are usually expectations of a sonnet. Additionally I think that students must receive help in recognizing the difference between a novel and a poem. In a sense, they must deal with the economic use of words in a poem. They must understand how a poem works and how poetry differs generally from prose.

Q: How do you help them to do that?

A-M.W.: I give presentations on this, and I also have students present. I help them, too, to understand form and structural devices. So, for example, in a play, when we look at a soliloquy, I help my students identify its features and "define" it. They need to know too how it functions. I ask probing questions, such as, "What does it tell you?" "How does it relate to the plot, to characters, to theme and all the other elements?" They then recognize how it helps them to understand the inner workings of the character's mind – what is going on in the character's head. When students know the basics, they are able to expand their interpretative stance on any given text.

Q: So is it that you have a set of questions, then, that you use to help them to probe?

A-M.W.: Yes, I usually provide a set of guided questions for the students. So when they look at a soliloquy now, or any other element that we focus on, they are able to relate that to the broader context of the text. What do you think will happen as a result of how this character thinks? How does what the character thinks/believes present a challenge based on other characters' viewpoints? How do you think this belief might affect setting – psychologically, politically, socially? Sometimes, too, you start in the middle of the text, in that kind of way, but I find that once they get a foot in, they can really work their way around the text, and I try to help them to do that.

Q: Is there any particular word or phrase that you would use to describe your teaching style?

A-M.W.: I think that I am predominantly student-centred in my style. I am the guide to push and to probe and to pull out and to help them make meaningful connections with the text, to kind of oversee and steer the process. Unfortunately some students do not like it when the teacher acts as a facilitator, as they simply want to be given information. They do not like the challenge of reaching beyond where they are merely satisfied. Sometimes they do not like doing the activities. Then there are those students who do not really want to read, and those who just want to access the summaries online. Others, however, see the fun side of reading literature. We have to find creative ways to encourage them to enter and to explore the text.

Q: What do your students really like about your classes?

A-M.W.: Students say they always learn from the classes. Most of them say the classes are fun; they believe I think outside the box, I present them with challenges and force them to think critically. They also like my selection of texts; they feel I am knowledgeable about the texts, and that forces them to prepare for classes. Some say that I set high standards. Others say I show the relevance of literature and how it benefits the individual. One student said the classes are not always about literature but also about life, and she is always enriched by the class experiences.

Q: Let's focus now on the teacher. Elaine Showalter has written a book on teaching literature, and she lists a number of anxieties she feels teachers have – for example, teachers teaching in isolation or not knowing exactly what method to use. So do you have any teacher anxieties in terms of teaching literature?

A-M.W.: As a teacher who has a deep interest in my students' learning, I sometimes experience some anxieties. Not the type that would incapacitate me or anything like that. I have found that the anxiety that I have with one group, I might not have with another group. For example, last semester, in particular, I was very anxious about the capabilities that a particular set of students had. And that particular anxiety didn't only come from the fact that I have a track record of good students' performance and that that could be derailed, but also from have being head of department and teaching them two courses. If as head I cannot teach these students, where am I going to get the moral authority to tell other lecturers, who have complained about these students, that the students can meet the demands of their expectations? I was particularly pressured – well maybe [it was] a self-imposed type of pressure to be a model, to make this work, and to prove that if these students could pull through this course, it is possible they could pull through any other course.

Q: My final question: What do you think is absolutely essential for teaching Caribbean literature? What do you think students really need to have, to know – whether you're talking content or method?

A-M.W.: I'm going to speak based on what I have observed from my experiences with teaching Caribbean literature. I think that in one sense, the literature itself serves as a type of historical representation of our experiences. Once you're studying Caribbean literature, you're always privileged to learn a piece of our history. So I find that it is essential that students have an understanding of our historical experiences and how these inform the works of Caribbean writers. The writing is rich, and sometimes the style is very complex, so younger and more inexperienced learners might find this challenging.

Sharon Phillip

"I think that what is most important is introducing literature
as something that is pleasurable."

Ms Sharon Phillip has taught literature at the secondary level for twelve years and has been teaching at the university level for seven years. Currently she is lecturing at the University of the West Indies' School of Education, St Augustine, in the bachelor of education and the diploma in education programmes. She is also a course coordinator for three language arts courses in the BEd Primary (online) programme.

Phillip was one of the key participants in the Caribbean Poetry Project, a collaboration of the University of Cambridge and the UWI Schools of Education (Cave Hill, Mona, and St Augustine campuses). She coordinated four Caribbean poetry workshops in Trinidad and Tobago, to expose teachers to innovative methods of teaching poetry in secondary schools. She is also one of the writers of the text *Teaching Caribbean Poetry*. Her research interests are Caribbean poetry, children's literature, language arts and literacy, and reading.

Q: Ms Phillips, could you please tell us about your interest in literature?

Sharon Phillip: Well, it stemmed from reading, but also, I guess, more of an interest was created when I did the literature courses at the UWI, and I had to go very deeply into the analysis of texts. I used to do a lot of reading before, but not necessarily think about the craft.

Q: So the university played a significant role in your becoming more interested in literature?

S.P.: Yes, I definitely think so.

Q: What do you see as important in getting students interested in literature or reading?

S.P.: I think one of the most important things is the teacher's passion for the subject, because if you have to teach literature and you're not even passionate about it, you don't really encourage your students. You might have few students in the class who might have a genuine interest in it, but if the teacher has passion, you can actually ignite in your students a passion for it. I think, too, the choice of books or the choice of materials is important. Sometimes we make selections based on our own taste, and we don't even consider the students' interest. I think, too, that at the other levels, such as the primary level, when literature is being introduced, especially poetry, you need to consider what the children might like. With their choices, we can still achieve our goals in terms of the kinds of understanding we want them to have about literature – and life, by extension. And I'm saying that because just last week, while supervising teachers on teaching practice, I observed a lesson in which the students were using a collection of poetry compiled by the English department. In it I saw poems that I had taught at the sixth-form level but in this case they were selected for first- and second-form students. This could be one of the reasons why students do not like poetry. If you are introducing them to poetry, and you use poems that are too difficult for them to understand, you're obviously going to discourage them from liking it. I remember when I was teaching at the secondary school, and we had to do an anthology, we tended to look for "lighter", more age-appropriate ones. We can introduce students to the craft through the lighter poems, and these would be more enjoyable for them. I think that the element of pleasure – eliciting pleasure or invoking pleasure in children – is missing in the teaching of poetry. We need to think about the pleasure of poetry and the selection of poems that would get the children interested.

Q: Yes, I agree with you about that pleasure. Many teachers think that pleasure should not be part of the teaching of literature. You know, it is thought that you should only focus on the "heavy stuff", the analysis of the elements.

S.P.: And I want to add another thing in terms of teaching strategies used.

Many teachers use literature, or they're using poems for comprehension, and again that element of pleasure is left out. They just focus on getting questions answered. So literature in some ways is synonymous with doing comprehension or comprehension-type exercises. I mean, it's such an unimaginative approach, and it certainly discourages students from learning.

Q: Knowing this, how do you actually prepare for your classes or for your lectures at the university?

S.P.: What I try to do is target the teaching of elements and the theories that appear in the English curriculum, because these are things the secondary school students have to know. So I try to focus on teaching strategies teachers can use in their classrooms. Yes, I would give them some articles or give them some links to the articles, but when I'm doing the actual presentation, I try to focus on those areas that I think that teachers have difficulty with, and more importantly, I show these teachers-in-training how they can use different strategies, different kinds of resources to help their students like and understand poetry. I try to break the tendency of treating poetry as a comprehension exercise. I also like to work with a variety of technological elements, so I scour through YouTube sometimes to find anything that is relevant. My way is to provoke them into thinking and then have them discuss what is on the video. I actually have used that as one of my assessments.

Q: How did that work?

S.P.: Okay, what I did is I asked them to watch a YouTube video, relevant to a particular piece of literature, and comment on it in terms of the criteria I provided, such as the teaching strategies used and the relevance to their specific classroom context. The students [then] presented a reflective piece on the video.

Q: I like that. Can you share with me memorable sessions in your teaching?

S.P.: One thing that I can recall is introducing a group of teachers to the concept of bibliotherapy. They started wondering about it. As we continued to explore the concept, they then responded, "This is something we do, right?" Well, I said yes. So they recognized at that point that the approach some of them use has a particular name, or label. More importantly, after

I introduced the concept and discussed it, they were able to think immediately of how they could use it in their school and classrooms. What I really liked about that particular session was that, you know, it was some kind of – well, I don't want to say epiphany, it's too powerful a word – insight, and the realization that they could have been engaging in bibliotherapy all along. The following day one of the students actually went and tried something, and returned to the class to tell us about what he had done in his class and how the children appreciated it. I think, times like that, you know, are really, really important, because it's good when they see the relevance of what we teach. So often, students say that we just introduce all of these theories and that they can't see the relevance, but they were able to see it then, and I think that was really good.

Q: I can imagine how you felt with that "aha moment". Tell me, though, is there anything particularly challenging about teaching literature at the tertiary level and how do you deal with it?

S.P.: Since my courses are focused on teaching literature, I don't spend much time on the actual analysis of literature texts. One of the challenging things is the limited background and experience in literature that some of the students have. You can suggest books, you can highlight articles and so on, but it is a challenge to have them actually read the texts. I can say that the challenge tends to be getting the teachers to prepare lessons that encourage a deep exploration of literature concepts that includes a study of the author's craft.

Q: Yes, I can understand that. I'm beginning to see a particular teaching style of yours emerging. Would you like to just elaborate on that?

S.P.: What I can say is that I do not lecture. I spend very little time lecturing actually, and we have, like, three-hour periods. I like to throw out ideas that would provoke them into thinking; then I get them involved in discussions on the different aspects of the areas that I've introduced. So I tend to have a lot of activities, including discussions and in-class group work, because I find that's more effective than when I just stand and talk. If they just write notes, that does not give them a chance to think deeply about the subject. However, when they are more fully engaged, they surprise themselves.

They come up with ideas, and then it's amazing to them what they had never thought about or never done. I like to bring in the technology too; I try to mix it so that the resource for the class is not just a PowerPoint presentation. I sometimes bring in a film or music, and I stress, too, that when we think about literature, we're thinking not only about the printed text. Basically my teaching style is more interactive; it's not just standing and talking.

Q: In what way does this pleasure come out? Can you identify any particular aspect in which you manage to make it very pleasurable? Is it through the interaction?

S.P.: I think it's through the interaction, and then I'm also passionate about literature. Also I try to choose activities that they can get some pleasure out of, so that they can see how they can do that with their students as well. That's sometimes challenging, though, because you're taking a chance when you're selecting an activity that you think that they would actually enjoy. I try to do that, because I want them to see that what they do in the class when they come to lectures would be some of the things they can do in their own classrooms and try to evoke that pleasure. So it isn't always about doing an activity for marks. Well, I suppose every student anyway always wants to know if it's for marks. But if we do things just for the fun of doing it, there will be learning, [and] also it will help their creativity to emerge. I've had my students write poems, and they came up with some interesting ones, even though they never even knew that they had the ability to do it. But I challenged them to do it, and I got some really lovely poems. And then they realized that this is something that they actually liked. Once I even challenged my students to write a palindrome, and I got two. That was great! They had never been exposed to that type of poem, so I was amazed at the results. I actually had a student who was more science-oriented, and she came to me and said, "You know, I really like literature. You know, now I'm really trying to find ways of doing more literature in my class." At least I reached one person!

Q: Sounds like you've reached more than one!

S.P.: Yes, so I think the interaction most of all, and my own enthusiasm for literature would add to the pleasure of their experience of literature.

Q: Is there anything particular you find about presenting literature to Caribbean students? Are there specific things you take into account or you make sure to introduce? Does the Caribbean context figure in any big way?

S.P.: Well, one of the things that I do is I actually give them assignments that would make them look specifically at Caribbean literature. I get them to talk about its complexity, the culture and how it influences what people have written. Because there are so many changes in the society, some of the younger children, like some of them in the primary schools, don't have much knowledge about the Caribbean cultural background. I think it is always very important to discuss the context of the literature text, the social and political context. Therefore, I try to model what I expect the teachers to use in their practice.

Q: Is there a particular genre that you like to teach?

S.P.: I think I started out with my preference being prose, but now I tend to do more poetry. I think it's because I recognize that it's one of the areas that is most challenging to teachers.

Q: Can you say why this is so?

S.P.: I think it's based on how it was presented to them when they were going to school. So they see poetry as something that is difficult and complex. They see it as requiring a lot of analysis, and therefore they have difficulty interpreting it. I have actually had students admit that they don't teach poetry unless it's necessary, so there may be a group of teenagers who have had very limited exposure.

Q: Given that situation, do you, apart from the strategies that you have mentioned before, have any other strategies that you use for poetry in particular?

S.P.: For poetry especially, I try to use a lot of songs and have students compare songs with printed poems. I also try to cover a range of poems rather than just simply the more popular forms. Also, one assignment I tend to give is to have the students list the poems they are expected to teach at a chosen level and locate resources they can use to support them. They locate songs, other poems, video clips, posters and objects that they can use.

When I give this assignment, I hope to encourage the students to create a repository they can share with their peers and use in their classrooms.

Q: Finally, what changes would you like to see made in the teaching of literature?

S.P.: I think that what is most important is introducing literature as something that is pleasurable. Also important, of course, is the kind of materials you use when you're introducing children to literature, because if you don't do that right, then you may start them off disliking poetry. Then it becomes more challenging to teach them at the tertiary level. I recognize that the traditional analysis of poems should not be totally abandoned because of the obvious merits, but that method should be balanced with more interactive and innovative ways that are motivating.

Aisha Spencer

"I find it important that we intentionally teach students how to interpret, how to read texts ..."

Dr Aisha Spencer has been teaching literature since 1998, first at the secondary level and since 2004 at the tertiary level. She taught at Mico University College, in Kingston, Jamaica, for eight years and is now teaching literature and literature education full-time at the University of the West Indies at Mona. A lecturer in the School of Education, she is also responsible for preparing students to become effective teachers of literature.

Spencer has been a member of the Teaching Caribbean Poetry project and is one of the authors of the text *Teaching Caribbean Poetry*, which emerged from that project. She is one of the editors of a new anthology of Caribbean poetry, *Give the Ball to the Poet*. Spencer has also published a number of papers on literature.

Q: Dr Spencer, what do you particularly like about teaching literature?

Aisha Spencer: Well, for me, I am very passionate about literature itself. I enjoy literature, the *experience* of literature, and I want to pass on the types of experiences I have had with literature to students. And, of course, because most students tend to run away from literature, one of my goals is to engage them and to help them understand the power of the literature experience.

Q: Perhaps students are running away from literature because they don't see it as having much value. So from your perspective, why is it still important to teach literature?

A.S.: I think that literature develops our ability to analyse, to look at things differently, to work out things in a way that you probably would not in normal circumstances. You go through a text and decide what the writer might mean or what a character is really like. Literature automatically engages the student in a level of critical thinking that I think is on parallel really with any other subject. I've found also that one of the main benefits of teaching literature is that it helps students, who would otherwise not open up, otherwise not express their feelings, become expressive. I find that students who I may not normally hear from at all, will, for example, suddenly speak up when they disagree with my interpretation of a character. And through that space, I begin to understand how they are thinking, and through the discussion that we are having, they begin to explore the text in a new way.

Q: What, then, about the pleasures of literature? Do we take this for granted?

A.S.: I think it is important, and it's something that we tend to miss because of our very academic type of focus on how students study and how they do in an exam. We tend to neglect the fact that the text can provide pleasure for the students. We take it for granted that they have had that experience in their childhood. Some of them have never really had that opportunity to just read for the sake of reading, for the sake of enjoyment. They've always had to do it for an exam, and so I think that the tasks that we give them should help them to personally connect with the text. They then enjoy the process of engaging with the text. The intentional ways we set up our methodology in a tertiary situation should, therefore, not be just lecture style but should include our actually teaching students to enjoy the text.

Q: So let's talk now about your teaching style. How do you generally prepare for your tutorials or your lectures?

A.S.: The first thing I try to do is to think about how the student expects me to come to the class, and I try to divert from that expectation. So I think about some of the activities I'm looking at but do so wearing the student hat. I try to see the activity from a student's perspective. I ask myself, "How would they expect me to come with this?" and I bear in mind that I'm teaching teachers, so they're automatically expecting me to do some of the same things that they may do or have been doing. Then I look at the theories on the aspect that I'm teaching; I find out what the theorists are saying. I also ask what skill sets are attached to what I am going to be teaching, and what I want my students to get out of the session. So my goals for the lesson are not just in terms of the theoretical content but in terms of the skill set, because modelling is important. And so if I'm expecting the students to model certain things and teach certain skills to their students, they have to understand how that is done. So those are two main things I would do. The third thing I tend to do now is merge the theory with practice, with application. So there's no point in going more than ten minutes into the theory without allowing for a situation where they can apply the theory.

I have simulated class situations, yes – but I also like to engage students first in literature. I feel that if the teachers can respond to literature themselves, then it makes them more confident and more aware of how their own students might respond to it. So sometimes I ask them not to put on a student hat – that is, to think in terms of their students – and also not to put on a teacher hat, because then they're trying to produce academic responses based on what they think you want them to say or what they believe they should be saying, whether as pre-trained or already trained teachers. I ask them, "Who are you now, sitting in this class, and what is your 'natural' response to the tasks assigned?"

Q: Well, you have moved into talking about how you get them involved or try to get them involved. I like the idea that you actually ask them to take off their hat as teachers and to think of themselves as individuals. Already you have engaged them mentally in terms of involvement. Where do you go from there? How else do you get them involved?

A.S.: One of the things I believe is that setting an example is really one of the best ways to get student teachers to understand particular methods, so I would utilize in class some of the very strategies that I'm teaching them about. I ask, "Does it work? Does it not work? Does it have to work? Is there something that has come up through using the strategy that causes us to shift from how the theory says it works, and does that mean I shut off because it shifts?" I explained earlier that orientation as a teacher is very important at this point. So while they're going through the strategies and activities in the class, I ask them to access how they're feeling as they're responding to it, because I think it is important. As I've said to them over and over, "You don't try to teach something that you haven't internalized yourself." When they do this, they may have comments such as, "But this is not working for me, but this is not the way that I feel; and that theory said X, but this is not what I find is happening." Getting them to understand that they have a right to question the theories and determine what works and what may not work is essential. So I think the bottom line for me is that we must practise what we preach, but we must not preach something that we do not already believe ourselves. So we have to internalize it. I found that the best way to help students do this is to actually engage them in the classroom, to practise teaching literature and not just have them listen to theories of teaching literature.

Q: It sounds like you've had many memorable sessions of teaching literature. Could you please share with us one of these?

A.S.: Yes. I'll share a session I had with teaching drama. I find that because drama is the "stage on the page", students do not respond to it as performance. I remember trying to get them to understand that if they're going out to teach it as performance, then they have to be able to see it themselves as performance. So we had had a session on drama as performance. At first students were quite shy and did not want to engage in role-play, and perhaps in their minds they were saying things like "Why doesn't she just lecture? Why is she asking us to do all of these things?"

They had a script about death, and the script was very humorous. It was looking at Death, as a character, encountering another character to let him know that it was time to go, and the character was resisting. Our goal was to explore how to teach the elements of drama without putting up a long list on the board for students simply to make notes and then regurgitate these later. At first, I couldn't get anybody to act; once one group got started acting, however, the class took off. They were so many different interpretations, and people were saying, "No, man, that's not how the character would act, he wouldn't be dressed like that, he would have a bald head" – just little things like that. And I didn't expect that. So we get students to engage with the elements on a face-to-face kind of basis. And by the time we get into the technical aspects of the drama, they have already "met" them. They are then no longer intimidated by concepts or definitions.

So that stands out for me as a memorable situation – the practical actually came before the theoretical.

Q: Let's talk now about the opposite of this memorable situation. Have you had a session that you would rather forget?

A.S.: Definitely! When I first started teaching at the tertiary level, I think I felt that in order to be "academic" and in order to fit the role of "lecturer", I had to stop "teaching". Unfortunately, most of the models I had had on teaching at the tertiary level were based on a lecture style.

My heart was crying out to get up, walk around and engage. I ended up having lively discussions, but I wasn't really talking a lot to the students. I was giving notes for almost the entire two-hour period, which drove me crazy! Though the students were nice about it, I think they wanted more, or even if they didn't realize it, they could have benefited from having more of an engagement with the concepts with which they were being presented rather than simply the discussion. In fact, it's something I tell my students all the time: they need to have more than an open discussion for the entire session, because the different skills are not being nurtured in a situation where only that is taking place.

Q: What skill set are you thinking of?

A.S.: This has come through my experience, really, as a teacher prior to tertiary as well as at the tertiary level. Some of us automatically love literature, and we have been blessed with a background of engagement with literature that allows us to continue to develop with literature without someone having to appeal to us to do so. But there are many students who do not have that natural inclination, perhaps because of background, and, therefore, I find it important that we intentionally teach students how to interpret, how to read texts through the tasks that we give them. I think at the tertiary level where I am training teachers to teach literature, this is crucial. So it is not just about, for example, some activities that you can give the students to do; it's about what you want to achieve in this literature lesson. Do the students understand the shift from literal to figurative? How can we get them to understand that shift without simply telling them *this is literal and this is figurative?* So the tasks and activities would be centred on engaging them in *an understanding* of how to acquire meaning, not simply assuming that they automatically house "meaning" in their brains. When I say skill set, that is what I mean; it's about helping them to understand, for example, figurative language.

Q: So it's a focus on the actual process of reading and understanding literature?

A.S.: Exactly.

Q: Given that focus, what methods, what strategies work best for you?

A.S.: I believe that throughout most of my own tertiary years, I was not taught literature in a reader-response–oriented manner, and so when I came into contact with Rosenblatt's ideas, I was floored. I asked myself how any student could possibly dislike literature, if they're engaged in literature with this kind of approach. With a reader-response–oriented frame to the teaching of literature, I automatically am able to create an activity quickly, because I know that the reader-response approach means putting the student in the centre, means understanding that it's a transaction between text and student, means having the student personally connect. So there are a number of tenets that automatically flow, once I think of a response orientation. So that's predominantly what I use, and I think it's a very eclectic approach. It combines so many things. So it's not that their literary knowledge is being thrown out; they're still engaging with it, but they're engaging with it in a way that will help them to remember and to appreciate the text.

Q: In a way it seems to me that what you are doing is helping the students experience literature. It's not about teaching them about literature but having them have an experience of literature, or rather you're doing a combination. Do you experience other major challenges in teaching literature, especially in this way?

A.S.: One of the challenges is how literature is seen on a broad scale generally in tertiary institutions like universities. I think we sometimes underestimate the value of literature and what it is able to produce in students. One of the big challenges is trying to teach student-teachers literature methodology, when they do not have the requisite literature background.

Q: How do you deal with this?

A.S.: I try to use the literature circle idea, where I place students in groups and then work with the groups based on their needs.

Q: How, then, do you differentiate your teaching of poetry, prose, drama?

A.S.: Well, I certainly believe that one of the things we need to do is help students to understand the features of each text so that they can better interpret what they're reading. Very often it's because they don't understand how to read the text, why they do not want to access the text. If you're going to introduce students to poetry, then they have to understand that the language of poetry doesn't work in the same way that the language of an article or an essay works. They have to understand that the language of poetry works differently from the language of prose or drama, and so they can't come to it with the same expectations. I think it's important that we acknowledge that there are distinctive features for each genre, even though some features overlap. We should teach these intentionally, so that students become familiar and comfortable with the differences in each genre.

Q: You've indicated that in teaching poetry we need to focus on the language and the way language is used differently in poetry. Is there anything else you want to say about the teaching of poetry?

A.S.: I think what is standing out for me as a kind of principle that I try to impart to my students and to myself as I read is, we need to allow the poem to be what it is. Don't impose your standards, conventions, rules and so on. Read the poem for what it is. I think a lot of students get frustrated because they're trying to read the poem in terms of the conventions they have been taught. There's a poem called "Introduction to Poetry", and I start every poetry class with that poem, because it speaks about what readers want to do with a poem. The poem suggests that all they want to do is tie up the poem to a chair and beat it until its meaning comes out. The engagement, the experience with the poem and how the poem affects us are all lost. So I usually start by asking them to change any orientation they may have, where they focus on "Where's the metaphor?" Where's the simile?" "Where's personification?" and just allow the poem to be.

Q: Is there any parallel to the way you teach a novel? Does the structure force you, or rather encourage a particular way of teaching? In the same way you talk about allowing the poem to be and using that as the springboard from which you teach it, is there a similar approach to teaching prose and drama?

A.S.: Yes, I would have to say that. I think the structure of a novel certainly matters and also of course the origin of that novel and the author of that novel – all of those things matter. However, I tend not to start with structure, because I find that students run away once I begin with structure. They tend to think, "Oh, she's getting technical now, we're going to be expected to know all of this." So at the start, I try to get them to connect with a particular aspect of the text. It may be the focus on a theme. It may be a particular character. The truth is there is never a set way, a set type of questions to ask. I try to feel out the class and see what their interests are before I proceed. But certainly, we have to move into structure, and I would use their connection to the text to help them move into structure. So I would ask them, for example, if it is because the novel has started with a flashback that we get a particular response, and if it matters, then, that this is an epistolary type of text, and how does that influence other aspects of the text? So I look at structure, but not before I allow them to connect to the novel as a whole.

Q: Clearly you use a number of approaches to get your students to experience literature. What have you found actually works best for them? What method, what setting perhaps, what instructional aids?

A.S.: I think the bottom line for me clearly is the response-oriented frame, as I said, and within that I try to have a task-oriented focus. I try to allow the concepts to be couched within the tasks that I do. I do introduce them to the concepts first, because I think they should always have an idea of where I'm going and what I'm trying to accomplish. So it is task-oriented with an emphasis on purposefulness and relevance. With every single class I ask myself, "Has my student left better than when they came? What is it that they know now that they did not know before that they can use?" Milner and Milner speak of it as the extension part of the teaching cycle – *enter, explore, expect* – and they say, "Okay, now that we've engaged students with the text, how can they match that to the outside world in the different situations they will encounter?" And so I try to model what I'm proposing, because I'm teaching teachers to use these approaches and strategies. I want them to have a practical grasp of how the strategies work.

Q: In an earlier conversation with you, you mentioned your use of music, your use of visuals to teach literature. Will you please elaborate on this?

A.S.: I think maybe thirty years ago, everybody read, or you tended to assume that most persons read. Now I'll get to a first-year or second-year group, and they have not read basic texts. I find, therefore, that you can't come expecting that they've already experimented with reading or with engaging with texts, and so I find they get bored easily if we only centre the classes on discussion. And even if you're soliciting their responses, which is student-centred, they're still not there, many of them, and so I have to get what I call "manipulatives" – hands-on material which enables them to engage with the tasks. The more they're asked to perform these tasks, the more they have to draw upon or nurture particular skills, as they are trying to access meaning or knowledge from the texts. I use that especially with poetry, because I find it works. It helps them to become engaged, and at the end of the lesson, they realize that they've accomplished a lot. Teachers often say that they cannot complete a literature syllabus unless they lecture the students and give them a lot of notes. I can recall one class in which I worked with a past paper from our regional examination CSEC, and I showed them that by the time we had finished with the tasks, they would have been able to respond to all of the set questions without my ever posing one of those questions. So my aim is to help students engage in the material in such a way that they have a holistic understanding, not a dissected, rigid way of accessing the literary texts.

Q: Tell me a little bit more about the tasks. It's interesting this idea of yours about using manipulatives.

A.S.: I find that graphic organizers are extremely important for poetry. A number of our students tend to be weak in their written expression, and sometimes we are, I think, expecting too much from them. The graphic organizers help them to generate and connect their ideas before they actually produce a written piece. At first, the ideas are segmented. The result is that students begin to feel confident as they participate in this process. They don't worry about how they're writing or what their lecturer expects. Another "manipulate" that I use to help them with the writing is a template. So I may begin the written response for them through the template; for example, "In the poem we see where" – and a blank space follows – "and that allows us to understand that" – and another blank space follows, and so on. They focus on the content, while the language is being modelled for them.

Q: What have been very interesting assignments for them based on all of this?

A.S.: I think one of the best ways is to try and look at alternative assessment forms. If they do have to get an essay, I try to incorporate things like the checklist, the rubric or the peer-editing process so that they again understand that the teaching of literature does not end with methodology or the steps that they'd be doing in their lessons (as teachers themselves), but they're to continue this response orientation in the actual assessment they give. We also look at journal entries and how to develop skills through those. They learn that it is not just about allowing their pupils to write, but also about how to move them from where they are with the journal entries. So we examine "prompts" that we can give and how prompts can help to change their level of thinking.

They also create posters or diagrams. They may, for example, create a poster with symbols for a particular concept, and [having them] work with their peers, I get them to create something new. They discover, then, that new ideas can emerge when working with their peers and not just from listening to their lecturer. This can be inspiring for them.

Q: Elaine Showalter in her book on teaching literature talks about teacher anxieties, which include things like the matter of isolation. When you think about your own teaching, do you have any anxieties at all?

A.S.: I think each time I meet a new class, there's one main anxiety that will surface, and it's about whether I will be able to reach them. I don't want to say the wrong thing. I may be getting students who hate literature. I don't want to come across as being so passionate about literature that they begin to pull back. I want everybody to be comfortable no matter what level they are at when they enter into that classroom space. Another anxiety is about ensuring that I am modelling what I am asking them to do. So I'm not just moving with my theory in my cloud space, but I'm actually providing them with enough exposure and experience in the classroom space to help them to engage with what I'm saying in a meaningful and practical way.

Q: And finally, what do you think is absolutely essential for effectively teaching Caribbean literature and literature in general?

A.S.: I think an understanding and a basic framework for reading literature. For Caribbean literature, a basic understanding of the history of the literature itself and where it's coming from – a history of the place. I think that would go for all literature. One of the things in one of the methodology courses that I teach on literature is to have students trace the history of English and then of literature. I help them to understand why people study literature and then encourage them to figure out what they think is literature's value.

Often we tend to dive straight into the content, not appreciating the fact that some students need a basic understanding of what literature is, how it can be useful, and what is its purpose.

Sandra Robinson

"And because they [the students] come with different experiences and perspectives, you sometimes have this wonderful 'callaloo pot'."

Dr Sandra Robinson has been teaching literature since 1986. Her experience spans secondary as well as tertiary levels. She taught at an all-girls school, then at an all-boys school. After this she taught literature at St Vincent and the Grenadines Community College Division of Teacher Education. Presently she teaches literature content and pedagogy at the University of the West Indies, Cave Hill, Barbados, where she has been teaching for about five years.

Dr Robinson has also published in the field of literature education and was most recently co-editor of a special issue of *Caribbean Journal of Education* on teaching Caribbean poetry.

Q: Dr Robinson, what do you particularly like about teaching literature?

Sandra Robinson: First and foremost, what I get from reading literature is the interaction with other worlds. I'm also fascinated by the language. I read, too, for pleasure and also for escape. These are experiences that I feel I need to give my students.

I think of my mother buying books for us – for example, bedtime stories. I recall at secondary school reading about other landscapes, whether it's Heathcliff on the moors in *Wuthering Heights* or Elizabeth going on her long walks in Jane Austen's *Pride and Prejudice*. So I enjoy the idea of moving students across different cultures and just showing them a bit of the world that is in a way different from where they are. But also I enjoy the idea of getting them to interact with the language, to look at the way in which somebody has written something and try, so to speak, to unlock that piece of text. And because they come with different experiences and perspectives, you sometimes have this wonderful "callaloo pot". I like that kind of interaction both with the cultural and heritage aspects of the text as well as with the language of the text itself.

Q: What do you mean by "callaloo pot"?

S.R.: Callaloo pot is a soup for us in St Vincent and the Grenadines. In the pot you have different kinds of food: yam, dasheen, breadfruit and meat. So it's a variety of stuff, and when you get into the pot of soup, you really love it. You pick out those things that you really like and eat first. So the literature class can be a lot like this.

Q: What a lovely image! So can we assume that the teaching of literature is still important? If so, why?

S.R.: I think it is, and I believe it is. Recently, I was reading an article which was looking at the offline and online comprehension skills of students, and it got me interested in the way students read texts. And I remember having a conversation with a class that focused on the notion of e-books, and whether students should buy books, and if they are going to read them and so forth. And one student made this comment: "I still like the feel of that paper, that book, you know, in my hand." The idea of cuddling up somewhere and feeling like I am away just for a few moments is not something that technology might allow me to do, though you could perhaps do that with a Kindle. But I understand what she meant in terms of just turning pages and just actually handling paper. However, I think the importance of literature goes back to what I was saying earlier; literature provides an opportunity to interact with language in a way that is not as practised at that stage. In an English language class, you're specifically focusing on certain aspects of the language, but the students encounter language in literature in a way that is spontaneous. And their reaction to it in the moment that they are reading is also spontaneous. Literature also offers, not just young people but all of us, a moment to interact and to have experiences in a way that is safe. You know, you might be reading something, and you connect with it in a way that if you were confronted with it in reality, you might have to engage with it differently.

The teaching of literature also helps students locate themselves in history. Literature can help resolve identity issues and get that historical rootedness. Literature is also important now because it facilitates teaching a particular kind of literacy – a literacy that helps students deal with the information bombarding them online, to question critically what to accept and what not to. Literature encourages students to question the text. Disrupt it. Ask, What is missing? Whose voice is violated? What is the truth here? And I think the truth here is that literature can offer students an opportunity to build a critical line of questioning.

Q: You have identified for us many of the reasons literature remains relevant. How, then, do you actually prepare for meeting these goals of literature teaching? How do you prepare for your tutorials, for your lectures?

S.R.: When I started teaching literature, I just wanted to cover the text, to make sure that it was completed. And what that meant really in terms of planning was deciding which chapters we were going to cover that day. But it always included a question on their views about what they had read and a discussion around that. Unfortunately, students came to see literature in a way that I didn't like. It was just simply about reading activities that many of them didn't like or enjoy, and neither did I. When I went to teacher training, something changed for me. It was no longer about the "what" of the teaching, "what" I needed to cover. It was a matter of how best these students learn and understand. I started thinking about the learning I was after, rather than the book I was going to teach. And that changed the way I thought about the process. I began to focus on the pedagogical process itself. It's more now about uncovering the text for and with the students.

Q: It's a process that requires that students read the text. It is, however, a fairly common experience that getting students to read the text is challenging. How do you address this? How do you plan? How do you actually get them involved and participating in classes?

S.R.: I embrace a lot of transactional theory, and part of that means valuing what students bring to the situation. I think it's important to enable connections instead of focusing on control, and by that I mean the students have to be given an opportunity to make connections with the text. This will enable them to make sense of the information that is emerging from the text. This leads to an opportunity for a lot of active learning now. So sometimes reading takes place in the classroom in a way that is different. I might use activities like "jigsaw", where I actually assign different portions of the text to be read in a particular time and with a particular learning outcome in mind. Another activity or strategy that I use to enable the reading is called a "dialectic notebook", or "double-entry journals". I ask students to quote from the text a sentence or two that they think are essential to understanding what they've just read. I then ask them to write a response to that sentence or quote. So on one sheet they write two columns – one column indicates the quotation, and the other column their response to it. Students also respond to each other's quotes. In this regard, a third column titled Peer Response is added, and the activity becomes a triple-entry journal. And this is followed by something called "doubting and believing". Here, again on a single sheet, the students make two columns – one to indicate their doubts, and the other to indicate their beliefs. They again identify and write a quote from the text and respond under the appropriate column with "I believe this", and in the other column, "but I doubt this". There are also activities which can be used to encourage active learning using sentence prompts, and these are just a few among many active learning strategies and activities. But the point is that through these activities we are enabling and encouraging the thinking process. And I am not just referring to the secondary level but also to the university level. I think too often we assume that students know how to learn, but this is not always the case. I think it [learning] is something that we need to demonstrate to students. There is value in the initial stage to demonstrate what thinking about a text can look like, and then you give them some other tools to use to get more engagement.

I really believe that "how to learn" is something that we should demonstrate initially. Our students can excel, but they don't have the tools. It's not a lack of knowing, but of how.

I am constantly revamping when I go to the classroom. I give myself permission to say, "Sandra, that was rubbish today." Then I go back to the drawing board and think about the learning that I'm after. I get the students to talk to me about the difficulty they encounter getting into a particular lesson. You have to make an investment in the strategies that they are going to need to get to where you want them to be.

Q: What is a concrete example of the learning that you want in the literature class?

S.R.: I may use a set of sentence prompts when introducing a concept. For example, if we are looking at particular traits of characters, I may ask students to write a five- or a six-sentence paragraph for me about this particular trait. So I'd start by asking them to begin with "I already know that . . ." This taps their prior knowledge. Then the other sentence might be about asking a question of this kind: "However, sometimes I wonder . . ." We continue like this until we have a paragraph. I then ask them to share their paragraph aloud, so they hear what they have written and also what other people in the class are thinking. I know it seems like a very unsophisticated thing to do at the university level. But we are still talking about a bunch of young people who we often assume come with a lot of experience. I don't assume; I also verify.

There's another active learning strategy that we also use. When students complete the paragraph, I ask them to go into pairs. In pairs they share their paragraphs. And so we begin to develop as a class a particular way of thinking about this concept that we can always refer to as the class experience.

Q: Could you please elaborate on how the jigsaw exercise works?

S.R.: You can tweak it in several ways. The jigsaw, I think, is an interesting activity to use. I think it works better with poetry and prose, ut it could be used if you have an entire chapter or two chapters on themes or characters, settings and plot. You can actually assign the reading that you want students to focus on with regard to setting. So the entire chapter can have elements you want students to see or read, so that they might understand elements of the setting. To do this, you divide the class, and you assign readings pertaining to the particular literary components or concepts you wish to be the focus of that particular class. And so, let's say you have divided the group, according to the size of the class, into groups of five. Group one will do that portion of reading that deals with setting. They will read the assigned section of the text and focus on setting; another group will read the chapter and focus on themes; another group will read the chapter and focus on plot and so on. Each group, because of its assigned focus in the reading of the chapter, becomes what we call an "expert group", because their discussion of the chapter is focused and specific; they are all reading the same chapter, but the focus of each group is different – one group may discuss setting and another plot, and so on. And when you're done, the members of each expert group, the setting "experts", the plot "experts" and so on, then letter themselves from A to E. So all the As from all the groups come together, all the Bs, all the Cs and so on. So what you have now is a second group with experts from all the groups sitting in; and in that subgroup, the experts will be teaching each other about the information that comes straight from their expert groups. That way, when they are done, everybody goes back and shares with the original group, and each individual student is then able to read the text with that added knowledge.

Of course, you have to be mindful of the fact that sometimes the information they are sharing may not be completely accurate, but the beauty about this strategy is that you can get the students to write afterwards – maybe write a response to questions about the setting, which gives you access to the kinds of thinking and engagement the students are making with the text. The information accessed from the students' writing can then be used to plan. And they can now go back on their own to develop understanding of, and have a more critical engagement with, text. In this way you get reading done in a more learner-centred manner.

Q: Given all these interesting activities, what has been a particularly memorable session for you?

S.R.: Believe it or not, there are two things that stand out in my mind. One was actually in Jamaica, where I was teaching briefly at Ardenne High School. I was using poetry as a response to the text *Shane*. We were looking at that text, and I felt I had used all the materials needed for the students to understand the text. There is this scene in the novel where Shane is taking his gun out of the holster, and the little boy, Bob Starrett, observes Shane, who previous to this does not carry a gun. So Bob secretly, out of curiosity, takes the gun out of the holster and, unknown to Bob, Shane sees him. So

I used the poem "Innocence" from Pamela Mordecai's *Sunsong 2* to encourage a response and connection to this particular scene in the text *Shane*. The poem tells the story of an adult persona reflecting on a childhood experience. The persona had gone into a shed to smoke a cigarette. The persona went to the shed to hide from being seen. But the adult persona ends the reflection with the observation that while the shed provided a hiding place from being seen by someone else and a feeling of physical safety, it could not hide him from himself. Moreover, the persona questions the notion of "feeling safe" and what it means; in other words, even if one feels safe because the world does not see, there is still that feeling of conscience to contend with; so doing things secretly does not save us from ourselves. The reading of the poem and the scene with Bob in the text *Shane* led to a very insightful discussion about how, sometimes, we hide and do things in secret and make choices that we know are not part of our value systems. And after we discussed it, I got them to write and reflect on some experiences that they had had. One student wrote about a very personal experience relating to an encounter that she had had with a sister who was an underage drinker, and she, the student, felt so burdened with the situation that the engagement with both text – the novel and the poem – led her to share the experience. Interestingly, she insisted that she didn't like literature, and she didn't like the book, but here she was responding in a very personal way as a result of how she had encountered the text. I suppose it was so personal she couldn't acknowledge that she had made such a personal connection with the text. When it actually happened, it just blew me away. It blew me away because it wasn't a connection that was superficial. The literature lesson and the texts used in the lesson had triggered something in this student that was so profound that she was actually able to write about it. So you know, that was quite memorable for me, because it reinforces the power of literature itself to enable us to make connections in a deep way.

Q: On the other hand, was there a session that you would rather forget? And why?

S.R.: Many! We all have them! One in particular stands out. But one of the things that I have become wary of is being overambitious with regard to what I am able to do in a forty-minute period. So you know, you have these gossip magazines that many people like to read. I remember using a Shakespeare play, *Romeo and Juliet*, and I asked the students to look at the opening scene. I asked them to imagine that they are going to write a gossip column about this scene. I wanted them to write an essay, but I didn't want to say to them, "Write an essay." I wanted them to write the essay in the form of a column for the gossip magazine, and to use the opening scene in *Romeo and Juliet*. Initially, I wanted to give them the option to write the column individually or in groups but decided against this. The thing is, though, I didn't think about the importance of giving students choice. I just went ahead and made the decision that they would do it in pairs. Even at the university level, you would imagine that there is always some degree of discord among students – some not talking to others, and the like. These were undergraduates, by the way. And we were looking at activities that could be used to get students "through the text". It was a take-home assignment. I came to learn that there was a pair who had a whole lot of "stuff" going on between them, involving a young man and a girl at the bus stop, and one big quarrel broke out. They did manage to complete the assignment, but the discord between them affected the sharing in the end. In effect, the opening scene of the play mirrored in some ways what they, too, were experiencing. What I learned really at that moment was that sometimes it is important to give students the option with regard to how and with whom they wish to work.

Q: You have been talking about strategies that you have been using, for example, the jigsaw approach and sentence prompts. Can you identify those that work best for you, or perhaps even what instructional materials work best for you in your literature class?

S.R.: I like a lot of visuals. You see that notion of critical literacy that asks you to disrupt the common understanding? I like that. And so how one begins a class is very important. Sometimes I use images, like a short clip from YouTube, a cartoon, a video that's related to the course, maybe five minutes long, with questions to think about throughout the process of listening or viewing. But I think during the introduction of a class, one needs to look at the fact that the students are an important part of what happens, and the introduction can help to establish the kind of thinking which is necessary for the discussions which often underpin the class's engagement with the text.

Recently, to begin a discussion about women in society, I used two images of the *Mona Lisa* – the usual image and another that disrupted the common view of the image. I got them to look at the first image. And then immediately after, I showed them the other image of the *Mona Lisa* smoking a cigar. I just showed it to them, and I waited. The response was that students started making comments, but, first of all, the first image evoked expected responses, the usual things you hear about the *Mona Lisa*, you know. Who is she? Who is she smiling at? She's so ladylike – perceptions of how women should be and that sort of thing. And then when they got to the second image, they were divided on the notion of how the female personality and perspective was presented. So I said, "Let's talk about that." So now you have them thinking about what they think, sort of activating their prior knowledge, and you are also getting them to question the text, which, in this case, was first the image. In this regard, the introductory activity challenged them to clarify their understanding of the texts being studied. We were at the time studying novels by Jamaica Kincaid and M. NourbeSe Philip. So for me the introduction, and how, as a teacher, you plan for the learning you are after, is central. It's something that you'll have to give lots of thought to. Whether it's asking the right kind of questions or looking for the right video clip or image to provide the kind of thinking that will lead to textual engagement.

Another video clip that I use is a scene from the movie *Mona Lisa Smile*, starring Julia Roberts. Roberts's character has been teaching for quite a while and has been assigned a group of young women to whom she is required to teach art. But this group of students is overconfident. And in this clip Roberts enters the room and begins the class with a series of slides depicting a variety of artwork. The first slide is an image called *Carcass* by Soutine. As the slide is shown, Roberts observes the students as they flip through their books in an attempt to locate the image, which is not a part of their prescribed text. "What's that?" a student asks in confusion, after failing to locate the image. Roberts responds, "It's art." The students observe that "It's not on the syllabus." And Roberts continues: "I know, but what do you think? What's your reaction?" The class, in the clip, is now silent, and again Roberts challenges, "Well, come on, think about it. There's no textbook now telling you what to think. What I want is your position." And that right there becomes the critical thing. There are some texts that are not part of the requirement, but they can have a profound impact on what you are teaching, and so they need to be considered. And in the movement and journey towards understanding, it is necessary and important to consider them. I use this to provoke a kind of thinking in students that someone else – including Cliff Notes – does not have to tell them what to think about the text. It's a moment to validate the perspectives that they hold and to make them feel empowered to share that perspective. I believe that this is a central responsibility of the teacher in the literature classroom, especially when you are just getting into the text.

Q: Yes, it is. You have been discussing your approach to teaching the three genres: poetry, prose and drama. Do you find any distinct differences in the way you approach the teaching of these, and in particular poetry?

S.R.: Not particularly. But sometimes the distinction is also based on how you read it. And it is possible that reading might still remain the same even if the form differs, because the language somehow leads you to a particular way [of] reading the text. Because poetry is so condensed, somehow the mind wants to fill the gaps. And how one fills those gaps is going to be very dependent on the kind of experience that one has had. The poet might use a particular image to communicate something that they are observ-ing and want to talk about in a way that is different from how the reader might have [observed it]. So how I approach poetry is different sometimes, because there is a certain way that students will read the language and en-gage with the language. Frank Collymore has this poem called "The Moth", which simply reads, "The moth / ate cloth." That's all. And it is sometimes useful in teacher education to communicate some of the things that you want students to consider in a poem. I usually don't begin by asking what the poem is about, because that raises other questions. I ask the factual questions like, "What is happening in this poem?" So we look at the facts. There's a moth, there's cloth. So let's pull out all the facts that we can, as we go through all of what that might mean. It's a matter of making sure that everybody agrees on what the facts are. And then we begin to talk about what this might mean and the various ways that we might arrive at how to get meaning, so to speak. Whereas with prose, I think sometimes the author places characters within a particular perspective to tell the story, to tell the narrative of that experience. So sometimes what I do with prose is, for example, use a fairy tale.

Fairy tales have themes which are similar to those in the fiction that we are studying. I remember once we were looking at a novel that had a lot to do with human relations issues in society, and for that particular text, as an initial response, I used nursery rhymes. It's about demonstrating the actions in the text.

Q: You clearly have a distinctive teaching style. How would you describe it?

S.R.: Very non-traditional. I have always been like that, very non-traditional. I have never been a teacher who did things by the rules and regulations. I suppose part of how I come to teaching is linked to how I learned too. So I am always aware that there isn't sameness. I am always looking for new and different ways to do the same thing. How I taught this text this year is different from the way I taught it last year, and I am always looking around me for things that I think I can bring into my practice that can give relevance to my pedagogy. Like a few days ago I went to observe a teacher completing the practicum component of the postgraduate dip. ed. programme. They were reading *A Midsummer Night's Dream*, and the teacher was using all the sets of flowers and those images that you see. But on my way from home I saw this sign that says "Fruitful Hill", but it wasn't spelt FRUITFUL; it was spelt "FRUIT FULL". So my mind starts to work. I'm thinking, you know, this is such a wonderful idea: use this to get the students to think about differences. I am always looking for ways in which I can activate their thinking. I use the environment and the stuff around me, and that includes everything. "Things" have a way of facilitating the teaching and learning process.

Q: You have identified and discussed how literature can address some of the needs of students. Will you please elaborate on this?

S.R.: What is it about the students I teach that makes me think they need to learn how to learn? They need to understand how to transfer and find meaning in what they know, because they're coming from a teaching–learning environment that focuses on knowledge acquisition and the recall of information and sometimes "model answers". And teaching, when you look into these classrooms, is often focused on covering the text or the information as opposed to uncovering that knowledge. It's challenging to focus on getting the students to acquire that knowledge. But it is also important to engage students about what to do with that knowledge and how to deal with it. These are things that the students are not so comfortable with. Sometime ago, I was listening to a broadcast on CNN, *GPS*, hosted by Fareed Zakaria, and he was making an observation about his early education, which began in India. He said, "I learned how to learn, how to look. But when I came and I saw what was happening in America, the education system taught me how to think, and that for me was the missing element." And I am not saying that we should spoon-feed students – because this is the reaction I get and continue to get every time I raise this issue – but scaffolding even for adults is necessary. That is why Vygosky talks about the zone of development. In many instances, I think what they need is the skill and competence with regard to knowing what to do with information if they are going to transfer from what is learned to meaning-making.

Q: How do you deal with the challenge of this?

S.R.: The interesting thing is that I think when students encounter me first, sometimes it's bothersome for them. Because they are so used to coming to class, sitting, listening, taking notes, getting them to change that perspective is difficult initially. So it's about establishing the culture of that class, and I say to them that in my class there is no such thing as having no opinion. Even if you don't like the text that we are using, that's an opinion too; so let's talk about it. I have had students who have said to me, "I don't like this set of activities. Please give me an essay to write and let me go away." And I am quite mindful of that too.

I start off by acknowledging that this is who they are and how they view the text. For example, I teach a course which is not a literature course, but it is an English education course, and I use literature to go where I want to go. This takes place from seven to nine in the evening. You can't sit before the students at this time and lecture to them. I teach in a way that requires them to think and not revert to a laziness of mind which, I think, limits them.

Q: What types of assignments have you given them that were particularly helpful, interesting or that worked for them in helping you achieve the goals you've just outlined?

S.R.: I think that same activity or assignment that I told you about earlier, the enquiry journal. That particular assignment focuses on getting them to think, getting them to think about the opening of the scene of *Romeo and Juliet*, for example. They are writing the essay, but now there is a context for that essay, which is the gossip column. They were using the knowledge and the information, but I think they found that quite interesting.

Another assignment that I gave and which I think is useful is journal entries, because I am teaching the content with the pedagogy. Using Robert Bolt's A *Man for All Seasons*, I got them to examine More's wife Alice's character more closely. To do this they wrote a series of short essays in the form of journal entries. To write these entries they considered and looked closely at her diary and, based on the play, made four additional journal entries up to and following her husband Thomas's death. The essays were entries that she, Alice, might have made from his, More's, time in jail. So I got them to write journal entries based on their reaction to the movement of the plot and stuff like that. And they found this quite interesting, even when they had to deal with issues, because when they got to this part in the play, a lot of them were very emotional; they liked that final scene in the jail. And this is one of the assignments in the teaching of literature course. I also use, often, Lorraine Hansberry's *A Raisin in the Sun* and ask them to consider the social implications, but this is really for a curriculum focus to develop a unit in social studies.

I think most of them liked the discussion of the social issues, because they are doing literature, and they have been given an opportunity to look at the text from a different perspective.

Q: Were there other challenges of teaching literature?

S.R.: Students don't buy texts, and so that is an increased challenge, I think, especially given their hesitancy when it comes to reading and learning. Reading is not something they come quickly to, but I try to find means and ways to get them to read. It also means that everybody is not able to read the text at the same time in the way that I would like.

It's for that reason that I try to structure adequate classroom activities and assignments in a way that they cannot get by without doing the reading.

What I find is that there are challenges, too, when it comes to students and how they negotiate university life and their personal life. A large percentage of our student population is students who are working, and so when they come to class, there is an element of distraction. It is a question of the extent to which they can invest in the learning experience, and this puts a burden on them in relation to classroom activities and assignments, because this is something that they cannot get by without doing. I also think that we have a responsibility to make sure that students understand that there are consequences to choices. Yes, there are economic issues and so forth, but there are some basic tools that one needs in order to facilitate the learning experience, and they have to take responsibility for that. Without knowledge of the text, students sometimes depend on other people's experiences, and so when we are talking about the text in tutorial, that's the time they join in the discussion, and I think, "I have to address this, how do I respond to such superficiality?" And there is also the issue that some texts challenge some aspects of their moral perspective. So you have students who will tell you they struggle through a text because of this. However, literature is literature because it challenges one's thinking.

Q: Elaine Showalter talked about seven teacher anxieties in literature to do with, for example, gender, isolation, teaching versus learning. My question to you now is what, if any, teacher anxiety do you have?

S.R.: I don't know if it falls under Showalter's list, but I have anxieties, too, about my own knowledge and how I transfer things to the students. I find that there are also times I come to the teaching of literature from different perspectives – a teaching perspective as opposed to simply an analysis of content perspective. I don't simply teach content and then get students to analyse. In planning to teach the text, my teaching strategy is not only a literature study – but also about pedagogy or teaching that will influence students' practice. Quite a number of my students are teachers coming from school, so there is that struggle sometimes in finding that right balance. I don't know if that answers your question.

Q: Yes, it does. Certainly! And my final question is: In teaching Caribbean literature, what is absolutely necessary in order to do so effectively?

S.R.: Passion – I think you should be passionate and value the traditional focus on heritage as it relates to discourse in literature content and teaching. It is about bringing alive a sense of who we are as a people, and enabling and empowering students to question texts. And I mean all texts, anything that communicates meaning, in the journey towards engagement.

Kelly Baker Josephs

"I think teaching literature allows students to see themselves more fully, more completely if only for a moment."

Professor Kelly Baker Josephs has been teaching for thirteen years in different locations. After attaining her degree, she taught literature full-time in Miami, first at Florida International University, then at Rutgers University, New Jersey, then York College, the City University of New York. She also taught for a year at Johns Hopkins in Baltimore. Currently she teaches at York College as a professor of English.

Josephs specializes in world anglophone literature with an emphasis on Caribbean literature. She teaches courses in anglophone Caribbean literature, Caribbean digital humanities, literatures of the African diaspora, and gender studies. She is the author of *Disturbers of the Peace: Representations of Insanity in Anglophone Caribbean Literature* (2013), and founding editor of *sx salon: a small axe literary platform* and the Caribbean Commons website.

Q: Professor Baker Josephs, what do you like about teaching literature? I mean, you've been teaching it for over thirteen years, so you obviously like teaching literature.

Kelly Baker Josephs: Yes, though I don't always teach literature. I like it. I like getting to teach literature, but I often also teach writing. So when I teach literature, I like sharing new ways of seeing the world with my students and new ways of seeing their own world as well, not just the large world out there, which is important, but also their own, more immediate world, particularly if they are of Caribbean descent.

Q: Why did you move into teaching literature?

K.B.J.: I love reading! I wanted to teach. I didn't start in literature. I started in communications and advertising, and once I got to college I knew that that's where I wanted to be, so I figured I would work for a while and then teach advertising at the college level. Once I got into advertising, I realized I didn't want to send anyone else into advertising, so I had to sort of rethink what it was that I loved, and literature was one of these things I loved. I had an English teacher for a professional writing class at the University of Miami, which is where I did my undergrad, and he had encouraged me to apply for graduate school fellowships. At the time I wasn't thinking graduate school at all, but it was my senior year, and I thought, Well, why not? If he thinks I can, I should try it. But the fellowships that he suggested didn't cover advertising, and so I had to think about what else I would do if I was going to do one of these degrees. And it became English, because it was the only subject I wanted to study at an advanced level. I didn't get those fellowships, but just the application process had me thinking about graduate school as well as English for graduate school. Then I went into advertising and forgot about that for a while. When I was thinking about going back to school, that came back to me, and I thought, Oh, I'll try for English – and that's what I did.

Q: Why do you think it is still important to teach literature? A lot of people, for example, don't see any value in doing a literature degree.

K.B.J.: Right, so I do have concerns when I get students who are English majors. I have concerns for some of them when they're not sure what they're doing, and they're just doing this degree because they can't figure out something else. And they're not particularly graduate school material in the various ways you have to be in terms of academia and commitment to that type of life. I question what they will do with an English degree if they are stopping at the BA level. On the other hand, I think it is important in the sense that no matter what your major is, you should take literature because of the open-mindedness it encourages towards ideas, cultures and people, and, among other things, the simple pleasure of reading and analysing texts. And doing a degree in literature enhances that and can prepare students for a range of professions in which analysis and empathy are necessary skills.

Q: I can understand that. I'm shifting our conversation now to your actual teaching style. How do you prepare for your tutorials or your lectures?

K.B.J.: I always have to read the text again completely. No matter how many times I've taught it, I find that it has to be firm in my mind so that I can walk confidently into a classroom. So, for instance, I just taught *White Teeth* last week, and *White Teeth* is not a short novel. I've taught it before, and I've written on it, and I've read it I don't know how many times, and I had to read it again, because there's just no way to really walk into a classroom with something that's even three or four months old in your head and be able to talk about the things that you need to. I mean, you will have things that you want to talk about, you'll be guiding students there, but there will always be tangential or unscripted conversations that the students bring in, and you don't want to stand there – at least I don't want to stand there – and say: "That happened in this novel?"

So my way of preparing is first to read the novel completely, and then I often go through page by page. When I go through, I mark it, I go back, and I write down everything I marked. Now if I've taught it before, I'll have that already done, so I just have to go back to that, but if I'm teaching it for the first time, I just create that the first time and then I organize those page numbers by ideas. I've just taught *White Teeth*, and I identified history, family, immigration as themes or ideas that I want to talk about in the class. I move the page numbers around based on that. Often I then create questions for groups. I print the questions out, make copies and divide the class into groups to discuss the individual questions, and then we discuss as a class.

Q: So how do you usually get your students involved? Well, I know you said you actually create questions for groups.

K.B.J.: Yes, I like group work. I often teach longer classes, maybe two or three hours, so for those longer classes I try to mix it up. I don't do group work all the time, but I find that getting students involved in the actual answering of a question engages them. It also helps those who haven't read the text and gets them in some way involved in just the conversation. So it's usually groups of three or four depending on the size of the class and how many questions I have, sometimes just pairs if it's a smaller class. There will be all the questions on the one handout, but they're only assigned one question. However, I do ask them to look at the other questions just to sort of fix in their minds what else is going on.

Recently I have found that giving exams is also a way of getting students involved; because they're so focused on a grade, I try and use that in some way to help them during class time. I give them a "test" that comes directly out of these questions. And it's not onerous, or at least I don't think of it as such. It's open book, open notes, and it's often the same question or a slight variation on something I asked in class. So if we're asking about an idea in terms of, for example, postcolonialism, I might not use *White Teeth*. I might use the book I'm going to teach next, but the question is the same. They are asked to apply it to different text. They know, then, that an exam will be based on what's going on in class; it's not going to be something completely out of the realm of what they've learned. They're, therefore, more engaged in answering the question in class. Sometimes they get too caught up in the "give me exactly the words you want me to use" sort of approach, but often there are enough people in the class where they get engaged in the question itself. So that works, most of the time.

Q: This is a very interesting approach – using the exam as a way to delve into the text. This is totally different, of course, from teaching to the exam.

K.B.J.: Yes, because I found that if you didn't have some way of coming back to things at the end, then you've just lost what happened during the semester. So you read a book, you talk about it, and then it's gone without any exam presence. When there's an exam, there's a reason to go back to it and think about the books in connection to each other.

Q: Yes. So they do the group work, they have a question, you have a discussion afterwards, and then you use that same set of questions with another text, so they begin to have a kind of tool. The set of questions becomes a tool for understanding literature books – am I understanding you correctly?

K.B.J.: It's not always the same set of questions. Sometimes that will happen. I also teach different types of classes, so if I have a theory class, which I teach quite often actually, then it is necessarily about the theory; it's questions about representation and narratives and whatever else I'm teaching in that class. So, yes, it is likely the same set of questions for a particular class, but it's a different set of questions for another class; it depends upon what the text or class requires. In any case, yes, they then have a tool which they can apply to another text.

Q: Have there been any memorable sessions?

K.B.J.: I don't know that sessions in themselves have been particularly memorable. I do have good sessions and not good sessions, I know that. I think, too, you remember that something that you did was successful when it's time to teach that text again. However, I've found that doing that doesn't work all the time. I mean taking one activity, one approach from one class into another doesn't always work, because classes have their own personality. What seems more memorable is the class [the students] as a whole, whether the class itself was successful or not.

Q: Can you recall anything in any literature lessons in any of the places you've taught that gave you particular pleasure? Or are there students that have made for a memorable session?

K.B.J.: Maybe it's my perspective on this, but it's very hard to answer that question. I had one student, my most recent honours student – so as an honours student, of course, he's memorable. He just defended his thesis, and watching his growth was amazing. I hadn't had an honours student for a couple of years actually, and this student grew through my classes. He came through my theory class, and then he started working with me on American literature, not Caribbean. He had a stutter, and so he learned to write instead of to speak. He had learned to sit and really think about texts as he remained quiet; therefore, his writing was very good. That is memorable. It's the way that he really was focused on trying to communicate that is always going to stick with me, but I don't know how much I had to do with this. I mean, I helped to shepherd the thesis that ended up coming out well, but I don't know how much I had to do with his focused attempts to communicate.

Q: From the way you're speaking about him, you probably created a very supportive environment.

K.B.J.: But I didn't know anything about stuttering. I was able, however, to

213

give him the opportunity to be the student speaker at the Dean's List ceremony. I had been asked to find a student speaker, because I was the director of the honours programme. He was my honours student at the time, and though I knew he was not a fan of speaking in public, I asked him to be our speaker. At first he declined, but it made an impression on him to be asked, and apparently he discussed it with his brother, also a student at York. His brother somehow convinced him it was an opportunity he could not turn down, so he came back to me and agreed. It turned out that if he practised and omitted certain words, he would not stutter. He worked really hard; he sent me drafts of the speech, and I sent back whatever I thought might need to be changed. It was completely a motivational as well as congratulatory kind of speech, which is what is needed for a Dean's List ceremony. He did an amazing job; he brought out the anecdotes, the right motivational words, the right inflections; and he did everything without stuttering. He was so proud of himself for that moment. I think teaching literature allows students to see themselves more fully, more completely, if only for a moment. I don't know if he would have been able to do so well if he had worked with another teacher from another discipline.

Q: As our only Caribbean American interviewee, could you please share with us what it is like teaching Caribbean literature to non-Caribbean persons? You are teaching primarily non-Caribbean students, aren't you?

K.B.J.: No, not in my current job – well it's about split in half. At York there are often immigrants of colour or children of immigrants of colour. So there are ways in which they connect to Caribbean literature. Even so, I do have a substantial Caribbean set; I'd say about a third of my students are Caribbean. I'll have also some Asian, Arab and Eastern European immigrants, or the children of these immigrants.

Q: What is it like teaching Caribbean literature to non-Caribbean students?

K.B.J.: It's interesting in that sometimes the Caribbean students want to claim authenticity and authority over the other students. So they will say, "That's not how you pronounce it", or "Let me tell you the backstory of this carnival moment", or something like that, and that's actually kind of cool, because I let them talk. And then if they're going overboard, or if they say something that doesn't quite fit with the text, then I can pause them and say, "Well, here's what you might want to think about with that case", and I often remind them that the Caribbean experience is not homogenous. It's also great to have some of them in the class, because it points out to the students who are not from the Caribbean that the Caribbean isn't one space – that the Haitians in the room may relate to things differently than the Jamaicans, and so, too, may the Dominicans and the Trinidadians.

So it's very important in my classroom to talk about the Caribbean as a space of multiples, to complexify the Caribbean beyond pictures of tourism. It's great having immigrants from different places; so my Bangladeshi students can speak about British colonialism with my Caribbean students, and also to my Caribbean-identified students who have never actually been to the Caribbean. It's interesting for all of us to see the ways that colonialism has shaped our lives even in this space.

Q: Do you incorporate technology in your classes?

K.B.J.: I prefer to be in a smart classroom in case I need it. I don't always use it, but I like to have it just in case I need to show a video or show students where to go for something, but I'm quite comfortable with the chalkboard. I haven't moved away from the chalkboard yet.

Q: Would you like to say anything more about the strategies that you use in general or particularly how organizing students in small groups works for you?

K.B.J.: I'm keeping the group work even with very small classes. I find that I hate when I talk too much; you lose them. I think students talking to each other, then sharing with the larger group, and me talking where I need to in those spaces, works best. It's not always great for timing – sometimes you run out of time – but I just tried something new last class, because when we were working in groups on *White Teeth*, we ran out of time. I had them type up their responses including page references, and I'm going to post it on our online Blackboard site. Because this is the senior seminar and they are going to be writing papers, I'm trying to set up the group work in ways that will move towards the paper writing. This is an experiment.

Q: Do you teach poetry at all, or is it just prose and theory?

K.B.J.: I've never taught a full poetry class, but I do teach poetry within classes. I teach the Introduction to Literature class, and so there's poetry on that syllabus. And the last two times that I taught Caribbean literature, I taught only poetry and short stories; so it was an approach through short texts using the Oxford anthologies.

Q: Is there any major difference in your approach between teaching poetry as opposed to prose?

K.B.J.: There probably should be, but no. I used to have students recite poetry – I haven't done that in a very long time because of time constraints. They used to have to memorize a poem and perform it. I did that with my first Caribbean literature class, and that's always interesting as well, because they can surprise you in so many ways. But for the most part, I treat them similarly in the sense that we look at language, we examine the use of literary devices, and we discuss historical context.

Q: Do you ever manage to get visiting poets into your class, or writers? I mean, you have a lot of contacts there.

K.B.J.: Yes. I haven't had any poets that I can remember. Last semester I taught *Sections of an Orange* by Anton Nimblett, and before I assigned it, I asked him if he would come and teach two of my classes. He writes poetry, but the class wasn't about his poetry; it was about his short fiction. That was great especially for the lower-level class, and he completely enjoyed the lower-level class. They were so engaged. They're mostly non-English majors, but they had read his book, and they had so many questions for him. This semester I'm having Robert Antoni come to talk about his work with my graduate class. I'm teaching a very interesting graduate class called The Digital Caribbean. It's not literature per se, although I come to it from an English professor perspective. We're reading *As Flies to Whatless Boys*, and Antoni has a website that goes with it; he's thinking about how to do an e-book in a certain way, and so he's coming to talk to the class. He's very good with language, with capturing language, and so he's trying to translate that to a multimedia presentation. It's a smaller class, and so it's a different approach at a graduate level to bring in a writer, I think, than at the undergraduate level class. It's going to be their having a conversation with him rather than his doing a presentation.

Q: That sounds like an interesting project, which suggests different teaching approaches. Would you say the style or structure of the novel affects the way you teach it?

K.B.J.: I often start the semester, sometimes even my Introduction toLiterature course, with theory or historical context or both. I get students to think about the theory through the text and not get caught up in what isn't applicable to how we are approaching the text.

Even if it's a short poem, I often stress setting and that setting has to do with the reader as well as the text, and not just where you are but what else you're reading at the time. Also, I let students know the focus we will choose for a particular text; for example, I will tell them that we're not going to talk about gender in this book at this time, because we are more concerned about religion. I let them know as well that it doesn't mean that these issues aren't in the book or important in the book, but that they're just not part of how we're approaching it right now.

Q: So you identify early what the focus of your text will be, what theoretical approach?

K.B.J.: Right, and I think we all do that. We don't necessarily use a specific theory, but we know that we can't talk about everything in the text. We might talk about the text in conjunction with what books we've read before, even if we're not thinking theory. I think of theory as a lens, as providing a lens for us to look at this new text. In my Introduction to Literature class, I often have large, broad themes that we're going to think through, because it helps the student. So we begin by reading and talking about the purpose of writing or why people write, or by discussing diaspora, or maybe both things; then that's what we're looking at when we read the text or texts. I find that the students feel more confident about the text as well, because they have a handle on it. They can say, "I know what diaspora means and here's how I see it at work in this text." So this semester I am teaching a twenty-first-century Caribbean diaspora class, and I began with essays on diaspora in the first class. But only one class and about two to three texts, because it's not a theory class. Then we turned to the fiction, and I could later introduce ideas of race and gender, maybe religion, or class depending on the book.

Q: How would you describe your general approach and your style of teaching?

K.B.J.: I try to have a discussion class rather than a top-down approach, where everyone views me as having the information that I need to "download" to students.

Q: Would you also say that providing the historical context is important for you?

K.B.J.: Yes, that's part of where I come in – to sort of provide relevant portions of that information to students, so that they can then use it to read and interpret the text.

Q: I am also noting that you're very concerned about giving your students a handle, some tool with which to approach the work.

K.B.J.: Yes.

Q: What specific help do you find that your students need?

K.B.J.: The first thing is that they need to recognize their abilities and their responsibility to exercise those abilities. I know that sounds simplistic, but often students just look at something and they think, *I can't read that*, or *I can't write that*, or *I've been told that I can't do that*. So I often start the class with a "This is up to you" kind of speech. I find that if they try, I try very hard with them, and that if they don't try, I can't afford to try either. So that's sort of my teaching philosophy de facto, in a sense. I will go to bat for you if you are going to bat. I'm not going out there by myself. And that's been part of the learning for me over the thirteen years: you extend energy for the ones who are themselves extending energy. I don't know how else to put it. You could have a student who writes very well, who you know is capable of doing way better work than they do, but you can't make them do it. That's still very hard for me to accept; I imagine it's difficult for everyone, but that's been especially hard for me here. As I mentioned earlier, at York College, the students are majority of colour, but the faculty are majority white, and the way some of them speak about the students sometimes has racial undertones. These racial undertones exist in the way that they speak about how ready these students are for college, how capable the students are of doing certain types of work, what they have to do with their own teaching style in order to meet students where they believe the students are. So I have to sort of tread a line between pushing the students too much and not enough. It's finding the words that give students the idea that they are capable of doing difficult work. Now if they don't want to do it, they don't want to do it – you can't do anything about that. That's another reason I start with more theoretical texts, to just sort of say, "Here is the level that you can work to; here is the level that I'm expecting you to work toward."

Since I began at York in 2006, they've raised the requirements for entrance to the college by about 3 per cent, or something like, from a 75 per cent to a 78 per cent. It was really small, and I could see a difference in the level of writing in my class but not necessarily a difference in the level of thinking. Often I can't do much about the writing level. I can encourage and encourage them to get tutoring for their writing, but I find I'm not as capable of improving their writing technically, because I just didn't get trained in writing, and I'm not as interested in that. I'm interested in their analysis of the text and their ability to make connections and think about the world that this book is bringing in. So I find that the help that my students often need is to know that they can make connections, that they are allowed to make connections, that we will entertain connections in class and that there are wrong answers. I have this in my guidelines somewhere; there are wrong answers, but there are many right answers in literature. So I will tell them when there's a wrong answer as well as help them find how the text might support their answer.

Q: So do you actually give them a set of guidelines?

K.B.J.: As I've done this more and more, I've built up an archive of documents, many of them guidelines for assignments. I do lots of responses that are formal writing. I assign sometimes six, sometimes even eight for the semester – it depends on what else is going on in the class – and they have to submit these before we talk about the text in class. And they often have a prompt. I found that writing clear guidelines for what I expect in these responses helps avoid confusion and frustration for both me and my students.

Q: Before you actually do the text in class, they have to do a personal response to the text?

K.B.J.: It's not a personal response; it's called a response paper. They're responding to a prompt. It forces them to think about the text before coming to class and "getting the answers".

Q: What assignments do your students find interesting? Are there particular assignments that they actually really like doing?

K.B.J.: I have different things that I do with different texts, so if we're doing a play, I sometimes make them act out short scenes. I learned this activity from another teacher: give students a section and have them act it out without any words. Other times I will ask them to do a complete production with the play, selecting a director and a producer and assigning other roles if necessary; it depends on how much time we have. I may also ask them to select a section of the text, choose a particular way to abridge it, and explain why they did it in that way. It makes them engage in the text in different ways. With poetry sometimes I ask them to get in groups and decide how to perform the poem – not like act it out but how to speak it out loud. They are forced again to think about the text and what the poet is trying to say. I've done things where I ask them to look for a word or phrase that a writer repeats and consider where it comes up, why it comes up so often and why at those particular moments. A lot of my exercises are often close reading exercises or formal/formalist readings of the text. Sometimes if it's a play I might ask them to see it as a movie and cast it with well-known actors. They love that one – the undergrad classes. They have to cast movie stars in a role and tell me why that person and why that role. This provides insight into how they are visualizing these texts. Students like to move a lot, you know, and be loud, and so when you can do that constructively with the text, it engages them.

Q: This is very interesting work. So you teach plays as well. Do you teach Caribbean plays also?

K.B.J.: I don't do Caribbean plays very often, because I've rarely found short ones, and of course they're not anthologized in the text. I think, too, about the cost of texts, because my students are often not getting financial aid for books. So I try to think about which anthology will serve my needs, but still be affordable.

Q: So is the cost of texts a challenge in teaching literature? How do you address this?

K.B.J.: You know individual books don't cost much, but when you add them together, they do. I try to give students enough notice, so if they need to get it from the library, they can. I am finding that several students are using electronic books lately, because they can get those free sometimes, but I emphasize in my classes that because we're doing so much close reading and moving between pages that e-books will put them at a disadvantage. I leave it up to them. I tell them that they can use them for class but not for the exam. What I'm going to try this semester is to bring extra copies of some of the books for the exam and see how that works.

Q: What other challenges do you have, especially since you are working with such a diverse group?

K.B.J.: Getting them to read. Yes, getting them to read before they come to class is challenging, which is again one of the reasons I have an online discussion board in my undergrad class. I try to think about the reading assignments in terms of whether it really is feasible or not for them to get it done. This semester I have a lot of "big" books, and I try to intersperse these with shorter texts and with a movie. So it's not like we read *White Teeth* and then we're going to read *The Brief and Wondrous Life of Oscar Wao* right after it. You can't do that. I try to arrange assignments so that it's not onerous, and I can focus in on what it is I need to get done.

Q: Elaine Showalter has written a book called *Teaching Literature*, and in it she lists seven teacher anxieties, anxieties such as isolation and covering the syllabus. Do you experience any anxieties related to your teaching of literature?

K.B.J.: You know, that first day is always one of anxiety! This semester has worked very well, but I've been challenged by my need to be prepared, which is not something I'm letting go of, but with the Digital Caribbean course, it just was not coming together at first. I like to walk into class with the syllabus that says, This is what we're doing for the whole semester. I couldn't do that with the Digital Caribbean course, because I didn't know, and I needed to pull together a set of readings for something that hadn't been done before (that I know of), and so it was proving very difficult. We've had a great two classes so far. But always, the first class is full of anxiety. Always, even thirteen years later. It's good to be at one place for as long as I've been, because they begin to know you – and you know, they get younger while you get older!

I no longer have to stand by the door welcoming people, which I had to do at the very beginning just to sort of, say, yes, I'm the professor. At the beginning, I was told to stand by the door and welcome the students, so that they know that you're the professor and they're not confused when you walk in. Now I have less anxiety about looking the part.

I don't know if in the Caribbean you have this problem, where they expect that you're the student because you're of colour. No matter how young you look, [they think] if you're brown or black you cannot be one of the faculty. Unless you're dressed in a suit or something similar, the automatic assumption is that you are not one of the faculty, and that happened to me quite often at the beginning of my time at York. It's not about how you look in terms of age; it's about what the student body is expected to look like and what the faculty body is expected to look like. I also recall my first class at York and my first course, which was a writing course. One of the students, who could barely speak English because she had recently immigrated from French Canada, a black woman, was consistently late to my class, and she couldn't write. I told her what she needed to do. Her response: she went to the office and told them, "I want a white teacher."

Q: What?

K.B.J.: Exactly. But that was my experience; at this college that was my welcome. So what students expect professors to look like and how to establish a certain amount of authority in my classroom are some of my anxieties. I think that the experiences of women of colour in the academy here led to particular anxieties about authority and about respect in the classroom.

Q: When you reflect on teaching literature and particularly Caribbean literature, what do you think is absolutely necessary for teaching it effectively?

K.B.J.: A knowledge of history, which, you know, is never complete. I grew up in Jamaica, and I had to learn a lot of the history as I worked through the literature. I think you need to be able to give your students context for the text; you have to let them know that this text doesn't just come out of the writer's imagination.

Q: So you clearly don't hold with the view that the meaning of the text lies purely in the text.

K.B.J.: No, I'm not a formalist, though I use formalist approaches. I'm a . . . historicist? I don't know what the word is, but I need historical context.

Conclusion

Teaching literature matters. In fact, it matters a great deal given the social, economic and environmentally complex world in which we live. How to make sense of this world, how to balance the needs of self with others, how to live well in these times, how to read the future – these are all questions very much within the province of literature.

How we teach literature remains an essential question. Much has been written on the *what* of literature, its content. Much less has been written on the *how* – how to teach literature effectively. *Caribbean Writers on Teaching Literature* has provided a space for the necessary reflection on this.

An "isolationist" culture, as Wilmot terms it, encouraged by our technology and a fast-paced society, requires more than ever a sense of community if we are to survive. A literature pedagogy of connectivity, which has emerged through the conversation with our eighteen teachers, creates this needed sense of community. It begins with the creation of a community of readers, as teachers connect students to text and context. Being so connected, students become more aware of their local and global world.

In this period, of instant messaging, of hyperlinking, we are becoming less attentive book readers, as Kingsley (2017) remarks. Kingsley, moreover, cites literature professors like Greg Garrad, who speak of having to cut back on their reading lists to accommodate students' lessening desire to read and contemplate books. It is evident that uncovering the process of reading for and with students as well as showing one's love of books have worked to a great extent in encouraging students to recognize the importance of reading. So, too, has locating the text in the students' context as well as in the larger space and time context. To counter more effectively the students' tendency to read a book only by reading its summary or skimming, perhaps teachers should engage directly with the "slow reading movement".

What the teachers interviewed here have made abundantly clear, however, is the realization of one of the key aims of literature: the development of self, or, as Wharton puts it, the "cultivation and celebration of [one's] personality" (Wharton as quoted in Young 2017, loc. 88). Living and working in a Caribbean society with its history of fragmentation, divided selves, multiethnicities and races – in effect, a microcosm of much of the world today – these teachers have, through the teaching of literature, enabled students to connect with themselves and to their society. No easy task. Yet it is one that emphasizes the value of literature, that answers "What is literature for?" – a question too often posed when discussing the relevance of courses, programmes or subjects.

Moreso, this connection to self and others, to life's "meaning", is effected through literature's sheer pleasure, beauty and mystery. And so "what looks like life [transposed] into a collection of written sentences . . . voices that come from nowhere and live on in our consciousness, . . . this magic" (Smith 2013) can be gifted to our students. They too can learn to hear "the singing . . . bigger than all of we / And making us better than we think we could be" (Baugh 2000, 37). The art and practice of literature – a gift that refines and heals us, transformative in all its diversity.

References

Baugh, Edward. 2000. *It Was the Singing*. Kingston: Sandberry Press.

Beach, R.D., S. Appleman, and J. Wilhelm. 2006. *Teaching Literature to Adolescents*. London: Routledge.

Beach, R., and J. Myers. 2001. *Inquiry-Based English Instruction*. New York: Teachers' College, Columbia University.

Collie, J. and S. Slater. 1990. *Literature in the Language Classroom*. Cambridge: Cambridge University Press.

Bonham-Carter, C. 2013. "Taking It Personally: An Approach to Teaching Caribbean Poetry". *Caribbean Journal of Education* 35, no. 2: 139–46.

Bowell, P. and B. Heap. 2001. *Planning Process Drama*. London: David Fulton.

Brubacher, J. 2016. "Teaching-Learning Process: Characteristics and Limitations of Behaviourist, Cognitivist and Humanistic Approach to Learning". http://www .scribd.com/doc/5769721/teaching-learning-process.

Bryan, B., and M. Styles, eds. 2014. *Teaching Caribbean Poetry*. London: Routledge.

Dance, D.C., ed. 1986. *Fifty Caribbean Writers: A Bio-bibliographical Critical Source Book*. Westport, CT: Greenwood.

Down, L. 2011. "Education for Sustainable Development: Latest Buzzword or a Paradigmatic Shift in Education". *Caribbean Journal of Education for Sustainable Development* 1, no. 1: 8–16.

Flaherty, C. 2015. "Major Exodus". *Inside Higher Ed*, 26 January. www.insidehighered .com/news/2015/01/26/where-have-all-english-majors-gone.

Haven, C. 2010. "Lit Class Under Attack?" Stanford Report, *Stanford News*, 7 December. http://news.stanford.edu/news/2010/december/humanities-defense-landy -120710.html.

Kingsley, P. 2017. "The Art of Slow Reading". *The Guardian*, 15 July 2010. https:// www.theguardian.com/books/2010/jul/15/slow-reading.

Kravis, J. 1995. *Teaching Literature, Writers and Teachers Talking*. Cork: Cork University Press.

Lambert, J. and P. Cuper. 2008. "Multimedia Technologies and Familiar Spaces: 21st-Century Teaching for 21st-Century Learners". *Contemporary Issues in Technology and Teacher Education* 8, no. 3. http://www.citejournal.org/volume-8/issue-3-08/current-practice/multimedia-technologies-and-familiar-spaces-21st-century-teaching-for-21st-century-learners.

Ledent, B. 2007. "Caribbean Literature: Looking Backward and Forward". *Vetas Digital* 5: 68–79.

Lombardi, M. 2007. "Authentic Learning for the 21st Century: An Overview". EDUCAUSE Learning Initiative, ELI Paper no. 1. https://www.researchgate.net/profile/Marilyn_Lombardi/publication/220040581_Authentic_Learning_for_the_21st_Century_An_Overview/links/0f317531744eedf4d1000000.pdf.

Milner, J. and L. Milner. 2008. *Bridging English*. Upper Saddle River, NJ: Pearson.

Rosenblatt, L. 1960. "Literature: The Reader's Role". *English Journal* 49, no. 5 (May 1960): 304–10, 315–16.

Pieper, I. 2006. "Teaching Literature". Paper presented at the intergovernmental conference Languages of Schooling: Towards a Framework for Europe, Strasbourg. 16–18 October.

Showalter, E. 2013. *Teaching Literature*. Oxford: Blackwell.

Sumara, D.J. 2012. *Why Reading Literature in School Still Matters*. London: Lawrence Erlbaum Associates.

Smith, Z. 2013. "Zadie Smith on *NW* – Guardian Book Club". *Guardian*, 1 August 2013. https://www.theguardian.com/books/2013/aug/01/zadie-smith-nw-book-club.

Walcott, D. 1970. "What the Twilight Says: An Overture". In *Dream on Monkey Mountain and Other Plays*. New York: Farrar, Straus and Giroux.

Young, D. 2017. *The Art of Reading*. London: Scribe.